Planning
America's
Communities

Planning America's Communities:

Paradise Found?
Paradise Lost?

Herbert H. Smith

PLANNERS PRESS
AMERICAN PLANNING ASSOCIATION
Chicago, Illinois
Washington, D.C.

Grateful acknowledgment is given for permission to reprint from the following:

Richard O. Baumbach, Jr. and William E. Borah, *The Second Battle of New Orleans History of the Vieux Carre Riverfront Expressway Controversy,* copyright 1981 by [authors. Published by the University of Alabama Press.

Allan Bloom, *The Closing of the American Mind,* copyright 1987 by the author.] printed with permission of Simon & Schuster, Inc.

Henry S. Churchill, *The City is the People,* copyright 1962 by W.W. Norton & Compa.., Inc.

William Fulton, "Visionaries, Deal Makers, Incrementalists: The Divided World of Urban Planning," published in *Governing,* June 1989; copyright 1989 by *Governing* magazine.

Bill Hornby, "At Best, City Planning Isn't Bureaucracy—It's Democracy in Action," copyright 1988 by the *Denver Post.*

Charles Henning, *The Wit and Wisdom of Politics,* copyright 1989 by Fulcrum Publishing, 350 Indiana St., Golden, CO 80401.

Jane Jacobs, *The Death and Life of Great American Cities.* Copyright 1961 by the author. Reprinted with permission of Random House, Inc. and Jonathan Cape, Ltd.

Richard D. Lamm, "Hard Choices," and "Colorado Government: Running on Empty," reprinted with permission of the *Rocky Mountain News.*

Simpson Lawson, "Baltimore Reexamined," published in the *AIA Journal,* November 1982; copyright 1982 by BPI Communications, Inc. Used with permission.

Roger K. Lewis, "Planning Is a More Sensible Choice," published in *Urban Land,* September 1989; reprinted with permission from ULI—the Urban Land Institute, Washington, D.C.

Daniel Mandelker. Reprinted from *Land Use Law, Second Edition,* by Daniel R. Mandelker, with permission from The Michie Company, Charlottesville, Virginia. Copyright 1988, 1982 The Michie Company.

Dwight H. Merriam, "Taking Remedy Finally Confronted in First Lutheran Church," published August 1987 in *The Law and the Land,* a quarterly newsletter on real estate, land use, and the environment, published by Robinson & Cole, a Connecticut law firm of which the author is a partner.

Michael Middleton, *Man Made the Town,* copyright 1987 by Bodley Head, Ltd.

Thomas J. Noel and Barbara S. Norgren, "Denver the City Beautiful," reprinted with permission of Historic Denver, Inc.

Jerry Norman, "There's No Substitute for Planning—But We Try," published in *The Caller Times,* March 19, 1988.

M. Scott Peck, *The Different Drum,* copyright 1987 by M. Scott Peck, M.D., P.C.; reprinted by permission of Simon & Schuster, Inc.

Neal Peirce, "Despite Its Wacky Image, Boulder is a Model for Urban Planning," reprinted with permission of the *Denver Post.*

Steve Raab, "Boulder Builders Mellow Toward Slow-Growth Policy," copyright 1988 by the *Denver Post.*

Copyright 1991 by the American Planning Association
1313 E. 60th St., Chicago, IL 60637
Paperback edition ISBN 0-918286-71-9
Hardbound edition ISBN 0-918286-72-7
Library of Congress Catalog Number 90-82670

To my wife, Nancy, for her persistent, ego-deflating, but most beneficial first editing of this manuscript and most of all for her encouragement, support, and meaningful love.

Contents

Acknowledgments   xiii

Foreword   xv

Introduction   1

1. **The Forces At Work**   7
   Federal Government's Role   8
   Examples of Other Federal Influence   10
   The Cumulative Effect of These Federal Programs   17
   State Governments' Role   19
   Conclusions   38

2. **Economics and Taxing Policies**   39
   The 1954 Federal Housing Act, Section 701   39
   The Effect of Taxing Policies   46
   The Effect of Changes in Society   47
   What Economic Pressure Has Done To Local Governments   49
   Economic Development Quality   52
   Building a Strong, Lasting Economy   56

3. **The Courts' Role In Land Use Planning**   65
   Interpretive Changes   66
   Public Health, Safety and General Welfare   69
   Police Power and Eminent Domain   69
   Land Use Attorneys and Expert Witnesses   71
   The Appeal Process   77
   The "Back-Room" Scenario   77
   Landmark Euclid v. Ambler Case   79
   The "Taking" Issue   80
   A Final Word   86

4. **Four Cities that Have Made Planning Work**   89
   The City Is the People   90
   Portland, Oregon   90

Charlotte, North Carolina   98
Minneapolis, Minnesota   106
Pittsburgh, Pennsylvania   111
An Editorial Summary   116

5. **Some Have Tried**   **119**
Baltimore, Maryland   119
San Diego, California   130
Denver, Colorado   136
Saint Paul, Minnesota   139

6. **Then There Are Others**   **143**
The Mason/Dixon Line and Planning Attitudes   143
New Orleans, Louisiana   144
San Antonio, Texas   149
Memphis, Tennessee   156
Corpus Christi, Texas   161
Albuquerque, New Mexico   164

7. **How We Got to Where We Are**   **171**
Horizontal v. Vertical Pattern: The New Corporation   172
Form and Structure of Government   176
Political and Community Leadership   180
Public Officials' Planning Attitudes   185
Major Influences on Policymakers   188
Three Major Factors Contributing to How We Got Where We
     Are   190
Evaluate Your Elected Officials   192
Lack of Coordination in All Levels of Government   193

8. **The Planning Profession: Past, Present and, Maybe, Future 197**
The City Beautiful Movement   197
National Planning Organizations   204
Interviewees' Critique of National Planning Organizations   205
The Planning Profession's Present—and Future?   211
Conclusion   219
Postscript   222

9. **Quo Vadis?**   **227**
The Importance of Urban Form Decision Making   228
The Bright Side   234
Planners and the Planning Profession   240

The Need For Change   247

Index   **251**

Tables
Table One - Profile of Persons Interviewed By Profession   188
Table Two - Interview Ranking Tabulation   190

Acknowledgments

This book would not have been possible without the cooperation and assistance of a great many people. My sincere thanks go to all of those who provided me with contacts in various cities and to those who were kind enough to share their knowledge, experience and opinions during the interviews. Special appreciation is expressed for several who, in some way, contributed directly to the manuscript production. They are:

Dixi Gloystein, for her computer expertise, patient understanding and invaluable assistance.

Thomas Grimshaw, who provided advice and helpful, but sometimes caustic comments on his favorite subject—special districts.

Linda R. Hall, for computer and printing assistance and for being available in case of emergencies.

David Herlinger, friend and mentor, provided encouragement, interest and support, as well as a constructive review of the manuscript.

Martha K. Johnson supplied an objective lay-person review, reaction and comments.

Steven D. Koch, for the expert computer programming and technical knowledge he imparted.

Gilbert McNeish furnished substantial information and materials pertaining to general legal matters included in the text.

Harvey Moskowitz, a willing and helpful source for details of the courts' role in shaping New Jersey planning and zoning and the establishment of "court appointed masters."

Marjorie Price was a source of candid and frank discussion that helped to keep me on track.

Carol Strathman, for her confidence in me and support of my work as well as an always-ready, encouraging smile.

Linda Tafoya deserves thanks for letting the preparation of this book occasionally disturb the smooth operation of her organization.

James Westkott, the first to urge me to undertake this project, for badgering me and encouraging the writing of this book, and for his patient review, suggestions and consultation.

Foreword

Is the urban planning profession enjoying robust health, or is it showing signs of infirmity? Are planners having an impact on the shaping of America's urban communities, or have other forces—economic, political, demographic—become so overwhelming as to render the planner's role increasingly insignificant?

Much has been written lately in response to these questions, and a variety of prescriptions have been offered for improving the profession's vitality and efficacy. Some writers urge greater emphasis upon the planner's role as a visionary or idealist; others stress the notion of effectiveness, viewing competent and timely service to clients as the key to the profession's survival; still others emphasize the political content of planning practice, and urge planners to become skilled actors in the political arena. Other roles—technical analyst, mediator, social activist, communicator, etc.—are commended with equal vigor.

Enter Herb Smith. His book is certainly a contribution to the literature mentioned above. Its style and tone, however, are uniquely his own. This is not a scholarly tome, intended solely for an audience of academics. It is, rather, a book to be read by all who care about the future of our cities, and about the roles that planners ought to be playing in the production of urban form.

Herb Smith is an urbanist. He cares deeply about cities and is a perceptive observer of the forces that have shaped them in recent decades. He is concerned about the negative impacts that various federal programs and initiatives have had on cities and about the records of state and local governments, which, in his view, have not been much better. At the local level, according to Smith's analysis, the key villains have been short-sighted and self-serving political leadership, civic apathy, a general hostility to the idea of planning, and repeated acquiescence to economic development pressures.

Unlike many books that are long on analysis but short on remedies, Smith's work is chock-full of suggestions. Many of these are of the "common sense" variety—his emphasis, for example, on the need for capable political leaders who have a "planning attitude," and therefore on the critical importance of ensuring that the right people are elected to public office.

The book is a deeply personal expression of Herb Smith's concerns and ideas, strongly informed by—and benefiting from—his 40 years of experience as a planning official, consultant, and educator. His observations also reflect, however, the viewpoints garnered from a number of interviews conducted during the course of visits to some 15 cities. In part, then, the book "takes the pulse" of planning as it is assessed by those involved with it on a day-to-day basis. In the final analysis, however, the views and ideas that give the book its identity and flavor are Smith's own. And that's what makes the book a pleasurable experience.

He has strong opinions, and states them vigorously. He also names names, and some of his characterizations are bound to prove controversial. He deeply admires the planning process in some cities (Portland, Charlotte) but is highly critical of what he has found in others. Along the way he also offers some views regarding our national planning organizations, professional publications, and planning schools.

In short, Smith has written a provocative, wise, and stimulating book, one that gives voice to many of the concerns that appear prevalent today among rank-and-file planners. Some readers will react with anger, others with cheers. But all will react. Once again Herb Smith has performed a valuable service for the planning profession.

Michael P. Brooks
Dean, School of Community and Public Affairs
Virginia Commonwealth University
Richmond, Virginia
July 1990

Introduction

Every day hundreds, perhaps even thousands of decisions are being made throughout the United States that have an effect on shaping the urban form—and thus on each one of us as individuals. Who is making these decisions and how are they made? The obvious answer is that they are the responsibility of our elected policymakers who may or may not be influenced by the recommendations of appointed members of planning commissions, zoning boards, and/or neighborhood groups. In some cases the decisions may be affected by an organized planning department's recommendations or a comprehensive plan. Conversely, in these times of economic crisis in many of our cities and towns, and with recognition of political realities, an important question arises: Are value judgments based on long-range considerations and sound recommendations being pushed aside, and crumbling under economic development pressures, entrepreneurial greed, or just plain old fashioned politics?

After more than 60 years of organized city planning efforts and the existence of professional planners' organizations, what has this planning concept actually accomplished? Where does the planning process stand today? Is it not time that someone with an extensive exposure to that profession take an objective, analytical look at this situation and suggest what might be done to help assure a more livable urban form for future generations?

Questions like these have been on my mind for many years, even before I reached the hallowed age that categorizes me as a senior citizen. For that reason, after retirement from teaching planning and community development at the graduate level for twelve years, it seemed logical to explore those questions further in a hard-hitting but objective and honest critical analysis. If weaknesses in the planning process are revealed, then changes in philosophy, emphasis and/or approach for planners, the planning profession and the general public should be postulated, so that a better job can be done in shaping our cities and our urban form.

1

Planning is an idea whose time came long ago, yet the lack of good planning is evidenced by the mess in which most of our cities and suburbs find themselves today. Simple observation of the built urban form speaks volumes that the idea has had great difficulty being accepted and applied. Although the concept of local government planning has been sold, in one way or the other by both federal and state governments, there has not been adequate education of the public about how effective planning should, and can, work. In other words, no way has yet been found to allow planning to prevail over the very powerful forces based upon self-interest and greed that are working endlessly against this process.

Planning is the most difficult concept yet conceived by humankind to sell to the public. Vibrant planning is a series of ideas. To convince another person of one person's, or even a group of trained professionals' ideas, is an almost impossible task when they have an opposite mindset. This is especially true when, as in most cases, this mindset is based upon a lack of accurate information, rumors, vested interests, personal political ambitions, dislike of government, etc. All these motivations are thinly or thickly veiled and are expressed in allusionary oratory highly colored by stated objections based on the ever popular platitudes of God, motherhood, apple pie, and country.

The governmental planning referred to in this book is general and conceptual, not a comprehensive master plan or a detailing of implementation tools such as zoning, subdivision regulations, and capital improvements programs. It is one I have developed over the years of what I believe lays a good base for beginning to understand the process. To me the planning process is a systematic means of problem prevention and problem solving for people in a democratic society, working together, through their government, for the institution of programmed governmental pre-action to direct and shape a desired comprehensive, coordinated result in all aspects of the urban form and urban society. It would be interesting to know how many professional planners reading this will agree—or disagree.

With that as a basic definition of my view of the term "planning process," a few words now on the reason for and the intent of writing this book. Until now only a few people, particularly those with planning experience in the trenches and with a true exposure to the vicissitudes of the planning process in a political society, have bothered, or been audacious enough, to take a penetrating, objective and analytical look at the successes and failures of the planning process. After forty years as a planning professional with experience in local, state, regional, and private consulting planning, as well as teaching at the graduate level, I believe that it is time to do just that. Some planning professionals such as Dr. Michael P. Brooks in his article, "Four Critical Junctures in the History of the Urban Planning Profession,"[1] and Melvin R. Levin, a past president of the American Institute of Certified Planners in his book, *Planning in Government,*[2] have, at least, raised the prospect that it is time for serious study to be given to the present effectiveness of the planning process and planning education. While applauding their thoughtful comments and using quotes from their writings, the approach I have taken has been somewhat different. This book focuses on three major areas which I believe have the greatest affect on the way the urban form has been, and is being, built in this country. These are:

1. The external forces of federal and state governments' influence on local governments' ability to shape their urban form.

2. The roles played by the planning profession and planning education in where we are in our urban form development.

3. The acceptance, or lack thereof, by local elected officials and the general public of comprehensive planning as an effective tool for building the future of their community.

By considering these major factors, all concerned public officials, private citizens, and those of us in the planning profession can reexamine who we are, where we have been, where we are now, and where we are going. We might find better ways to do what we have been trying to do, new ways to involve more people, so that all of us, working together, can do a better job in building our urban form so it once again is "Paradise Found" instead of, as we are doing now, descending further into today's "Paradise Lost."

Among those who have decried our inattention to shaping the form of our cities with the future in mind, Dennis O'Harrow, executive director of the former American Society of Planning Officials, had no peer. In a guest editorial written for *Kiwanis Magazine*, June 1958, he summed up our tendency to ignore the long standing "Paradise Lost" trend in city building better than anyone else before or since. He said: "In spite of the enlightenment of some manufacturers, business, and developers, it takes no trained aesthete to know that development since World War II has produced square mile after square mile of ugliness, desecrated land, and despoiled landscape. This is not democracy; this is anarchy!"[3]

In the meantime, we need only to reflect on the billions of dollars spent by the federal government, and some states, in encouraging local communities to plan. These taxpayers' dollars have gone into the support of planning departments, consultants, and reports over the years to help us realize the importance to each one of us of a well-conceived planning process. In addition to money, hundreds of thousands of volunteer hours have been contributed by members of planning commissions and zoning boards in trying to understand this thing called planning and to make it work. All of these efforts emphasize further why we each have a stake in what is going on and in examining ways to do it better.

Although not one of my most favorite authors in view of her indiscriminate application of the term "planner" to all those faulted by her, Jane Jacobs accurately summarized our failures, especially those resulting from urban renewal disasters, in preserving and building urban form. In *The Death And Life Of Great American Cities,* she wrote: "But look what we have built with the first several billions: low income projects that become worse centers of delinquency, vandalism and general social hopelessness than the slums they were supposed to replace. . . . Cultural centers that are unable to support a bookstore. Civic centers that are avoided by everyone but bums. . . . Promenades that go from no place to nowhere and have no promenaders. Expressways that eviscerate great cities. This is not the rebuilding of cities. This is the sack of cities."[4]

Thus taking this current drastic situation into account, I decided to undertake the research, interviews, and the writing of this book. From the time I began writing the first of my other books on planning and zoning for urban development, I had been convinced that writing a book is very much like the production of a baby: The only real fun is in the conception! My experience with this book, however, makes me think I might change my mind since I have had many pleasant experiences during its preparation.

My research enabled me to revisit a number of familiar cities and to update my knowledge about them as well as learn a great deal about some that were new to me. Secondly, it afforded me the chance to meet a great many interesting people and to observe politics at work in varying ways and in differing structures of government. And though there are a large number of concerned, dedicated people out there doing the best they can to make their community a better place and to preserve or build a better urban form, I have definitely concluded that planning will work only in communities where it is made a major point in every election campaign.

Thirdly, my previously faltering belief as to whether planning can ever work in a "democratic," capitalistic society has been greatly restored by this swing across the country because I saw that planning can be, and is, meaningfully effective and successful in a few places—not many, but thank God for those few. It was most heartening to me to experience the interest and enthusiasm of elected officials, planning professionals, developers, planning commission members, neighborhood activists, and the general public in seeing a book such as this available to stimulate discussion, possibly debate, and perhaps even involvement. That has been my prime objective throughout this entire project.

One conclusion I drew from these trips and the material gathered is that there is no question that the system of democratic local government planning *has not failed!* Instead, from my examination it became clear to me that it is we, the people, who have failed in operating that system. This is a disturbing omen for both planners and planning, as well as our cities, unless we change our tactics so that we are doing a much more effective job of educating and selling the planning process and its value to the general public.

Finally, an explanation of the methodology used in the research will be helpful to the reader. Thirteen cities were selected for investigative visits, not just for geographic distribution, but also with an intent to look at communities with varying economies, population compositions, and planning attitudes. In each city, interviews were conducted with from four to nine actively involved people. Persons to be interviewed were selected from six professional areas representative of those participating in some way with the shaping of urban form and who could thus provide comparative viewpoints. These six categories were composed of an elected official and/or planning commissioner; a planning staff member; a major private developer; an economic development agency official; a planning consultant; and a neighborhood activist. In addition to the forty-five minute or longer interview, participants were asked to complete a ranking form (discussed in chapter seven). Also, a locale inspection was conducted in each city and newspaper articles, publications and other research materials were collected. In the discussion about four of the cities personal experience, past and present, provided a large amount of the basic knowledge, although updating of information was accomplished in all.

The frequent references to Denver and Colorado are the result of my period of residency in Denver and my serving on state study committees as well as being a board member of the Colorado Housing and Finance Authority. Some of these references provide a comparison to other places while others provide worthwhile examples of generally applicable forces affecting urban form development both constructively and adversely.

NOTES

1. Michael P. Brooks, (Chicago: *Journal*, American Planning Association, Spring 1988), pp. 52–58.

2. Melvin R. Levin, (Chicago: Planners Press, American Planning Association, 1987).

3. Marjorie S. Berger, ed., *Dennis O'Harrow: Plan Talk and Plain Talk* (Chicago: Planners Press, American Planning Association, 1981), p. 109.

4. Jane Jacobs, *The Death and Life of Great American Cities* (New York: Vintage Books, Random House, 1961), p. 4.

1

The Forces
At Work

In order to understand fully just where local government planning is today, and how it got there, it is essential for us to examine some of the forces at work over which local government has had no control whatsoever. Careful reflection provides irrefutable evidence that these forces have vastly influenced the shape of urban form in this country and, to a large measure, the way in which planning is viewed by the American public. These outside forces in many ways have been responsible for some of the successes of the process, but more importantly have been the prime contributor to far more failures of planning at the local level.

There is a shibboleth frequently mouthed in this society, but not often applied in meaningful policy adoption and subsequent action: that is, our expressed belief in local control, the favorite canard of every politician from the federal to the state and county level. When the subject arises of where responsibility for control of land use should lie, any suggestion that greater effectiveness in solving intergovernmental metropolitan problems of urban form building would result if responsibility were broader based is immediately met by elected officials at all levels loudly proclaiming, "That's a local government responsibility." The examination in this book will show just a few of the ways that this has been ignored, either by action taken or inaction, when it has been politically expedient to do so by local, state and federal politicians. Expressed belief in local control thus becomes a sanctimonious escape route for higher government elected officeholders, a means of protecting political power and fiefdoms by local officials, and a political hot potato to be avoided.

From the beginning, the task of adopting, enforcing, and administering land use regulations relating to private land has been vested theoretically with local government—the counties and incorporated municipalities—with relatively few exceptions. Noteworthy innovations in this last category are the application of state land use controls in Hawaii, some of the broad enactments of the Oregon and Vermont legislatures and more recently reactive legislative measures by states such as California, Florida, and New Jersey in attempts to protect areas such as coastal zones, wetlands, and flood plains where further development is deemed to be of critical state concern.

FEDERAL GOVERNMENT'S ROLE

Actions taken by higher levels of government in attempting to fill voids left by local governments' failure to take corrective action or to impose policy direction is almost always based on a meritorious idea when conceived. The end result, however, is often destructive or obstructive instead of constructive. This can be credited to many factors. Primary among these is the failure of higher level legislators and administrators to fully examine the spin-off consequences, especially in the area of added financial burden, on the local governments who must deal with the resultant impacts and/or problems built into the general enforcement or policy implementation requirements. No two communities in a state and no two states in this country are exactly alike, which is a truth frequently unrecognized or ignored by higher level government programs. All of these points are most applicable as criticisms of the federal attitude as exemplified by a few examples to be discussed in this chapter.

Lack of Federal Government Coordination

First, however, there is one other disturbing element that should be obvious to any careful observer of both the history and the operation of our federal system. For years Congress and federal administrators have stressed the need for and the importance of local cooperation and coordination. Any number of legislative acts and administrative fiats have sought to enforce such interrelated effort. These have included most of the programs dealing with housing and urban renewal, highways and urban transportation, environmental protection, and any one of many others relating to the distribution of federal dollars. It might be said that the feds have become masters at the use of the "carrot and big stick" technique. One example is the coercive action resulting in the creation of councils of governments with authority to review local requests for federal dollars ostensibly for the purpose of achieving local coordination. It can be pointed out in instance after instance how these policies and programs have done more to shape, or misshape, the built urban form than all local planning lumped together.

The irony of this is that not since the first 100 days of President Franklin Roosevelt's administration, when Department of Interior Secretary Harold L. Ickes created the National Planning Board (later, the National Resources Committee and, in 1939, the National Resources Planning Board), has there been any attempt on the part of the federal government to achieve centralized coordination and sensible allocation of resources between Washington and the states. Given the task assigned to it as well as the power it had to interfere with pork-barrel practices, it hardly seems necessary to wonder why Congress abolished the board in 1943.

To be brutally honest, it is doubtful that any student of our national system of governmental operation can dispute factually the statement that the most uncoordinated, noncooperative, and least interactive level of government in this country is the one operated in Washington, D.C. This is evident throughout the departments including each division and bureau of which they are comprised. As one example, within the Department of Interior there are five major agencies, each charged with various aspects of administration, management, planning, development, and acquisition or disposal of public lands. Past performance has illustrated a lack of willingness to work together under one policy or to cooperatively coordinate among themselves. Instead there is constant defense of turf, in-fighting for authority and control, and a resultant struggle for protecting funding allocations and seeking additional appropriations. The same is true within the Department of Transportation, the Department of Housing and Urban Development, and any other you may choose. Probably the best example of all is the wonderful "cooperation" between the Department of Defense, the State Department, and the Office of Management and Budget!

The Interior Department is one example that reflects outside forces at work that directly or indirectly affect the efforts of all local governments in attempting to shape their urban forms and, in essence, their future destiny and quality of life. There are many such forces around, some of which are not recognized by local officials as having the impact they do on their day-to-day functions.

The Absence of a National Land Use Policy

The fact that no national policy exists on resources or land use for public or private lands can have a detrimental effect on local planning and shaping urban land when properties under the control of Washington agencies are sold, leased, or developed. The closing of a military base, for example, not only can affect the character of surrounding private development, but also the overall community economy. The reverse of this, creation of a new federal facility in the immediate vicinity, does the same thing in an inverted way. A good illustration of this was the location of the Air Force Academy and some space development facilities near Colorado Springs, Colorado. The potential for future growth of the city contributed heavily to the reasons why a European developer purchased some 22,000 acres between the eastern edge of the city and the site of possible additional space facilities development. This developer succeeded in convincing the city to annex his entire parcel. Immediately the comprehensive plan for the city, its zoning, its capital improvements program, and the preservation of a quality, central city business area all needed major rethinking and revision. Several years later, lending institutions foreclosed on this developer's land and it is now questionable whether the planned development will ever occur. An even more vivid example is what will happen to nearby urban form when the 60-square-mile site of the Superconducting Super Collider Project is under construction or is completed in the chosen location in Texas.

EXAMPLES OF OTHER FEDERAL INFLUENCE

As was implied at the beginning of this chapter, the greatest generator of forces over which local governments have no control are the result of legislation, policies, and administrative fiats imposed by the federal government. To emphasize the lasting adverse effect of some of those actions on local government urban form, it is only necessary to address some examples that can be considered as having the most far reaching and lasting influence.

Philosophy of Land As A Commodity

It is appropriate to reach back into the 19th century to remind ourselves of an action that changed the attitude of this country about land ownership in general. This was the Homestead Act of 1862 in which the U.S. government provided 160 acres of land to settlers for development as farms. A measure with a lofty and commendable objective but one which can be directly credited with beginning a change in our society which has reached its vertex during recent decades. In the simplest terms, this was the change from considering land as a community asset in which there was a well-recognized community interest to thinking of land only as a commodity with no recognition of any form of community interest.

The devastating result has been the tacit acceptance by far too many elected officials of a sophistical idea of land ownership carrying with it the "right," more correctly the privilege, for the owner to use it in any way he or she sees fit, regardless of its societal effect. Carried to the extreme as seen in today's resultant urban form, this can only be interpreted by a careful observer as including the maximum profit, even to the point of exploitation, from the sale thereof. Such action can eventually necessitate a subsidy from the public sector to correct the problems and damage resulting from the lack of the existence or proper enforcement of appropriate public controls. This public subsidy can range from bond issues needed to pay for infrastructure additions, improvements for schools or general operating budget increases for police and fire protection to more intangible effects, like loss of quality of life and increased environmental problems.

This change of attitude to the point where land is treated only as a commodity and the concurrent failure to accept that there is a vested public interest in the way land is developed is a strong reason why we have permitted the creation of the mess we have today in much of our urban form. This is what Dennis O'Harrow had in mind in 1958 (see Introduction) when he included an excerpt from a letter he had received from a local planning commissioner in an editorial he wrote for the American Society of Planning Officials newsletter: "Our chief trouble is that the planning commission is very largely composed of, and certainly dominated by, realtors, developers, and large property owners. To them land is a commodity, the owner of which is entitled to squeeze out the last possible dollar. They hardly realize that land is a national resource, and that every parcel is vested with a public interest."[1]

Federal Model Enabling Acts

After the World's Columbian Exposition of 1893 in Chicago, which was the beginning of the "City Beautiful" movement, local governments became more interested not only in adding aesthetics to city form, but also to recognize the need for land use controls and future planning for more orderly, organized urban development. Public controls of private land use development had not been considered as an appropriate function of government until the late 1800s and then were enacted only as regulations pertaining to uses considered to be a nuisance or a danger to public health and safety.

An ordinance reputed to be the first attempt at zoning was adopted by Modesto, California in 1885, followed by height restrictions established by Congress for Washington, D.C. in 1899 and by the city of Boston in 1904. By 1921, zoning land use controls had been enacted in 48 American cities and Secretary of Commerce Herbert Hoover proudly reported that this number had increased to 218 by 1923. Planning as a local governmental function also began to increase as a result of the creation of the first official commission for planning, authorized by an act of the Connecticut state legislature changing the charter of the city of Hartford, in 1907, to permit such an agency.

With the growing interest in both zoning and planning by cities, including the creation of planning boards or commissions by several states, some form of enabling legislation had been adopted in ten states by 1919, and in 1921 ten other states did likewise. Having a personal interest in encouraging zoning activity and recognizing a need for some standardization of state enabling legislation, Secretary Hoover in 1921 appointed a committee to draft a standard state zoning enabling act. By 1922 the committee had prepared a draft document that was circulated in mimeographed form with a final version later issued by the Government Printing Office. This was followed by a suggested Standard City Planning Enabling Act in 1927 with a final form printed and officially released in 1928.

With the highly laudable objective of seeking to encourage zoning and planning action and to provide model guides for doing so, why is there any justification for discussion of them in a chapter on superimposed forces that may well be of adverse influence on shaping of urban form by local governments? Careful study of the original provisions and its imprecise wording together with the benefit of some sixty years of experience can provide several logical reasons for doing so.

First and foremost is that in spite of all good intentions, the pattern set by the model act was that of putting the cart before the horse. The 1922 zoning model encouraged state legislatures to enact zoning enabling legislation that allowed local governments to adopt zoning ordinances without having a planning function. By doing so the implication was made that there was no necessity to give any consideration to comprehensive planning, something that was not precisely corrected by the 1928 planning model. The result of this was to create the unfortunate impression that zoning and planning are totally separate functions, independent of and not necessarily related to each other. The failure of a federal agency to resolutely tie together these two fundamental instruments for shaping the urban form has proved to be most unfortunate. Giving the appearance of sanctioning this separateness of zoning from planning has made much more difficult the task of developing the understanding that total comprehensive planning should be an essential basis for all land use controls. More detailed evidence indicating that we continue to struggle with the problems passed on to us by the models has been provided in Mel Scott's scholarly review of city planning in this country in his excellent book, *American City Planning Since 1980*.[2]

The Major Adverse Forces Affecting Urban Form

There are many other outside forces that have played an important role in aiding or hindering comprehensive planning for local urban form which could be discussed in equal detail but will be mentioned only briefly. These include military mobilization for wars and war itself, the Great Depression and federal action to achieve economic recovery, several of the federal housing and urban renewal acts, and the divisive Model Cities Program. More recently we have felt the effect of the Environmental Protection Agency's (EPA) requirements as well as, in some cases, the lack of effective action and sufficient enforcement authority by that agency. More will be said about a few of these in later chapters.

This summary of federal forces directly affecting America's urban form concludes with references to the three actions by federal branches of government that were the most destructive of existing urban form as well as strongly contributive to the inefficient, uneconomical development patterns carved upon the landscape over the last several decades: the policy of encouraging housing construction and assisting homebuyers by both the Federal Housing Administration and the Veteran's Administration; the 1956 Federal-Aid Highway Act; and the institution by federal courts of enforced racial integration through inner-system school busing.

Again, no one can fault the worthwhile objectives and grandiloquent ideas present in the conception and development of these programs. The obvious lack of serious consideration of the difficulty of administration, ultimate impact and spin-off, however, is readily apparent in the results evident today. How can a statement charging destructiveness be justified as applying to action taken to meet pressing needs and high ideals? The answer is not in the intention, but rather in the lack of comprehensive future-oriented thinking regarding basic policy and provisions for general application, which if addressed from a broader viewpoint might have avoided the resulting problems for impacted local governments and even achieved the commendable objectives.

Federal Housing Administration.   This is not the first time that the Federal Housing Administration's (FHA) policy on housing during the earlier days of its operation has been criticized as a destructive force on inner-city stability. Several well-reputed planners and other contemplative urbanists began to express major concerns about the agency's program soon after the conclusion of World War II. The central focus of this concern was the FHA policy of promoting new single-family housing primarily for the suburbs with no regard for the potential exodus from the center city encouraged by this action.

An example can be found in one of the reports prepared by Harland Bartholomew Associates in formulating the 1945 master plan for Dallas, Texas entitled "Your Dallas of Tomorrow: A Master Plan for a Greater Dallas." Comments made by the consulting firm were referred to and quoted by Mel Scott in *American City Planning*:

> Indeed, their report singled out the Federal Housing Administration for special criticism for pursuing a policy of promoting the construction of nearly all housing in suburban areas. This policy has hastened the process of urban decentralization immeasurably, they observed. The federal government, through its influence over housing policies and programs, is not encouraging comprehensive planning in cities, but on the contrary, is making more difficult its achievement.[3]

The result of this policy over an extended period needs little evidential support other than a simple observation of the rapid increase in urban sprawl, the degradation of center cities and the drained vitality thereof, along with the billions of dollars required to be spent by the public sector in providing the extension of public facilities and services. Unfortunately, this policy, to some extent, continues today in both FHA and the Veteran's Administration. The resultant travesty of ill-conceived urban form in the suburbs and the weakening of the economic and social strength of our cities is something for which everyone here today and those who come after will pay dearly, not just in a financial sense, but also in an irretrievable loss of quality of life.

Federal-Aid Highway Act. As if the policy of the FHA, and to a lesser degree the VA, was not enough of a threat to the inner urban areas, the 1956 Congress enacted a new Federal-Aid Highway Act. This legislation contained the largest appropriation of money ever to be earmarked for one federal program relating to aid for both states and cities, a total of $130 billion over a thirteen year period. While containing a provision for over $2 billion as federal aid to help states update primary and secondary highways as well as minor roads in general for the period from 1957–1959, the far reaching effect of the act did not stop there. It included an indication that additional money would be available thereafter.

The crux of the legislation, however, was that it charged the Bureau of Public Roads, armed with $2.5 billion, with the responsibility of constructing 41,000 miles of the original interstate highway system authorized in 1944. This earlier legislation called for 40,000 miles, however the 1956 act not only added 1,000 miles, but also greatly increased the appropriation for getting the program moving forward. It is worth noting that the justification for the 1944 act was highly touted as being primarily for the construction of a much-needed defense road network across the country. Because of strongly misconceived political pressure, the 1956 act was changed from that of an open country defense system to one that would provide access to cities containing state capitals as well as the vast majority of urban cities with populations of 50,000 or more. Included was a provision for some 6,700 miles of limited access, multilane highways through those urban areas.

As has been seen over the past forty-five years, Congress and the Bureau of Public Roads, working with autocratic state highway departments, superimposed this escape-route program on the cities without their planning agencies having any say about what the result might be to their cities. The result was about the same as if the federal and state agencies had taken a razor and opened the most vital artery of the life-sustaining support system of those cities, permitting the blood to flow without hindrance. No longer was there any restraint for those who, for one reason or another, preferred to escape the city for what developers depicted as "open country, freedom of life style" in the suburban and ru-urban areas.

The second silver spike had now been driven into the heart of the cities by forces over which they had no control and almost no input. The consequences were that those forces greatly enlarged and accelerated unguided urban sprawl, created an environment spawning suburban shopping malls which sucked the lifeblood from established central business districts, and, most importantly, did more to change land use planning and development in those cities than years of planning could prevent or undo. Intensification of development around every interstate interchange became inevitable, stable residential neighborhoods in the immediate area were blighted, and financial difficulties magnified for local governments by having to cope with and absorb the increased local traffic going to and from each interchange. Today most of the original urban interstate system has become nothing more than an elongated parking lot during peak rush hours.

It boggles the mind to think what that $130 billion could have done to preserve our established cities had it been made available to provide rapid mass-transit systems worked carefully into each city's future-oriented comprehensive planning. Again, this is well summed up by a quote from John T. Howard. "If a highway is so designed and built that it produces a pattern of land development and population distribution that worsens the livability and efficiency of a metropolitan area rather than bettering it, that highway is a disservice to the community—even if it carries traffic to capacity and all of the traffic seems to want to go where it is carried."[4]

From the damage done to cities over the years by highways superimposed without any consideration for comprehensive planning, the conclusion could be reached that highway engineers are often problem inventors, not problem solvers. Carried further this might suggest that efficiency ratings and promotions for these people are based on their ability to invent problems. How prophetic Frank Lloyd Wright was in 1906, as quoted in *Prairie Rambler* magazine, when he said, "The outcome of the cities will depend on the race between the automobile and the elevator, and anyone who bets on the elevator is crazy."

School Desegregation. Finally, the last of the triumvirate of programs mandated by federal authority that had an impact on urban land use in our metropolitan areas came from another branch of the national government and began with the Supreme Court's decision in the case of *Brown v. Board of Education*. This was followed by the passage of the Civil Rights Act of 1964 and the Elementary Education Act in 1965, both intended for the purpose of eliminating discrimination nationwide with the second specifically directed at public education. Again, a most admirable objective; however, the effectuation lacked thorough analysis of just what havoc the application procedures in some cases could have on America's inner cities. Using these authoritatively effective tools, the executive branch of government, through policies adopted by the office of the U.S. Attorney General, began a campaign to eliminate dual school systems where they existed and halt segregation in all school districts.

Unfortunately, the policies were implemented by court-mandated busing in the central core of some urban cities only. Soon after the Brown case, the filing of antisegregation suits in the federal courts became common practice throughout the country. The ultimate result was decisions by federal judges forcing school districts to achieve better racial integration by court-mandated busing where, in the court's opinion, it was deemed necessary. The actual determination of when and if a district had achieved equitable integration sufficiently to allow discontinuation of court-mandated busing also was placed entirely in the hands of local federal judges.

THE CUMULATIVE EFFECT OF THESE FEDERAL PROGRAMS

As I have pointed out in the discussion of the federal highway program and FHA mortgages, there is no doubt that suburbanization in the United States began in earnest after World War II. At first it was just the lure of the wide-open suburbs, mostly for well-to-do white families. A myriad of influences quickly led to an increase of the suburbs' attraction. Included were the impact of real estate sales and finance industries by their promotional activities, central-city financial disinvestment policies "red-lining" neighborhoods, and the quality of education in inner-city schools. It is obvious that the later application of school integration, especially the busing of children from a neighborhood school to one a far distance away, was only one further factor that may have contributed to the exodus.

If it is true that school busing, where it actually has been ordered, has contributed further to the decline of established urban areas it is a regrettable condemnation of our society. Nevertheless, many persons living in the inner cities have told me their convictions that busing contributed to urban decline probably more than the housing policy favoring the suburbs and the interstate highway system put together. Several white families told me that their major reason for moving to the suburbs was because they didn't want their children to be bused away from a neighborhood school. This has been the reason expressed most frequently, while others have stated openly that they did not want their children placed in a class with Black, Hispanic or Asian children.

The Cumulative Results

It is certain that for one or more of these reasons people have fled the cities like rats leaving a sinking ship. The more they fled, the more the sinking of that ship was guaranteed. As residents forsook the cities based on the effect of one or all of these three federal programs, the economic capability to maintain the existing infrastructure and public services already in place was drained off. Instead, the new suburbanites created demands for a repetition of those same urban services in the urban sprawl rapidly being created. Cities were left, to a large measure, with those who could not afford to move, had no school-age children, remained out of loyalty to the homes of their ancestors, or were the desperate urban poor.

The most unjust and devastating aspect of forced busing has been that it was applied to school districts within the center city while schools in the exploding suburbs were left to their own devices, inviting even more of those who disliked the city to escape the central urban area. In Detroit, where area-wide integration by busing students from the suburbs across district boundaries had been instituted, an appeal to the U.S. Supreme Court by disgruntled suburban interests resulted in an opinion declaring this illegal. It is difficult to argue against the contention that these three programs and policies have, one way or the other, contributed to the decline of America's urban form since the 1950s and 1960s.

The Root of The Problem

Again, I want to make it clear that I personally do not disagree with the desirable objective of any of these programs, especially with that of achieving racial integration in all our school systems, but I do disagree with the lack of comprehensive long-range consideration of the application designed to carry them out. I cannot believe that more applied foresight could not have devised effectuation methods which would have achieved even better the desired results with less disruptive affect on all inner cities. In fairness, it also should be noted that many social scientists do not place the weight on court-mandated busing as being the great influence on the flight from the cities as the opinions of some present inner-city residents and those who did leave have indicated to me.

There is no doubt that residential segregation is a complicated, complex social studies problem for which there is no easy answer. Opinions vary even among the social scientists themselves. Some believe, for example, that the drop in white enrollment in inner-city schools has been caused not only by court-ordered busing but by general population trends. Among these trends are the fall in the white birth rate and the aging of the white population in cities.

In a collection of papers written by various authors and presented as "A Consultation" to a Hearing of the United States Commission on Civil Rights in November 1985 entitled *Issues in Housing Discrimination* and a paper prepared by William A. V. Clark, Professor of Geography, University of California, Los Angeles entitled, *Residential Segregation in American Cities,* the effect of forced busing is evidently considered of such insignificance as not to have been given any mention. However, be that as it may, among many people, the debate on the influence of forced school busing, along with the federal interstate highway program and the federal housing policy, on the flight from the cities will very probably continue for some time.

STATE GOVERNMENTS' ROLE

Many state governments however, should not be held blameless for similar legislative action having an adverse influence on the ability of local governments to plan the shaping of desirable urban form in an orderly fashion. In these cases, however, it is far more difficult to excuse such legislative acts as having originated with high ideals and lofty motivations when, in actuality, their long-range consequences are simply not considered. Instead, even though the policies apply statewide, they are often the result of a desire for political retribution against a single entity of government, usually the state's largest city, or they are the product of some maverick legislator who is subservient to a vested-interest pressure group or a group that contributes heavily to that individual's campaigns.

Prime examples of these actions are found in states with a home-rule provision where a home-rule city takes some localized taxing action to benefit its economic base or the reshaping of its urban form. Some members of the state legislature may feel this action encroaches on a power of control that they want to retain for themselves. They immediately ram through a bill prohibiting such action to any city larger than a designated population, such as 250,000, of which there is only one in the state and thus the only one affected by the legislation. Though obviously discriminatory and in violation of the home-rule principle, the largest urban area in the state has no recourse other than probably an unsuccessful court appeal. This is just what occurred in Albuquerque, the largest city in New Mexico, shortly after the adoption of statewide home-rule authority. Such arbitrary action is always justified by dragging out the principle, frequently ignored at other times, that all local governments are creatures of the state and thus entitled only to do that which has been granted to them by a state legislature and conversely unable to do that which the state body denies. In other words, the legislature giveth and the legislature then taketh away.

Action Or Inaction Can Bring Adverse Results

State governments, like the federal government, have direct and indirect effects on the local development of urban form in a number of ways, some by action and some by inaction. The building of a new state highway or the improving of one by changing a two-lane road to four lanes can add to the potential for urban development or it can result in the loss of homes or other desirable structures and features like trees, shrubs, and even parks that contribute to the quality of a community. This direct effect also exists when the location of state facilities is decided without coordination with the local planning process. Conversely the removal of a state facility that is an employment generator affects both the stability of urban form and the economy of the area from which it was removed and, if relocated, the place of that relocation.

A state's failure to act when faced with an issue or an obvious problem can sometimes be more detrimental to a local economy than the passage of ill-conceived legislation. This applies to all levels of governments from federal to local. For example, the failure of Congress and the executive branch to be willing to adopt a national land use policy and to adequately protect our dwindling resources, including open space, is resulting in an irretrievable loss for all of us and our children. Equally, the lack of courage and sufficient concern for the future to bite the bullet and revise totally the taxing structure to a more fair and equitable one—as well as solving the deficit and national debt problems—all have serious consequence now that will increase significantly for generations yet to come. Although these serious problems will affect future urban form, their impact is obviously much broader and far reaching.

Inaction on the part of state government frequently contributes to the inability to resolve problems of major importance. This reflects the continuing conflict between rural, suburban, and urban legislators. Unfortunately the blame more frequently can be placed on powerful vested interest groups, the apathy of the general public, and the refusal of legislators to accept their responsibilities to look at the larger picture and act in the best interest of the public at large. Far too many state legislators are either obligated to organized, self-interested lobbying groups on a major issue, or else their view of that issue is limited only to concern about its effect on *their own* constituents who elected them from their district. My traveling around the country has shown me that this difficulty is present in a number of states although, fortunately, a few have been able to rise above some of these pressures.

Withdrawal of Federal Funding

Of even greater importance to the well being of some states is the failure of their elected officials to accept that the withdrawal of the federal government from financial aid programs related to planning, urban development, public facilities and social programs carries with it the implication that the resulting gap will be filled by state legislatures accepting responsibility to fill that gap. Such has generally not been the case. Instead, some legislatures, convinced that any proposal to increase the revenue base other than additional economic development is automatic political suicide, have acted as if ignoring the problems will make them go away. This has left counties and municipalities in a financial crisis as well as festering continued deterioration of education and transportation facilities, infrastructure, state services, and social programs.

A prime example of this is seen in the state of Colorado. In the late 1970s, the economy of the state was booming with state revenues increasing by approximately one third each year. With a surplus of approximately $140 million, instead of taking the long-range view and taking care of needed improvements then, the legislature sought to endear themselves to the tax-paying public. First they approved a tax refund to all tax-paying citizens with much publicity even though the actual amount returned to each family was not much more than a pittance. Next they eliminated the food and inheritance taxes and began income tax indexing that resulted in a loss of state revenue of $3 billion from 1980 to 1989. In the meantime along came 1981 and the changed federal policy about revenue sharing and federal aid programs.

In what kind of position has this placed Colorado today? With the bust that followed the lowering of oil prices and the cancellation of gas and oil experimentation on the state's western slope, a realistic analyst can only conclude that the state is in a desperate situation. To bring the existing capital improvements up to proper standards and to provide adequate assistance to meet lower-income housing needs, it was estimated (by a report entitled *Private Choices, Public Strategies*, prepared by a task force appointed by former Governor Richard D. Lamm in 1980) that between 1982 and the year 2000 a state investment of $234,425,000 would be required. Since then inflation has continued and the economy of the state has taken a drastic turn for the worse. In the intervening time period very little has been done to meet any of these needs.

In a five-part series of insightful articles, under the title *Colorado Government: Running On Empty*, the *Rocky Mountain News* stated that the costs for a catch-up in prison needs alone by the year 2025 would be $300 million and that public education had an immediate need of at least $44 million.[5] In a follow-up article it was reported that to upgrade the existing transportation facilities and provide the beginnings of a much-needed rapid transit system for the Denver metropolitan area alone could require as much as $6.19 billion dollars. To sum this up, two quotes appearing in the *News*'s five-part series in March 1988, seem to be appropriate here.

In that series a University of Colorado political scientist, Robert S. Lorch is quoted from his book, *Colorado Government*: "State budgeting in Colorado seems preoccupied with today to the excessive neglect of tomorrow." In the same article former Governor Richard D. Lamm was even more blunt. Speaking of the budget system and the state general assembly's fight over how $44 million for public education should be spent, Governor Lamm said, "They ought to be smart enough to know that Colorado faces big problems, and it isn't worth their time to mess around with all of this."[6] During Lamm's three terms as governor, the general assembly with their complete control of the budget abolished any semblance of a state planning agency by specific funding reduction, emasculated most of the authority of the State Land Use Commission, and completely killed a far-sighted executive order of the governor called "Human Settlements Policy." That policy's purpose was to encourage new urban development in existing urban areas and to discourage scatteration and urban sprawl. The choice of the policy's name was an unfortunate mistake dooming the order before it was even read—something of which no doubt most of the more outspoken opposing legislators were guilty. Colorado is a vivid example of the importance of the need for greater education for long-range planning, what it is, and why it is necessary, and the selling of this idea to each state legislator by all of us, particularly members of the planning profession. My visits to different cities made it obvious that this same effort is needed in several other states, especially in the southern part of the country.

Petition and Referendum

Before discussing more specific forces outside of local government easier to identify as having a direct relation to where we find ourselves today in planning, there is one other broad general force, applicable also to state government, that cannot be overlooked as one with which local government must contend. This is the greatly increased growth of "government by petition and referendum." I offer the disclaimer that it is not my intent to argue against the principle of this fundamental right in our society's governmental system. Rather it is for the purpose of providing two more examples of the need for planners, the planning profession, and appointed and elected officials with vision and a sense of the future to strive for clearer communication with people. This should be done with easily understood facts about planning the urban form, what we are trying to do, and why it is important to the future of each of them and their children.

Case Study #1. The first example is an illustration of the abuse of the petition and referendum process, certainly in the minds of those directly and adversely affected by the results, but to the reader it may, at first, not seem to relate seriously to the planning process. Hopefully the relationship will become clear as the story unfolds.

A lobbyist living in one of the Denver suburbs whose major employment came from apartment building owners and other interests contributing to the rapid growth of the suburban areas recognized a golden opportunity for expanding her power base. Capitalizing on an anti-Denver attitude she devised a scheme to end the city's horizontal expansion. She used the petition and referendum technique which, if successful, would lock Denver into its then existing municipal boundaries.

In 1902 an amendment to Colorado's state constitution was approved that allowed a consolidated city and county of Denver to be carved out of Arapahoe County, the county of which the original city of Denver had been a part. The attitude of the state's voters at that time obviously was quite different from what it had become by the early 1970s. By then the suburban and rural voters usually were against anything which might benefit Denver and it made no difference what issue was involved. Contributive to this attitude was the creation over the intervening years of surrounding suburban incorporated municipalities and the growth they had experienced as well as the action of Denver's Board of Water Commissioners in successfully achieving transmountain diversion of water from the more rural Western Slope lying west of the Continental Divide to the Denver area.

In the 1902 constitutional provision creating the consolidated city and county, Denver had been permitted to continue to annex contiguous areas even though all other counties in the state had previously been prohibited from taking over land in another county without a vote of approval by the voters of the county from which the land was to be annexed. The lobbyist, Freda Poundstone, recognized that concern about this feature of Denver's charter could easily be sold to people in the three surrounding counties as well as rural counties as an unfair special privilege which Denver should not have. She was aware also that Denver had one consolidated school district. The Denver Public School District was created so that its boundaries would be coterminous with that of the city and county of Denver. Therefore, each time Denver annexed land, the boundaries of the school district were automatically extended into the absorbed area. Therein hangs the tale.

As has been noted, to achieve desegregation, many cities in the country were ordered to initiate busing of school children from one school to another to obtain a better balance between races. Denver was one of these cities and presently remains under federal court jurisdiction. None of the school districts in any of the other twenty-one incorporated municipalities in the surrounding, fully urbanized metropolitan area were ordered to provide desegregation busing.

The situation gave Poundstone, her supporters, and all suburban and rural advocates of ending any further Denver expansion exactly the selling tool needed. Capitalizing on the innate prejudice and dislike of Denver by a large number of the state's population, Poundstone and her troops were successful in obtaining the necessary number of signatures to a petition to force a referendum by state voters. At the next general election in 1974, an amendment, referred to by most Denver residents as "that blankety-blank Poundstone Amendment," was passed by a majority of those casting ballots and Denver, as a consolidated city and county, was prohibited from further annexation by a constitutional amendment. The "Poundstone Amendment" gave Denver the same status as any other county of the state with respect to the law of annexation in Colorado. Therefore, except for a 1989 annexation of some 45 square miles approved by the voters of Adams County to allow the construction of a new airport, Denver became a totally horizontally landlocked municipality.

The sad commentary about this amendment is more than the strict limitation placed on the major central city of the metropolitan area along the Front Range. It is that the prime motivation of many of those in adjacent suburban counties that voted in favor of the amendment was a biased, emotional objection of court-mandated busing. Many of those were former residents of Denver who, when it appeared that this requirement was pending in the city, had fled to those suburbs so that their children would not be forced to be bused long distances or, in some cases, to attend school with minority children. While there was a contingent of voters who simply reflected their long-standing resentment against Denver, the prime motivation was the fact that the Denver Public School District followed the lines of any annexation and would have to impose desegregation on any area annexed. Naturally, the Poundstone promoters and advocates lost no time in seeing that this ember was fanned into a conflagration.

The effect of this action on the planning process, urban design, and urban form development should become obvious by now. In 1973 the city structures including those in the central business district still displayed a relatively low vertical profile. At about the time the Poundstone amendment became effective, Denver found itself becoming one of the centers of the rapidly growing oil and gas industry, and it was boom time again in the Mile High City. Newly constructed office buildings shot up like giant mushrooms, each trying to outdo the last one in reaching skyward.

Other than a floor area ratio (FAR) requirement, there is no height limitation specified for the central business district in the zoning ordinance. This FAR of 10 square feet of usable floor area for each square foot of lot area has been made meaningless by a list of "floor area premiums" containing nine ways to obtain bonuses of additional floor area by providing specified "amenities," all of which would have been standard requirements in a good zoning ordinance. In addition to this, a transfer of development rights from any parcel containing a designated historic structure to another location in the Central Business District (CBD) allows an increase in building square footage of up to 25 percent of the 10 to 1 floor area ratio specified for this district. Using these two methods of obtaining more bulk, some of the new construction exceeded the already generous basic ratio by as much as double, most of which went into additional height.

These generous construction "requirements" can be credited to, or blamed for, the lack of a strong planning attitude in Denver from 1968 to 1982. The mayor, the city council, and the city administration were all infused with the philosophy that there was no public interest in how land should be developed by governmental regulations. Consequently, the policy followed was that effective design standards were an infringement on private rights and the city had no responsibility or right to tell a property owner, especially commercial property developers, what they could or could not do with their land. The result was that during the boom period downtown Denver became the exploitive developers' paradise with the results from their increased density and towering office and apartment structures in the CBD and the adjacent neighborhoods furthering destruction of a sense of planned urban form in the central city.

From 1973 to 1982 the entire character, profile, and quality of development was transformed while Denver became known, as San Diego later was, as the nesting place of the construction crane. High-rise after high-rise seemed to appear almost overnight in the downtown area as well as in adjacent residential areas allowing multifamily buildings. The entire face of Seventeenth Street in the heart of the central city, referred to as the "Wall Street of the West," was changed with the demolition of many well built, sound, older buildings that reflected excellent traditional and historic architectural design. They were replaced by nondescript, tasteless structures copied from out-of-town architectural firms' previous projects in other cities. Since urban design standards were taboo to Denver's leadership, no building related to another or to the character of the area in its design. Perhaps because of the overstated fear of crime prevalent in our society, the ultimate appearance of these buildings presents a mausolean character that repels pedestrians instead of exhibiting a human scale that invites people inside to enjoy them. The resulting canyons of steel, concrete and glass are uninviting, unattractive and provide no reflection of the western heritage of the city in which they are located.

In other words, by the city's neglect of its responsibility to the public and the community, the quality of life and the opportunity to build a quality urban development character have been irretrievably lost. The travesty of all this is that had there been anyone in the city leadership with a sense of vision and a concern for the future who had been willing to fight for enactment and enforcement of standards to assure quality development the image of downtown Denver would be quite different today. In just ten years Seventeenth Street, the Sixteenth Street Mall, and even Fifteenth Street could have had areas of development emulating San Francisco's Embarcadero Center, the section of the downtown area near Harbor Place in Baltimore, and the fantastic urban development design of Portland's center city.

Instead, the ravages resulting from permitting speculative exploitation to prevail over established city standards are vividly apparent today in more than the nondescript high-rise monstrosities. The vacant parcels and blocks of land used only for parking lots in the very heart of downtown Denver are the results of another boom-and-bust cycle to which this city should have grown accustomed and been prepared for, but was not. At the height of the 70's boom, land in the central city was priced as high as $1,000 per square foot. Developers paid as much as $850 per square foot on behalf of Canadian, Japanese, British and Arabian investors, and then the bottom fell out and it was bust time again.

These investors, as well as the local land owners, either lost interest, could not arrange favorable financing, or decided to just sit tight and wait. During the worst of the economic recession the downtown office vacancy rate reached a high of 80 percent in some buildings with an overall downtown average of 30 percent. As a result, the asphalt paved parking lots came, serving as stop-gap measures while creating aesthetic scars in the urban environment. The economic conditions improved slightly in 1988 and began looking brighter with the construction of the new downtown convention center, but the economic health of central Denver still has a long way to come before its future as an alive and healthy business center can be assured.

Did the Poundstone Amendment cause all this? While the general recession cannot be blamed on Poundstone, you can bet your bottom dollar that it significantly affected the ensuing development that took place during the boom. The mental attitude of the administration and leadership of Denver after the amendment passed was one of panic and desperation. An already existing conviction that all growth, regardless of quality, is good was amplified many times over, becoming even more entrenched. When anyone questioned this high-volume vertical development, the answer was that nothing else could be done except permit greater height and intensity on the land area that we have, since we have been stopped from expanding our economic base by horizontal annexation. We cannot take the chance of discouraging those developers who have an interest in investing in our downtown by even thinking of strict standards. No idea of long range quality of urban form existed.

Case Study #2.   San Diego offers another example of the importance of planners and elected officials maintaining a close relationship with the electorate, keeping them well-informed, and listening to them before taking action to which there probably will be strong reaction resulting in petitions and referenda. In California every local government has been severely affected as the result of this citizen revolt technique. Seldom is there a general election in that state without a plethora of petition-initiated referenda, many concerning the way local governments can conduct their business, especially the levying of taxes. The most devastating of these was the infamous Proposition 13 passed in 1978. Those familiar with it know that it sets stringent limits on how much local taxes can be increased each year and, in addition, it lowered the previous base for real estate property taxation. Due to this referendum every local government was forced to tighten budgets, decrease services and reduce staff. Since planning, in the minds of many, is considered to be one of the more intangible functions of government, it usually has been one of the first programs targeted for reductions, not just in staff, but also in equipment, publications, consultants, etc.

The situation in San Diego illustrates how devastating this proposition, credited as the example that started taxpayers' revolts across the country, has been to planning programs. In 1979 the San Diego Planning Department staff consisted of 125 people. After Proposition 13 this number was cut to 80 where it remained for two or three years. As is usually the case, the first to go were those professionals involved in long-range planning. In the last few years the department has been able to make a few additions. All during this time, however, San Diego has continued to grow and in recent years has experienced another boom period with the resultant increased demands on the time of the staff. The planning function also had to adjust to another state-enacted provision, the California Environmental Quality Act, which requires every city to have an environmental quality agency with almost autonomous powers.

In San Diego specifically two major changes in planning policy were both the direct result of citizens petitioning for and successfully passing referendums. To begin with, comprehensive revision of the city's master plan was undertaken in 1965. After two years of work, dozens of meetings with citizens and public hearings, the plan was adopted unanimously by council in 1967. Almost immediately a group of disgruntled people started a petition for a referendum vote on the plan. Using the usual negative campaign techniques (such as this will hurt economic development, raise the price of homes, discourage business, and prevent job creation), the petition to question the plan's adoption was successful and at the next election the entire plan was overwhelmingly rejected, forcing it to be shelved by council.

Two years later the city adopted a growth policy containing a very advanced technique. It established "urban limit lines" around areas within which the city had infrastructure or felt that they could add the necessary facilities in the near future. Beyond that the more open fringes were placed in "urban reserve areas" where urban development was not to be permitted for several years. As is frequently the case, a developer proposed to build a community of 5,000 housing units in one of the urban reserve areas. Controversy arose over this and after a bitter battle the city council voted to approve it by a five to four vote. Citizen reaction resulted in a referendum that prevented council from approving anything in the urban reserve areas unless submitted to and approved by a vote of the people. Although seemingly representing a different public attitude than the one rejecting the master plan, this issue once again displays the power of citizen initiative and referendums in changing action of a city council.

These examples are but a few of the instances in which the ability of concerned and aroused groups of people working together have effected a change in everything from a zoning amendment to a change in form of government. As has been seen, the potential of this tool in affecting the planning process, both directly and indirectly, is unlimited. Even though sometimes used for a purpose detrimental to good planning and frequently by those having a personal axe to grind or a hidden motivation to gain publicity that serves personal political ambition, it is an essential privilege that should be preserved, but not abused. This power of the people should be recognized as a prerogative available also to those who are concerned about the future and the failure of political leaders to exercise vision, good leadership, and the manifestation of far-sighted policies.

The referendum technique can, and should, be used in a positive way rather than resulting from a negative public reaction. It is unfortunate that there still are so many community organizations and neighborhood groups that have yet to recognize the changes for the better that utilization of this privilege can offer them. For example, where a council has failed to adopt policies supporting a comprehensive plan, a referendum and a favorable vote of the people could achieve this worthwhile objective. This is but one of the many examples where inaction to protect the quality of life in the urban form can be overcome through positive action by the people themselves.

Special Districts' Role in Where We Are

Earlier mention was made of what has been permitted to occur in our metropolitan or "messopolis" areas and the influence of federal programs in contributing to some of the major problems of blighted urban sprawl. Over the last several decades there has been the growth of another serious contributor to the encouragement of this inefficient, uneconomical, and wasteful carving up of open land and green space. This time, while HUD and V.A. programs have aided the process, the major responsibility rests with state and local officials for the attitudes and policies that brought on yet another obstacle to good planning.

This newer problem is wholesale permission to form special districts for just about every function originally conceived to be that of elected government. As is the case with all governmental authority, except for the few specific functions allocated to the federal government by our Constitution, the states have the power to permit or deny local government functions either by legislative action or inaction. The abdication of responsibilities by state governments to the federal government during the more than forty years following the Great Depression left cities feeling more like orphans from lack of positive legislative action and leadership from their own state governments. State legislatures were all too eager and happy to have federal agencies take difficult problems and the provision of financial aid out of their hands. When the federal policies changed in 1982, few states were willing or financially able to step in and pick up the load and local government has suffered. Over the intervening years instead of positive state help, state enabling acts were adopted which further weakened the ability of municipalities to extend their boundaries by annexation and economically provide needed urban services.

The first such acts took place in states where municipal annexation laws were tightened up to drastically curtail horizontal expansion of incorporated physical boundaries. In almost every instance this was a result of agitation of rural and suburban legislators and their constituents who resented city expansion and wanting to avoid inclusion in incorporated municipalities (thus protecting themselves from what they believed would be the sharing of the tax burden of city dwellers). The irony of this lies in provision of public services. As the suburbs grew, in order to continue to have adequate urban services which new residents demanded, especially police and fire, these same areas were frequently incorporated into new separate municipal governments causing greater lack of unified, coordinated growth.

Autonomous Authorities As Special Districts. The concept of special districts has been deceptive and divisive enough to merit additional discussion. First it is important to understand that the separate and autonomous school districts are special districts, just as are all of the other various authorities created. The difference is that in the majority of school districts the members of the board of education running the schools are elected and directly responsible to the entire electorate within that district.

Such is not the case for many authorities in other types of special districts where governmental power is placed in the hands of an appointed board of directors. Their powers include the issuance of tax-free bonds, levying of property taxes to repay those bonds and, in some cases, even the power of eminent domain. Some of the larger authorities became so powerful that they have been known to defy the legislature that created them. This was the case on more than one occasion with the Port of New York Authority. People are still not aware that major projects such as the Pennsylvania Turnpike, the New Jersey Turnpike, the Garden State Parkway, the New York Expressway and hundreds of other similar projects were built by (and are still under the control of) a special district authority with governing bodies not elected by or directly responsible to the public. Special districts are now being used for nearly everything which originally was considered something only local, county, or state elected representatives were empowered to do.

Special districts come about because states required to operate under a balanced budget feel they must look for ways to undertake major projects outside of borrowing limitations or prohibitions. Unfortunately, the creation of authorities and special districts also frequently results from a lack of courage on the part of local, state and national officials when it comes to tackling difficult and sometimes controversial problems which should be a part of their elected responsibility. The method used to escape this responsibility is to establish a separate, autonomous authority or special district. This gives them an out when people complain about some unpopular action the district has taken by being able to say, "We can't do anything about it. It is out of our control—that is a separate agency." They fail to mention the fact that they created that entity and that they still have ways available to exercise control of what it can and cannot do.

The same has been true for counties and local municipalities. Where local and county governments are limited by state law in the debt they can incur and are becoming more tightly squeezed in their capability to finance the operation and services necessary to serve a growing number of people, they have turned to the authority and special district as the way around neglect by state legislatures. Like state governments, in so doing they engender a monstrous threat to the survival of representative government because of the loss of opportunity for coordinated growth as well as an economic, centralized delivery system of public services. Governments have succumbed to the temptation of using this illusory special districting technique for such diverse undertakings as soil and pest control districts, fire districts, park and recreation districts, library districts, drainage districts, regional transportation districts and just about any other governmental responsibility you can think of other than law enforcement. It could well be that the time will come when our descendants reach the point of regretting the day we opened that Pandora's box; in fact, some of us already have.

Where the two policies of (A) making it difficult for cities to annex and (B) passing loosely-drawn legislation permitting the creation of special districts were followed by states, an additional vital tool for achieving planned urban form was lost. The creation of regional systems for water and sewer services, interrelated highway and road patterns, coordinated recreational facilities, open space and land use planning were made much more difficult, if not impossible. Certainly the opportunity for metropolitan or regional government with an integrated system of public facilities and services was cast aside and probably lost forever. One notable exception was the action by the Minnesota legislature mandating metropolitan coordination by creating the Metropolitan Council in the Minneapolis/Saint Paul area. By subsequent legislative amendment even this organization has been made less of a mandating force and now serves more of an advisory and recommendatory function.

The Why and How of Special Districts.   In times of good economic conditions and rapid growth, developers see the opportunity to counter the arguments against leapfrog development as well as add an additional opportunity to make money. They seize upon the special district concept to create subdivisions and establish one or more such districts to provide water, sewer service, road construction, and even school construction. Should a state require an elected board in special districts, as some do, it is no guarantee of a genuinely representative board, since most special-district legislation allows the board to be small in numbers. Membership qualifications usually require only that each member be a property owner in or a resident of the district. It is the developer or the development corporation which forms the first board. Elections then, and even after residents move in, are frequently a sham. Assume the required number to constitute a board is only five. Who do you think is going to comprise that board? Obviously it will be composed of the developer and four associates or cronies who, one way or another, immediately become property owners.

When the development is being created by a corporation the board members are officers or employees of that corporation. As voter apathy is even greater in special-district elections—especially since many residents do not even know that they have a voting right—this inner-circle control can be manipulated for years. Some major corporations go so far as to create a "pocket" special district covering only the area where they have installed the water and/or sewer plants wherein they can maintain control of these services and the fees charged for them for the life of the project. If any developer, corporate or otherwise, wants to get out, the district residents are expected to buy those facilities, which is certainly a hidden expense to those homeowners. The potential for increased financial return to the developers and others involved frequently comes from the retention of ownership of the servicing agencies for which property owners must pay fees. In many subdivisions the purchaser of a home is automatically tied in to the services provided, for which they will pay a separately levied property tax to the district for retiring the bonds as well as a charge for this monopolistic service. Thousands of home buyers have gone into a new home without ever realizing that in addition to the normal county property tax and other local government taxes, they will be faced with a rather hefty additional charge for any special district services provided. There is no county or state governmental control over the charges enacted by the board of directors of a special district unless a state public-utilities commission is given the power to regulate them.

Illustrations of Special Districts.   Again using Colorado as an example, the Colorado Public Expenditure Council in a report released in 1987, noted that the state had 1,856 governmental entities when special districts were included. Of these, there were 63 counties, 286 incorporated cities and towns, 176 public school districts, and 1,331 special districts, each with taxing authority. Of the total property-tax revenue collected by all local governmental units in 1988, 10.24 percent went to special districts, a substantial increase of 6.21 percent from the 4.03 going to these entities in 1970. Very few people recognize that the steadily increasing bite of the taxing potential of any area served by a special district can have a serious adverse effect on representative governments in any taxing jurisdictional area, in other words any incorporated municipality or county.

The residents of Douglas County, Colorado, one of the state's fastest growing counties, found this out after it was too late to do anything about it. In establishing their ratings bond rating companies like Moodys and Standard and Poors look at the total of assessed valuation taxable and the taxes levied in any governmental taxing unit, whether governmental jurisdictions or special districts. When they conclude that the real estate tax burden has reached a point which property owners will not accept, their rating of all bonds issued within that jurisdiction is lowered. The result is that while bonds can still be sold, they will be harder to sell and will carry a higher interest rate thus again penalizing the entire tax-paying public. There were eighty special districts in Douglas County in 1987 whose total debt on bonds issued had risen to $375 million. This was of sufficient concern to the bond rating companies that they lowered the rating on any bonds to be issued by the county's school district and incorporated municipal units.

This situation is an example of speculative developers forcing the public sector to provide a subsidy while they continue to generate their profits. As a result of the tax load described above, Douglas County residents are paying in two ways. The first is by having to pay more taxes due to the higher interest rate, that is, if brokerage houses can find buyers for the lower rated bonds. The second is the increased risk of having all bond issues rejected by the voters since school and general purpose municipal bonds, unlike special district bonds, must be submitted to a general public vote. In the case of schools, if a negative vote occurs, much-needed facilities throughout the county would not be built to the detriment of the students and the parents in this burgeoning county. Occurrences like this also can increase taxpayers' resentment of continually rising taxes and lead to stronger support for petition and referendum efforts to secure an established statewide limit on the amount of any form of tax increase local governmental units can impose.

Needless to say, this adverse effect does not stop just with the schools. Incorporated municipalities will feel the pinch in their planning in terms of the further restrictions on the revenues that can be raised for public facilities included in their capital improvements program and in the resistance generated against further development by the present residents. Pressure for development in Douglas County, or any similar booming county, will not disappear because of the lowering of the rating of bonds the schools and municipalities probably will have to try to issue. The county planning department then will be faced with the choice of continuing to approve subdivisions and contribute to the worsening of the situation, or seek to get the county commissioners to agree to a moratorium on new development or adopt stricter regulations to achieve a slowdown. Should either of the latter possibilities occur it could be a perfect example of poetic justice for the ones creating the problem—the developers and their special districts.

Look Before You Leap. One caveat to suggest is that each of us become aware of the laws governing special districts in our state—it is to be hoped that the state in which you live has better laws limiting and controlling them than we do in Colorado. Even more importantly, when thinking of buying a new home, find out whether ownership will involve monthly payments to one or more of what is classified by many as an invisible level of local government—special districts. A property owner in Cherry Hills Village, Colorado failed to do this and, when she received her tax notice, discovered she owed $10,885 to eight different governments including $3,717 to the special district that had been created for the subdivision. She will be faced with paying this amount and quite possibly more, each year, as costs continue to rise, unless she sells the property provided she can find a buyer.

An even worse situation has arisen for some farmers in Adams County, Colorado. There, smooth-talking developers sold the county on approving a fancy, well-presented plan for a subdivision to be known as Barr Lake Village. To finance the public improvements they also obtained approval for the creation of the Barr Lake Village Metropolitan District, the broadest possible kind of special district which can issue tax-exempt bonds for water and sewer facilities, roads, and other public improvements. The developers convinced several farmers with land within or near the subdivision area that the sale potential for their properties would vastly appreciate as the subdivision was developed and persuaded them to allow their farms to be included in the metropolitan district, seemingly a very logical thing to do.

To finance the district the developers issued $14.3 million in bonds and succeeded in selling them, after which they proceeded to install improvements costing an estimated $3 million. The usual developer's happy success story up to here. However the unexpected that can happen anywhere, anytime, did. As a recession hit Colorado in the mid-1980s and the bottom fell out of the market for new suburban housing, the project never got off the ground except for the improvements installed. The sad part is that the farmers, without even knowing, or having any say about the bond issue, suddenly found they had been hit by the lightning bolt present when any special district goes under and defaults on the payment of principal and interest on the bonds. The property owners, those who bought lots with or without structures, and in this case the farmers who allowed their farms to be included in the metropolitan district, all became immediately responsible for paying any delinquent unpaid amount as well as all future payments due to the bond holders. Their only alternative was to call the bonds, provided they were able to raise sufficient funds to pay off the investors. Certainly not the kind of situation in which any of us would like to find ourselves.

This delinquency already amounts to over $3.5 million and is growing every day. One of the farmers has just received a real estate tax bill of $80,582.56 while a nearby farm of similar size, not in the special district, was billed for a total of $638.70 for the same year. Naturally the first farmer appealed to the courts for relief only to be told by a county district judge, "If a special district encumbers itself and the bonds don't get paid, people who can get stuck are the landowners." This is known as learning a lesson the hard way. Now there are over twenty lawyers charging sizable fees involved in the court action trying to straighten out the mess.

The principle of individual property owner responsibility goes to an extreme of which, again, most homeowners are unaware. Even if an area lying within a special district is annexed by an incorporated municipality, the individual property owners continue to be responsible for payments to the holders of the special-district bonds until they are fully paid either by continuing to pay the principal and interest or providing sufficient funds to call the bonds and pay the bondholders off. Should they default on the bonds they face the danger of losing their property or, at the least, have a lien placed on it.

As further proof of the dangers of this "shadow government," the residents in one of the Douglas County metropolitan districts have suddenly become responsible for the $4.45 million, twenty-year, general-obligation bonds issued by a development firm that has now declared bankruptcy. To try to salvage some of the damage, the development firm and the board of directors of the district have offered the bond holders forty-five cents on the dollar to try to prevent defaulting on the bonds. Should this Upper Cherry Creek Metropolitan District default on bond payments, residents of the district will be forced to bail it out through higher taxes.

These are but a few illustrations of how planning for efficient, quality urban form can be made almost impossible by an overabundance of governmental units especially when there is no means provided for assuring coordination between them. This results from carelessly drawn, ineffective state regulations and, in these cases, from what might well be considered negligent action on the part of the local county officials in allowing the creation of this potential for damage to their counties and residents.

CONCLUSIONS

In his book, *Planning in Government*, Melvin R. Levin stated:

> Since the 1960s, many cities have been in deep trouble. Unemployment rates are high, a sixth or an even larger fraction of their population are on welfare, crime rates remain intolerably high, public schools are in difficulty, and since the cities don't collect enough in taxes to pay for services, they have to rely heavily on subsidies from state and federal governments. It has been said that in the United States federal system, the states have the power, the feds have the money and the cities have the problems.[7]

What Levin does not point out is that federal subsidies now are almost nonexistent, a large number of states have not accepted the added responsibility for city survival and the plight of our cities has grown worse and more desperate with little being done about it. Perhaps it is as Rousseau stated in his *Social Contract:* "We must put up with a bad government when it is there; the question is how to find a good one."

NOTES

1. Marjorie S. Berger, ed., *Dennis O'Harrow: Plan Talk and Plain Talk* (Chicago: Planners Press, American Planning Association, 1981), pp. 193–194.

2. Mel Scott, *American City Planning Since 1890* (Berkeley: University of California Press, 1969), pp. 193–194.

3. Ibid., p. 401.

4. Ibid., p. 539.

5. "Colorado Government: Running On Empty," *Rocky Mountain News* (Denver: March 1988).

6. Ibid.

7. Melvin R. Levin, *Planning in Government* (Chicago: Planners Press, American Planning Association, 1987), p. 125.

2

Economics and
Taxing Policies

There are two important components basic to everything government does at all levels: economic forces and taxing policies. While each of these is generated from different sources, they are, nevertheless, interrelated. Fluctuation in economic trends, while stemming from the availability and use of private capital, is often strongly reflected by national governmental policies, particularly actions of the Federal Reserve Board and Congress. While levying taxes clearly falls within the public domain of government, the influence of these two components affect each other since national taxing policy must relate to the health of the general economy. When there are good economic periods, government can approach budgeting in a more optimistic manner and increase public-improvements spending and federal aid grants to states and local governments. It is imperative, therefore, to take a good look at national and state economic and taxing policies in order to understand the full gamut of forces at work outside of local government that influences planning and urban form.

1954 FEDERAL HOUSING ACT, SECTION 701

Without a doubt, the best way to illustrate this at both the national and state level is through an overview of the provisions found in Section 701 of the Federal Housing Act of 1954, which made federal funds available to aid local community planning. This, together with the Federal Highway Act of 1956 and the Model Cities Act, 1966, are the most vivid examples of an affluency of governmental policies that we have experienced since the Franklin Roosevelt era. All of these acts espoused the conviction that the federal government had a responsibility and a role to play in rebuilding America's urban form, including the provision of affordable housing for low- and moderate-income people. The contrapositive shock treatment of this occurred, of course, during the Reagan years from 1981 to 1989. It has to be left to history to show which was the better approach.

Section 701 of the 1954 Act began with a report prepared by a professor of city planning at the University of Pennsylvania, Robert B. Mitchell, for a subcommittee of President Dwight D. Eisenhower's Advisory Committee on Government Housing Policies and Programs.[1] Mitchell contended that federal agencies had never really understood or dealt with the problems of cities and they should do so by adopting policies to provide financial aid to help solve these problems on a broad metropolitan basis. Mitchell's position was that the federal government should not do the job itself, but should make aid available for this purpose and, with state encouragement and support, insist that cities and metropolitan areas demonstrate that they were actively involved in long-range planning and improvement programs. These recommendations were included in the report of the subcommittee with the strong backing of its members, most of them highly reputed business and financial persons, who were insistent that President Eisenhower support, and Congress pass, legislation to implement the recommendations. Such provisions were included in Section 701 of the housing bill and, together with greatly broadened urban renewal powers, were passed as part of the 1954 measure.

Another Carrot and Big Stick Approach

With the advent of direct financial encouragement for cities and metropolitan areas to organize new planning programs or expand master-planning activity where planning agencies already existed, a new plateau of federal involvement in shaping urban form began. This was made more emphatic by the broadened urban renewal provisions requiring a Workable Program for Community Improvement (WPCI) to be prepared by each jurisdiction participating in or applying for urban renewal funds. Under WPCI, each community applying for 701 planning grants had to meet seven requirements assuring that the local administration was prepared to be supportive of planning and the renewal process, or that this was already underway. In addition, the expanded law required that the WPCI must be certified as acceptable by the Urban Renewal Administration (URA) of the Housing and Home Finance Agency (HHFA), the predecessor to the Department of Housing and Urban Development (HUD). Thus the use of the "carrot and big stick" approach by federal agencies was further perfected with a corresponding increase in the intrusion of bureaucratic opinion and policy in shaping local urban form.

The Impetus Was Provided

The scene was set for these developments after the end of World War II with the return of the troops and the resultant accelerated lava-like flow of urban sprawl. Housing, roads, schools, shopping centers, and infrastructure were all needed. As usual, local governments, given only their own limited financial resources, were not able to meet the urgent demands, much less finance them or take the time to find guidance through comprehensive and coordinated planning.

As had been true since the economic recovery days of the Roosevelt administration, when a void existed as a result of inaction on the part of state and local governments, the federal government stepped in to fill that void. In the almost thirty years since Secretary Hoover's noble effort to encourage and promote local planning with the model acts, planning and zoning activity had continued to grow in states and cities in cyclical spurts related to broader national economic forces. There were major voids, however, in the lack of comprehensive master planning, interrelated planning, zoning and urban redevelopment, as well as inter- and intra-government coordination. These were the targets at which the 701 cannon was aimed.

Although there was a series of national legislative housing and redevelopment acts beginning in the mid-1930s, some of which contained federal financial assistance, it was the 1954 Housing Act containing Section 701, together with the 1956 Highway Act, which firmly placed the federal government in a partnership position with state and local governments in planning for urban form. This position was strengthened by a series of congressional and administrative measures over the next twenty years including the Demonstration Cities and Metropolitan Development Act (Model Cities, 1966), Operation Breakthrough Program (1969), Urban Growth and Community Development Act (New Towns–In Town, 1970), General and Block Grant Revenue Sharing (President Nixon's "New Federalism", 1973), and the Housing and Community Development Acts (1974 and 1977).

The theory of the 701 program was initially rather simple and its objectives were commendable: that states should be involved more in metropolitan and local government planning, that regional and metropolitan coordination should be increased, and that local governments should do more comprehensive long-range planning, even though the feds recognized that cities could not afford to do so on their own. To accomplish this, the 1954 Housing Act established federal funding of fifty percent of the costs of master plan preparation by metropolitan agencies and local governments. A state agency, approved by HHFA and later, HUD, would act as the conduit for this federal funding to local areas. At first this assistance was confined to cities with populations of less than 25,000 and "official" metropolitan planning agencies. Through political pressure, subsequent amendments to the legislation increased the population limit for cities to 50,000 and included cities, counties and groups of adjacent communities with a total population of less than 50,000 as well as state planning agencies that were conducting statewide planning studies.

Within a few years of the start of this program, states realized that they were funnelling federal dollars to local communities without having any meaningful review or approval provisions. In essence the national housing agency was contracting directly with local governments through the states without any say about the content of the plan material from a state viewpoint. To overcome this, many states started a grant-in-aid, frequently referred to as a "buy-in," program of their own and began to contribute twenty-five percent of the cost to each locality approved. Thus, by the time the 701 program hit its peak, the expense to a local government for having their planning staff or a consultant prepare a community master plan had fallen to one quarter of the total cost.

Everything was very simple during the first three or four years after the passage of the 1954 act. A local council decided, or a planning commission persuaded it, to have a plan prepared. If there was no planning staff, a consulting firm was hired to do the job. The consultants or staff planners knew the rules of the game and the firm or staff presented a scope of work within the guidelines and price limits set by Washington. The planning commission then approved the workplan and recommended acceptance by the governing body. When it was approved by council and the local share of funding was made available, the application was forwarded to the approved state agency, which assembled it with other applications to form a state program and sent them on to the federal agency. Eventually the entire scope of work was approved, the planning staff or consultant started work, and as progress was made, reports on the project were filed with the state to be sent to Washington for final approval.

The Rolling Ball Axiom. However, it was not long before the adage comparing federal programs to a rolling ball in a street came into play: after every rolling ball comes a running child. Applied to federal financial aid this is amended to "after every federal dollar of aid comes federal regulations and fiats of bureaucratic administration." So it was with the 701 program.

First, there were relatively nonrestrictive guidelines, then more detailed procedures were developed, and finally there was a long list of required "elements" that had to be included in every plan developed regardless of the size or character of the community for which the plan was being prepared. The places where effective planning for the future could be of the most importance—smaller cities and towns— could not see the need to prepare elaborate surveys and studies relating to elements which were more appropriate for a metropolitan area or larger city. Eventually the procedure and the processing became so cumbersome and time-consuming that city planning staffs and consultants began to lose interest in promoting the program and looked for other ways to advocate planning activity to local communities. The ultimate result of the demise of the 701 program, however, like almost all other federal grant programs, was the eventual elimination of money appropriated as a result of changes in political philosophy and constricting economic trends. It is obvious, however, that increasing controls and bureaucratic intervention contributed heavily to discouraging aggressive support in Congress for continuation.

Was It Worth The Money and Effort?

What has been the result of all of this? Are our cities and metropolitan areas any better planned or more efficient, and do they provide a better quality of life because of interrelated and coordinated land use patterns? How many workable programs were rejected completely by the Urban Renewal Administration as being unacceptable? Were the ones certified really effective tools for making our communities a better place in which to live and work? Or was O'Harrow right as usual when he said "What we need is fewer workable programs and more programs that work"?

Unfortunately, the answers to the above are not a clear "yes" or "no". Answers to judgment questions such as these always depend on personal opinions, likes and dislikes, and our own interests. Each of us sees life around us differently. Were this not so, local governmental comprehensive planning and the enhancement of the urban form would not be such a slow, painful, and frustrating process! The only litmus test, therefore, that seems appropriate for evaluating all efforts to reshape, preserve, construct, or enhance our urban form is that of honestly answering two simple questions: "Is this the best that we could have done?" and "Is this the best we can do for our future?" If we start from this two-pronged base it becomes easier to arrive at an understanding and a consensus whether we are evaluating our own neighborhood structure or judging federal endeavors like the 701 program or attempts to devise an effective urban renewal effort.

Approaching all of the issues proffered above with this basic test, how much simpler it would be to arrive, if not at complete agreement, at least to an acceptable common concern that could lead to greater unified action. Is there anyone with any degree of reflective ability who can honestly reply with anything but a resounding "NO!" to the questions put forward when they are couched in the terms of "Is this the best we could (or can) do?"

Having provided a somewhat philosophical method of evaluation, let us now return to evaluation of the 701 program and its related economic impact on urban form and the building and rebuilding of our cities. Here again, we have an example of federal legislation with a laudable fundamental objective, but lacking a meditative implementation process. For thirty-five years, debate has taken place about the value of both the 701 program approach and the earlier urban renewal efforts. Many have argued that both of these have done more harm than good to the creation of workable urban form. Just as many others, while recognizing that mistakes were made and some bad planning took place, still argue that accomplishments and increased interest in future planning outweigh the justifiable criticism.

Some of the More Notable Fallacies

One of the worst features of 701 was dangling the federal carrot of financial aid before uninformed, ill-prepared local officials and citizens. Other than the institution of the WPCI, which was often not understood, accepted, or supported by local governmental policy adoption, no attempt was made to educate the public about planning:

what it was, how to make it effective, and what necessary policy decisions were called for if it was to work. Even more frequently, enforcement of the intent of the WPCI was abrogated by political pressure through a call from a senator or congressperson representing a state where a specific community was having difficulty getting its application approved because of a faulty or inadequate WPCI. The buzzword of this period became "gamesmanship." How well you knew how to play the game with the appropriate review authorities and the connections you had in Washington and state governments could be the determining factor in whether you got approval for both 701 master planning and/or an urban renewal project. Professional capability took a back seat to the ability to cut red tape and get some "free" federal money for local governments.

During the height of the program in the 1960s, the most unforgettable illustration of lack of understanding of the planning process and the ludicrous extent to which the misconception of federal aid for this purpose as "free" money occurred. As a consultant I was invited to be interviewed by the elected officials and planning commission in a small New Jersey community that was interested in having a master plan prepared. Not long into this interview it became apparent that none of them knew anything about the 701 program, almost as little about an effective planning process, and further, they were not interested in learning. When I asked, after politely questioning their preparedness for undertaking a plan, just why they were interested in a master plan, the answer was honest and straightforward, but frightfully shocking. The mayor responded, "All our neighboring communities have gotten some of that free federal money and if we don't get some our people will think that we're not doing the job we should for them." Not one mention was made of correcting existing problems, stabilizing community growth, or preparing for the future. Needless to say, the request for submitting a proposal with a scope of work and a price was declined and that nice planning job was left for some other consulting firm to add to its list of clients.

What the 701 Program Did Do

On the brighter side, it must be said that there were some good things resulting from federal and state programs like the 701 program. Prior to 1954 there was little understanding about local planning and zoning and their role in building urban form and the word "planning" as applied to local governments was bewildering to many more people than it is now. There was no understandable or generally accepted definition of planning and, therefore, interpretation was the result of each person's previous contact with the term. While it cannot be said that such a definition now exists or that a universal consensus of the local-government planning process has been reached, there is certainly more awareness of the word. More people are talking about it, more politicians bandy the term about, and many more planning and zoning programs have been undertaken, some good and some bad, as a result of the federal approach contained in the 701 program.

For the purposes of this book there can be no doubt that the 701 program and the broadened urban renewal programs reflect dramatically the influence of federal economic policies and direct intervention on planning for and building local urban form. It is for that reason that extended discussion of this federal program is important.

THE EFFECT OF TAXING POLICIES

History may prove well that the most influential effect on our building Paradise Lost instead of Paradise Found has been the tax structure and taxation policies of the country, states, and local communities. Even though frequent band-aid remedies have been undertaken and delusionary revisions have been enacted, the truth is we have continued to allow an unrealistic, archaic attitude to prevail about an antiquated general taxing structure. Instead of coming to grips with the need for a drastic, more modern approach to taxation and having the courage to accomplish it, we continue to rely on the same theories and approaches that have existed for more than two hundred years.

The only real change for a brief period in the past was somewhat less reliance on real estate property taxes, although these are still very much with us and are now continually being increased. Add to this the income tax, sales taxes, transfer taxes, inheritance tax, user fees, license fees, and every kind of hidden taxation, including "sin" taxes that the fertile minds of the tax experts can dream up. Underlying this has been the fundamental theme of "No, No!" to any suggestion that the best thing to do is to rethink comprehensively the entire tax system based on economic and societal changes that have taken place, throw the old system out entirely and devise something that will work in the twenty-first century. "If it ain't broke, don't fix it" won't work anymore with our taxing policies and system. The system *is* "broke" and the proof of this is the national debt which can bankrupt the federal government and the evidence of thousands of local communities struggling to remain financially solvent. What is needed is a system based on equitability with everyone paying their fair share of well-justified expenses of running government, providing services, and preserving the environment and the quality of life. The old saying, "If you want to dance, you have to pay the piper" is a simple truth we seem to have forgotten, or prefer to ignore.

THE EFFECT OF CHANGES IN SOCIETY

As this country has grown, urbanization has expanded, societal life has become more complex, there are deeply ingrained social problems, and we find ourselves with several generations who have a new personal philosophy. That has been described as "me-ism," but this philosophy is more deeply devastating than that. It reflects the conviction of such people that, regardless of where they live, how little they invest of themselves in their community, and how little they can get away with in paying taxes, government owes them the provision of efficient services and the preservation and enhancement of every aspect of a good quality of life. At the same time these are the people who advocate and support the destructive force of taxpayer revolts, never pausing to reflect on their contribution to ineffective leadership and inefficient government by their failure to involve themselves in anything other than obstructive, negative endeavors. Their credo in life is always that it is someone else's responsibility and fault and "Why don't they do something about it?"

In our society there will always be those with this spectator attitude. The only way to overcome this is for those of us concerned about the future to resolve to increase our educational efforts, unite together, and strengthen our objective of improving the quality of leadership of those we elect to public office. We should do more to encourage these representatives to recognize that organized local planning—properly instituted—is the most effective tool available for building a community spirit. Bill Hornby, senior editor of the *Denver Post* summed this up very well in a column about Denver's latest master plan and the planning process. Headlined, "At Best, City Planning Isn't Bureaucracy—It's Democracy In Action" he wrote:

> This is democracy at its best. Party politics, ethnic and generational rivalry, commercial hopes, ego and id, and the many other human concerns

that are always on the civic table are mostly laid aside in this planning process. People really try to visualize, out there beyond immediate self-interest, the future of their place on earth.

The scoffers and the naysayers think this planning is a waste of time. The path from the plan to concrete political and economic action is so tortuous, so often taken a halting step at a time, that only the optimistic and the patient see much value in the dreaming. They do not realize that this dreaming creates the political dialogue and agenda of eventual action."[2]

In dealing with the spectator problem and our need for quality leadership, each of us would be well advised to keep Hornby's sage advice in mind.

Another aspect of the relationship of economic forces and taxing policies to community planning for urban form comes from the mobility of our population. When the east coast and the west coast areas undergo periodic colder weather, and are suffering an economic slump, the influx of population into the Sun Belt communities has a major effect on both the community they leave and the one into which they move. The receiving town or city must adjust to the unexpected population increase, bringing with it the need for increased municipal services, while the place from which they came loses a proportion of its tax base and purchasing power.

This problem is further exacerbated by our lengthened life span and the resultant increase in persons over age sixty-five. A larger portion of those reaching retirement age are looking for a less harsh environment and are choosing to spend their later years in warmer climes. This is especially true for Florida, Texas, New Mexico, Arizona, and southern California. Both the Florida and California legislatures have been forced to recognize this mobility as a problem and have passed rather stringent laws pertaining to local community planning, environmental protection of sensitive areas, and other measures mandating local government action with provision for state intervention in the event of inaction.

Writers such as John Naisbitt who depend upon trend observations for their material have contributed to this situation with their predictions. In his book *Megatrends*, Naisbitt named "Ten Cities of Great Opportunity" extolling these to be the areas offering the greatest opportunity and the promise of prosperity.[3] It would be interesting to be able to tabulate the number of people moving to the Sun Belt area based on these kinds of predictions, although it should be noted that

Naisbitt was very wrong about Denver, San Antonio, and Albuquerque. In fairness to him it should be mentioned that he did comment rather strongly about the adverse effect of major migration on the infrastructure demands of both the losers and the winners in the population derby.

In the late 1980s, when the full effects of the federal financial aid retreat and serious economic recession resulting from the oil and gas industry slump were felt, some of these "opportunity cities" have had to face the greatest economic crises they have ever seen. With inadequate state budgets, a crumbling and decaying infrastructure, financial institution failures, and rising unemployment rates—coupled with taxpayer revolts—some of the Sun Belt states such as Texas, Oklahoma, California and even Colorado now find themselves between the proverbial rock and a hard place.

WHAT ECONOMIC PRESSURE HAS DONE TO LOCAL GOVERNMENTS

The repercussions of these economic forces have not only been obvious at the state level. The most devastating effect has occurred at the local governmental level—the stepchild of our governmental structure. Towns, cities, and villages are placed in the dilemma of searching desperately for direct and indirect means to increase the tax base while maintaining quality growth in their urban form development. If a way is found to encourage growth and protect quality, the problem then arises of finding ways to provide the front-end financing for the upkeep of present services and infrastructure as well as increasing them in response to new growth demands.

Consequently, where states have failed to provide additional financial support to fill the gap left by federal aid reduction (and in some states like Colorado, where state assistance has instead been decreased), local communities have been forced into an almost war-like position among themselves. Each locality starts digging trenches and calling out its combat troops in the fight to attract the next shopping center or for that matter, anything a developer postulates will create jobs and generate additional tax income—what is referred to as "economic development." The long-run effect of these conflicts, generated by the fear of losing anything that may provide economic development, may well be that we are building a basis for a future bust cycle through overexpansion of unstable uses of land. This is especially likely in the case of multitudinous, ill-planned, ill-located shopping centers and other highly speculative commercial and industrial enterprises.

The Fable of "Prosperity Shopping Center"

Developers are very quick to learn the advantages that this "war" generates for them. When added to the already prevalent trend of turning the planning and zoning process into a bargaining and negotiating procedure, both good and bad developers operate as if they had all the aces. In other words, because of myopically conceived taxing policies greatly influenced by economic trends, a situation has been created enticing local governments into the "all growth is good" attitude—never mind the long-range public costs or any question of quality standards. Given this, the stage is set for the generally practiced developer technique of ignoring present zoning, obtaining an option on the cheapest land to be found, engaging an architect or landscape architect to whip up a quick development sketch and, then zooming in on the local planning commission or governing body.

Prior to this presentation the best known local attorney is hired to aid and abet the pitch which usually goes something like this: "Have we got a deal for you! We are going to build Prosperity Shopping Center. Here is a sketch of what it will look like. Ain't it a beauty! It will have 750,000 square feet, two anchor stores, fifty other stores and shops, add some $30,800,000 to your valuation taxable, create 500 to 600 new jobs, and produce $5,500,000 in additional sales taxes for your town. Off the record, we can tell you that we have had an expression of interest from first-class outfits for leasing more than 85 percent of the space even before we break ground. Now I know it is not zoned for a shopping center, but I have three real estate experts who will testify that this is *the highest and best use* for this land, so I am sure that getting the right zoning will be no problem. Oh, by the way, I should tell you that four of your neighboring communities have been after us to do business with them, but, if we can get quick approval on the zoning change, we would rather locate here. Just think of the adverse reaction of your residents if they should hear that you have turned down this golden opportunity!" The trap has now been set!

The esteemed attorney adds bait by erroneously citing several court cases purporting to show that denial would be unreasonable and illegal, even bordering on the taking of property without just compensation. The final bullet is fired when he or she righteously declares,

"Certainly, I would hate having to take my own beloved community to court and upset any adverse decision you might render." The trap has been set, baited, and is ready to spring.

Now we are at the moment of truth. The community developed a comprehensive master plan three years ago; it was approved by the planning commission and endorsed by the governing body. The zoning ordinance was revised, updated and sold over the objections of a few vested-interest people as being necessary to preserve the quality of life and provide more zoning stability for the entire community. At this moment the validity of both the planning and zoning processes are at stake because of heavy pressure to keep taxes down and presumably improve the economy.

At this crucial point, the vital questions are what kind of individuals have been elected, will they recognize that the moment of truth has arrived, how will they respond, and are there enough thoughtful, informed people among the voters who will support them if they take the action necessary to say, "No, we have a plan, we know where we are going, and we support it. What you are proposing does not fit our plan, will not be the best for all of us in the long run, so comply with our planning and zoning or take your project somewhere else!" How many of us, if we were in such a position, would do that?

Decreasing Stability of Planning and Zoning

The above situation is one reason we have a trend away from comprehensive planning and, when joined with the currently popular opinion that a plan hampers expedient political action and power building, planning principles stand little chance of survival. In times of economic stress the rationalization for emasculating the stability of planning and zoning is the delusionary concept that all growth is good, or in its worst form, the belief that it doesn't really matter whether it is good or bad so long as it produces jobs and tax collection opportunities. In addition to this rationalization, a broader view provides every reason to believe that many local elected officials and a large portion of the general public, motivated by dislike of "big government" and enamored with the credo of "no more taxes," have turned their backs completely on the planning process. They perceive it as boring and have fallen instead for the siren song of the product (pragmatic projects) because they can see results quickly and consider the pragmatic approach exciting and sexy. Where this happens in larger cities, much of the credit for development of such an attitude can be given to earlier short-sighted action by federal urban-renewal administrators and local urban-renewal authorities and their isolated project orientation.

As a consequence, we are faced with the development of two unfortunate conditions. The first is that of local policy-makers bargaining away long-range standards and the birthright of future generations under the guise of generating economic development and political expediency. In so doing they have passed on to those yet to come the burden of an extended subsidy from the public sector to correct problems created by their present irresponsible action—which contributes primarily only to private exploitation and excessive profits. There are untold examples of this in a number of the cities I visited. The second unfortunate development is that planners and planning departments are being relegated to a support role, and are becoming confrontation and conflict buffers who serve as negotiating agents and are therefore ripe for becoming the scapegoats when things go wrong. Further substantiation of this will be found in later chapters detailing some of the interviews in each city.

ECONOMIC DEVELOPMENT QUALITY

One other contributing factor to the woes of state and local governments, especially in states with distressed economies, can best be described as the "cheerleading" facade. The thesis is that all involved must talk positively and be excited and cheerful, regardless of the existing substandard quality of the product we must sell to overcome any economic slump. Optimism is one thing, but delusionary nonreality is something else. This attitude is represented by the sales pitches of chambers of commerce, economic development agencies, and elected officials in states experiencing troubled economic times. The fallacy in this is that it ignores the cardinal principle of successful sales managers and salespersons: first you must have your own house in order, have a good solid product, believe in it, and *then* you can sell what you have to reputable buyers and investors. Psuedo-optimistic salesmanship is successful only with schlock opportunists seeking the biggest bargain or best deal with very little investment of their own. It is a certainty that such an approach will not get very far with solid, long-term economic investors who ask penetrating questions and expect factual answers.

There is little possibility of any state, metropolitan area, or city selling itself as long as it operates with an inadequate public funding budget; has a decaying infrastructure; is neglecting the protection of its environmental quality at the expense of future generations; allows a continuation of a neglected and distressed educational system; and has no plan of where it is going or how it is going to get there. You cannot delude sensible, reliable investors into assuming an unfair portion of the cost to correct the problems which they know exist and expect them to buy your sales pitch that "This is the place in which you should invest, because we are telling you that everything is rosy."

Overreaction and No Action

Many references have been made above to our antiquated taxing structures and the taxpayer rebellion craze. As these have probably had the most influence on inadequately financed programs essential to attractive, quality urban form, one more comment about taxpayer resistance is not too redundant. In no way do I argue that there is not waste in government or that careless spending does not take place, nor should this be condoned. The position taken here is that everything possible should be done to identify wasteful or unnecessary spending, isolate those responsible, and organize support to throw the rascals out. In this way the specific irresponsible action is directly attacked and the entire system is improved, something that shotgun, knee-jerk efforts epitomized by taxpayer revolts will never do.

The fact is that such an overreaction to any problem almost always causes an even greater adverse effect than the ill it is intended to cure. Time already has proved that arbitrary mandatory tax-limitation measures forced by disgruntled taxpayers have caused such adverse effects and will continue to do so for some time to come. This ill-informed, emotional reaction is analogous to saying that because the Titanic sunk we should drastically restrict or eliminate all passenger ships, or because an airplane crashes we should do away with air travel. When the false front is removed from the expressed motivations of tax limitation advocates, it becomes clear that this is a rationalizing excuse for not wanting to be deeply involved and work to improve the quality of the people we elect to public office thereby improving the system, not destroying it.

Another process that does almost as much harm as overreaction to our achieving more effective and efficient government is the sin of sloth and omission rather than commission. We only need to reflect on a few of the revisions and reform proposals advocated over the years that contained excellent ideas which have been ignored under the mistaken time-worn reasoning that what we have now is the best we can do. The discouraging reflection is that the true motivation for this is always that the problem is too controversial and we don't have the courage to bite the bullet and take it on.

Let us turn again to Colorado as an example. Surrounding the city of Denver are five county governments. Some of the unincorporated areas of those five counties are just as urbanized as any of the incorporated municipalities of metropolitan Denver. Yet, the county enabling acts of the state, operating under laws created for rural county government over one hundred years ago, do not allow these governments to deal with the urban problems they have now. This is another reason for the development of the large number of special districts about which so much was said earlier. Through lack of foresight, narrow-mindedness, and fear of taking any action that might be controversial, the Colorado legislature has chosen to ignore a number of proposals that urged legislation allowing the creation of urban county powers for all or any part of the counties. The sin of sloth and omission by inaction can be, and in this case is, just as detrimental to achieving efficient government, capable of guiding coordinated urban-form development, as are misguided overreactions such as mandated taxing limitations.

The Colorado Front Range Plan. An excellent example of such lack of response and inaction occurred in Colorado some eight years ago. Governor Lamm was concerned about legislative inaction and the failure of government to adjust to changes and meet the growing needs of an urbanized society. To study the problems he established by Executive Order "The Colorado Front Range Project." The Front Range is that portion of the state lying just east of the Rockies and their foothills and extending from the Wyoming border north of Fort Collins to the New Mexico border south of Pueblo. This area contains about eighty-five percent of the state's population. Several hundred concerned citizens were appointed by the governor to serve on county committees and the overall coordinating committee of this project. These volunteers labored long and hard over a two-year period to study the Front Range–area problems and to make recommendations for planning for the future, including how governmental organization could be improved.

One of the subcommittees (called work groups), which I served as chairperson, was that on "The Roles of Government." From this work group, with final approbation of the total project committee and the governor, came some very fascinating, far-sighted proposals. The first was to revise Colorado statutes to authorize creation of urban counties and to allow such designated counties to provide urban services in specified urban-service districts. The second, even more imaginative and far reaching, was to convene a state constitutional convention for the purpose of creating an entirely new governmental structure within the state. The proposal was to abolish municipalities and counties and in their stead to create locality, district, and regional forms of government based upon population distribution and to establish a completely revised taxing policy and capability.

It is doubtful that even those of us with enough foresight and vision to offer such proposals dreamed that they could be immediately accomplished, but it is more certain that we at least hoped the recommendations would be sufficiently controversial to generate some thoughtful and constructive conversation and discussion. How wrong we were! Neither of these proposals ever got beyond being printed in the final report and presented at the project's wind-up conference. With all the publicity given to that conference and the reports submitted, not one newspaper, radio or television station gave these highly imaginative proposals more than three or four lines of space or comments. No editorial comments were made, no articles were written, and no radio or television follow-up took place. The legislature went the media one better: none of its members ever acknowledged that such a recommendation had been made. Several thousand copies of the final report were distributed and no voice was raised to advocate or question, so the general public was just as guilty of inaction as the legislature. The entire scenario is a perfect example of how to kill an imaginative, future-oriented proposal by ignoring it and pretending that it never happened.

This brings us back to the basic questions of how we can do more to preserve a desirable urban form and build it even better. Just what can and should be the role of planners, the planning profession, and the planning process in doing this? Do we leave the preservation of Paradise Found to splintered, struggling municipal governments or should the states assume a stronger role of leadership in policy and action programs? Would we be better off with a more standardized approach to taxes by putting the responsibility entirely on state government for all taxation and raising the necessary funds for providing local government, in whatever form it may be organized for the future, with equitable redistribution of operating funds, including those for education? Should there be mandated regional government with taxation authority and the requirement to institute equalized distribution of tax benefits from major economic development tax generators? Will such action overcome local municipalities' self-destructive warfare?

These are difficult questions, but they need to be asked, discussed, and thought through, and action programs need to be designed. Even if this does not happen, one thing should become more and more clear to all of us: we must seek stronger leadership in government and to achieve this we must elect political candidates who have proved they are not afraid to face up to those moments of truth that inevitably arise. Then, and only then, will we be able to stop the slide into Paradise Lost, a slide that unfortunately is already underway in a large part of the country.

BUILDING A STRONG, LASTING ECONOMY

The only way to build a strong, lasting economy in any community is to build sound, well-designed, attractive, livable communities with an efficient, well-planned land-use pattern and the necessary infrastructure system to serve it. All of this should be based on a community-supported planning process, the foundation of which is an adopted capital improvements plan and program. Without this approach we can never build strong, stabilized, economy-producing communities. Based upon the observations made and interviews conducted, with few exceptions, we are not now operating under the kind of planning support system that provides us the opportunity to build these stronger, economically sound communities.

The most important aspect of the planning process should be that of building durable-quality urban form. To make this happen each of us needs to become more involved with our local planning process. We need to support planning as being the only means available for us to work together toward making our future better and our urban form more livable. Building understanding and support for that premise is the one thing that the planning profession could have done effectively in the past and could now do, but has never done in a meaningful way. This education process to achieve planning's true objective of a better world for all would help make planning in all communities more successful, and also would meet the somewhat vested-interest objective of justifying its existence and gaining general public understanding and support for planning and the planning profession.

If you have read this far you know that a lot has been said about the realities we must face to build a better America. It has not been my intent to be pessimistic, but only to help us all face facts. One of the greatest problems we face is that too many of us don't want to do that, don't want to be reminded that things just are not what they should be, for fear that the thought might occur that we should accept more responsibility, be involved, do more. To encourage this, several examples will be given along the way relating success stories, showing that people can make a difference, and that planning can work to build a better urban form.

The Boulder Story

There is no better way to prove a point than by providing an illustration or an example. While it somewhat deviates from the body of the rest of this chapter, an examination of two cities' actual experiences with which I am familiar serves to dramatically make a point that I have argued for years. Upon reflection it will be easy to see the pertinence of inclusion here as the motivation in the action of officials of each of the cities has been based on economic and taxing considerations. The difference is that one took the long-range view with a determination to preserve what they had built up over the years and their quality of life. The other succumbed to what appeared to be an easy quick fix to immediate problems with a resulting sacrifice of community quality.

How often in the recent past I have heard elected officials and others express the opinion that imposing standards to assure a reasonable quality of product on developers will drive away economic development potential. This was the theme of Denver's administration when the quality of design of the central business area was permitted to be destroyed during the 1970s and the early 1980s. There are many examples to prove just how wrong this irresponsible attitude is. When the name of Boulder, Colorado, is mentioned, most people reading this book will envision a pleasant, attractive, desirable place to live and work. A number will say that they have thought of moving there. With its delightful mountain backdrop to the west, university atmosphere, and peaceful tree-lined residential areas, the city of Boulder and Boulder County have been cited by the media for their exemplary planning attitude, with local governmental administrations that know where they are going and what must be done to get there. This reputation is justified and it did not come easily or just happen. For a good number of years Boulder and Boulder County have been progressive and have had elected leadership with a sense of vision who have kept their eyes on the future community they wanted to build. Everyone seeking public office in the city or county knows that they must understand planning, be supportive of it, and have a plan for maintaining the quality of life in their platform to be elected.

There has certainly been an opposing force to this from the Boulder Chamber of Commerce and the developer community which have criticized the stringent standards established for planning, zoning and urban design. The greatest attack from the developers came in 1976 and 1977 when Boulder was one of the first cities, along with Petaluma, California, to adopt a growth management plan including limiting the number of building permits to be granted each year. This policy was first passed by voter approval in 1976 with a slim margin of 500 votes out of 37,000 cast. The next year the ordinance was adopted by council, revised twice, and withstood a test all the way to the Colorado supreme court; it is now serving as a model for cities and counties across the country, especially in California where growth management controls have had the greatest acceptance.

The most interesting part of this success story is that now, particularly because of the slack homebuilding market, the same developers who initially led the opposition have mellowed to the point of saying the idea is not all bad. In an article in the *Denver Post* written by Steve Raabe, one developer is quoted as saying, "My own thinking has softened quite a bit. Initially, I was quite resistant, but I am not sure I totally disagree with the concept now. The development community, to some extent, has accepted the argument that limited growth enhances real estate values and maintains economic strength by preserving the city's attractive environment."[4] That is quite a concession for any developer to make.

In the same article, former Councilman Paul Danish, the member who initiated the idea of limiting growth by building-permit control, said, "The single most important thing Boulder can do to maintain a healthy economy is to maintain a healthy environment. It is tough for the corporate culture to admit that, but they understand it." The proof of the pudding is that during boom times Boulder was the place in Colorado that could pick and choose from any number of highly rated companies wanting to locate there, and even now when the rest of the state is feeling the depths of an economic slump, the city is suffering less than any other community. While all the rest of them go looking for whatever they can get that purports to contribute to the economy, Boulder can, and does, still pick and choose. In fact, a lot of other Colorado cities rush to gobble up the development crumbs that Boulder has brushed off the table as being unsatisfactory for community character and standards—a fact the grabbing city will probably regret within a few years.

Boulder County has not failed to grasp this concept either. Several years ago, with the support of the city, the county commission turned down a major industrial corporation proposing to employ up to 5,000 people which had insisted that it would not locate in any place other than an area which had been earmarked for open space on the county plan. When the moment of truth came, the company was told that they could take their plant and go somewhere other than Boulder County. The philosophy of doing what is right for the future prevailed and, hopefully, will continue to do so.

Just a few years ago the county revised its master plan and rezoned a large quantity of land from intensive light industrial to a more restrictive zone for the reason that the county was overzoned for light industrial, in the opinion of the county planners. An out-of-town developer who owned 130 acres within the rezoned area petitioned to have the master plan and zoning revised again to allow him to construct a 1.6 million-square-foot office park where 3,000 people would be employed, even though the more restrictive zoning would allow 331,000 square feet of such use. According to the developer, this was not enough to justify his economic investment. The county planners and the planning commission opposed his request on the grounds that it would create a traffic overload on the servicing highway, have an adverse effect on sanitation, and would insert a major employment center into an area of sparse population. The county commission supported the planners' recommendation and again said either conform to our planning and zoning or go elsewhere. An appeal taken to court by the developer was of no avail and the county action was sustained. The case for effective planning and zoning maintaining quality environment rests!

For reasons such as these it is a simple fact of common sense that quality development looks for those places maintaining high standards, having a planning attitude, and knowing where they are going. Only the crumbs rejected from the quality table look for those areas with no sense of the future where, therefore, they know the policymakers can be hoodwinked and taken for a ride, because they have no idea of where they are going and no established standards allowing them to go anywhere other than downhill. Quality urban development, whether it be residential, business, or industrial, wants no part of an unstable, unplanned, uncontrolled environment as they know this is not a place to make a long-term investment. It is most difficult to try to understand why the vast majority of local governments do not accept and apply this basic truth.

The Contrast Between Two Cities

This section contrasts how Boulder has successfully protected its character and quality of life as compared to Littleton, another smaller city in the Denver metropolitan area. This comparison shows the value of maintaining an effective community-planning attitude in spite of the fluctuations in the general economy. On one hand, Boulder provides a perfect example of what I have been saying about the constant necessity of having people and leadership willing and able to make planning work. On the other hand, Littleton illustrates the fragile intangibility of maintaining the strong leadership and the community spirit necessary to support a continuing planning attitude in the face of economic-development pressures from both developers and people who become convinced that all growth is good.

Boulder is an oasis of quality in the desert of imperfection spread along Colorado's Front Range. I have visited there numerous times, lectured to classes on the Boulder campus, and observed the city with the growing feeling that what the people of this community have done can and should be done everywhere. Unfortunately the return trip to Denver and a view of the messopolis spread out for miles and miles against the foothills (from which Boulder has wisely shielded itself), provides a discouraging realization that "it ain't easy." However, such trips always serve to strengthen my belief that the tragic drama of the Denver metropolitan area didn't have to happen. *Planned change instead of changed plans can and will work.* Unfortunately, this will not occur until enough people realize the route into which we have been seduced to follow leads to a dead end.

Recently Neal Peirce, a nationally syndicated columnist noted for his interest in urban-form development and the environment, expressed some of these same views under the heading, "Despite Its 'Wacky Image,' Boulder is a Model for Urban Planing":

. . . A university town hugging the Front Range of the Rockies, Boulder prizes a lifestyle a few compass points off the American norm. . . . Everyone is into avoiding stress, living 'naturally' and healthfully. . . . Snicker if you will. Boulder also has a vibrant downtown and breathtaking mountain views unmarred by ugly billboards. A constellation of open lands constantly soothes the eye. The population has soared from 12,000 at the end of World War II to 85,000 today. But there's scarcely a touch of the ticky tack development that has blighted so many American communities.

Why? For 30 years, Boulder has developed and nurtured the most serious—and maybe the smartest—set of growth-management principles of any town in North America. The movement began when citizens recoiled at development creeping up the scenic mountainsides. It matured into a fervent belief that citizens can protect and control their natural environment.

Has slowed, managed growth hurt Boulder? No way! The jobless rate is minimal. And the city has spurned massive deals that would make the average business recruiter salivate in anticipation. One example: a high-tech firm that promised 5,000 jobs but wanted a piece of the city's open space. Yet when U.S. West recently was seeking a research-center site near open space, Boulder guided the big regional communications firm to an acceptable location. On its terms, without a penny of the tax write-offs or free land other towns were offering. Boulder won out.

Here's a town that has grown and prospered even while preserving its exquisite natural setting. The method is altogether replicable: Citizens relentlessly insisting on keeping control of their own destiny.[5]

The Littleton Story

Equally true is the fact that a community with a proper planning attitude and high-quality standards can lose both should its people fail to be diligent in seeing that they are retained—and if they instead become panicked or bamboozled into believing that a short-range economic development attitude is the better way to go.

When my students would ask for examples of where planning worked in Colorado, my response several years ago was Boulder and the city of Littleton, a southwestern suburb of Denver. At that time Littleton too had people and leadership who made certain that policy decisions were based upon long-range planning and implemented by excellent enacted standards. Not only did outstanding leadership come from the mayor and council, but the city for several years had had one of the best city managers in the country and a good director of community development. The people were supportive and insistent that the quality of the community as a good place to live and work be a prime objective.

After the bottom fell out of the oil shale energy boom in the early 1980s, most communities along the Front Range became infected with the short-sighted, quick fix, economic-development virus, and even Littleton did not escape the epidemic. For several years the city administration held a "Leadership Littleton" three-day retreat to which interested, involved citizens and potential leaders were invited. A number of years ago they asked me to be the keynote speaker on the opening day of the retreat. Under the title of "The Game of Life Is Not a Spectator Sport" I said:

> You are very fortunate in that you have had dedicated public officials, great leadership, and people with a sense of community.
> However, I believe Littleton today is facing its greatest challenge ever. You have arrived at a most important "Y" intersection and you must make the choice of which way to go. One choice is to recognize what you have and continue the commitment to preserving a quality livable community of a controlled size using only planned change. The other is, under the pressure that will be placed on you as this recession increases, to allow yourselves to be fooled into thinking that the only way you can survive economically is to accept any and all kinds of growth under the delusion of encouraging economic development, become a larger city instead of a delightful village, and lose all you have worked and fought for in the past. The challenge is that the choice is up to you.[6]

Regrettably I must state that Littleton became one of those places that panicked and chose the latter option. Elected officials, attitudes, and leadership all changed. The city manager referred to has departed and while the former community development director is now city manager, he is having to play under a new set of rules. Littleton still has the remnants of an attractive community, but changes can be seen that threaten quality and it is no longer referred to as an outstanding example of a city that knows where it is going and is going to get there through good planning policy decisions. The only people who allowed this to happen to them and their future are the people of Littleton.

These two smaller communities provide an excellent example of a lesson to be learned everywhere. One community stuck with its sense of direction, maintained its principles, and not only survived economically, but is thriving; the other decided either from fear of the future or being high-pressured by development interests to open the gates and lose that which had made it great. In several of the larger cities studied and discussed later in this book some similarity can be noted between their response to economic development pressures and the Littleton story. This example of these two smaller cities and the larger ones visited will also serve to point out that regardless of the size of the city the answer for building a quality urban form lies in leadership, community spirit and a recognition of the importance of vision.

The late Edward Abbey, devoted environmentalist, author, and raconteur once said

> The only thing more dangerous than getting between a bear cow and its cub is that of getting between a member of a chamber of commerce and a dollar bill.

NOTES

1. Scott, *American City Planning*, pp. 499–500.

2. Bill Hornby, "At Best, City Planning Isn't Bureaucracy—It's Democracy in Action," *The Denver Post* (January 17, 1989).

3. John Naisbitt, *Megatrends: Ten New Directions For Transforming Our Lives* (New York: Warner Books, Inc. 1984) pp. 250–258.

4. Steve Raabe, "Boulder Builders Mellow Toward Slow-Growth Policy," *The Denver Post* (November 21, 1988).

5. Neal Peirce, "Despite Its 'Wacky Image', Boulder Is A Model For Urban Planning," *The Denver Post* (May 28, 1989).

6. Herbert H. Smith, "The Game of Life Is *Not* A Spectator Sport!" Keynote speech, Leadership Littleton Retreat (October 11, 1985).

3

The Courts' Role in Land Use Planning

There is one principal source of external influence that is not given sufficient consideration by many of those serving on planning and zoning boards and commissions, or even by some elected officials. Failure to do so is an unfortunate oversight since it is the one influence that determines just what can or cannot be done through local government action effectuating future urban form. This force is the judicial branch of our government at local, state and federal levels.

Any court decision rendered establishes not only the legality of a specific action, but also sets a precedent for other courts to follow, unless upon an appeal that decision is overturned. Decisions of the U.S. Supreme Court continue to be precedential unless and until the personnel on that court or its members' viewpoints change to the point where a different opinion is rendered. For these reasons, those of us who are not lawyers need to develop an awareness and understanding of just how much the courts, through their interpretation of local land-use policies and action, have shaped the direction from which we have come as well as what we may be permitted to do in the future to build our cities.

The intent here is not to delve into this legal subject in detail, but rather to consider a few major milestones that are helpful in understanding where we are in the application of legal precepts in our day-to-day policy recommendations and decisions. Hopefully, this may be of benefit to those thousands of planning commission and zoning board members who make decisions or recommendations affecting the development of our urban form and our individual property values in every such action they take. As most people think of zoning when they think of land-use guidance, anyone interested in a more detailed discussion on this vital tool is referred to my book, *The Citizen's Guide to Zoning*.[1]

INTERPRETIVE CHANGES

Just as the ideas and attitudes regarding the role of planning in American society have changed, so have those of the courts in interpreting cases concerning the ability of local governments to guide, regulate, and restrict the development of private land. When regulation of private land use is challenged through a suit filed in court, the case usually is heard by a judge or, in appellate courts, by several judges without a jury being involved in either case. Consequently, it becomes evident that decisions vary depending upon the philosophy of the judge or judges rendering the opinions, even though the U.S. Supreme Court may have already set a seemingly different legal precedent in a similar case. One of the most interesting things about cases involving local government regulation of private land is that, no matter how many cases one has been involved with, either as an attorney or expert witness, there is almost always, in spite of precedent, some new wrinkle, technique, or procedure which offers a slightly different opening for either side to argue.

Not only do interpretations vary based on differing judges' viewpoints, but there is also a considerable difference in the attitudes of courts by geographical region in the country. A municipal action upheld in California may well be declared illegal in a similar case heard by a Georgia, Texas, or Idaho court. An overall generalization about any court's philosophy, especially state courts, is not something that can be safely stated. As an illustration of this, as late as 1945, while other state supreme courts had long upheld the basic concept of zoning, the New Jersey Supreme Court continued to declare it invalid because there was no adequate state zoning enabling act. Corrective legislation was passed followed by a gradual change of attitude that evolved over the years as urban and population density increased, municipal services were overrun, and new personnel appointments to the court were made. Excellent leadership was provided by then state chief justice Richard Hughes, a former governor, along with outstanding jurists such as justices William Brennan, Frederick Hall and Harry Heher.

Today, under the brilliant, far-sighted, and future-oriented chief justice Robert Wilentz, the New Jersey court is considered to be one of the most progressive courts in the United States. It has rendered some of the most far-reaching state and local regulatory decisions of any state court, all indicative of their motivation for expressing the protection of community interest. Not only does this illustrate the variance between state courts, but also emphatically substantiates the philosophy that courts can and do alter their judicial attitudes based upon changes in personnel as well as social mores.

New Jersey, California, Vermont, Oregon and a few other state courts have advanced from a hardline conservative view of the protection of the "right" of individuals to do whatever they choose with their land to a progressive view that recognizes the increased complexity of an urban society. They are giving increasing consideration to community interests and community rights in the development of land. Many state courts with a different philosophy still retain an ultraconservative view that "private rights are still supreme" as reflected in some of the southern, midwestern, and Rocky Mountain states.

The United States Supreme Court, however, is the final arbiter with authority to determine the legality of any action of an individual, a corporation, or a unit of government. Although we are taught, and we want to believe, that our rights are clearly established by the U.S. Constitution and the Bill of Rights, there are those who argue that the only right any of us have is the right or "privilege" tested and sustained by Supreme Court action. A study of the Supreme Court's interpretation of the Constitution and the effect of the different philosophies of its members over the past sixty years would show there is no guarantee that what was considered legal or right yesterday will still be true tomorrow, or vice versa. This fact is actually evidence of the elasticity, resilience, and pliancy of our Constitution, some of its greatest attributes.

Support for this supposition can be developed by a look at just a few illustrations of such interpretive changes. The first of these resulted from the Civil War (although we native southerners still prefer to refer to it as "The War Between the States"). Prior to this war, the idea of states' rights, a fundamental theory of the founders of this country, was considered to be a sacred, inviolative right. This changed drastically after the conflict between the states and was tempered even more after the Great Depression and the stacking of the Supreme Court by President Franklin Roosevelt, with the approval of Congress, in his effort to restore the economy of the country through federal intervention.

Could any drafters of the Constitution ever have foreseen the Supreme Court declaring as constitutional the myriad of federal aid programs, the control of state banks, and the assumption of federal authority instituted in the 1930s? This is certainly doubtful, but it surely shows the adjustability of that court based upon its composition and societal changes. Other illustrations include legislation upheld pertaining to school discrimination, fair employment, the refusal of private clubs to accept women and minority members, and even the usurpation of the largest tax source, the income tax, by the federal government. These examples vividly illustrate how what was once believed to be an inalienable right can be reinterpreted and designated an illegal privilege by the changing philosophy of the judicial arm of our government.

When Governor George Wallace stood in the doorway of an Alabama school refusing to allow black children to enter, there is no question that he and many others throughout the South believed that his action was clearly protected by the fundamental constitutional theory that the sovereign power of government is vested in the states and states' rights would prevail. Some of the more avid segregationists even believed they had the right to choose with whom their children could go to school. Their argument also included the position that blacks were provided "equal educational opportunities" throughout the South's segregated schools. The Supreme Court decision in *Brown v. Board of Education,* together with the Federal Civil Rights Act again placed this right in the privilege classification and established that it was illegal.

The same thing continues to happen today with the idea of private rights in land ownership. In the early days of this country's history, its vast unsettled territory and the sparsity of population allowed people the right to do anything they chose with land. As the nation expanded, cities were built and population density increased; this change is reflected in the greater number of decisions courts were called upon to make regarding land-use regulation. Their findings that upheld restrictions on private use of land increasingly sustained reasonable municipal action in the public interest.

PUBLIC HEALTH, SAFETY AND GENERAL WELFARE

As the country grew and cities developed, long-range planning was established to shape the physical form of land-use development and the supporting infrastructure to preserve and protect public health, safety, and general welfare. Shaping future land use, after the initial planning stage, means the utilization of legal tools that cause the plan to become a reality. These tools are zoning, subdivision regulations, and to some degree capital improvements planning and budgeting. Even though a community may have adopted a comprehensive land development code or a growth management plan instead of separate ordinances for zoning and subdivision control, their legality will depend upon the test of whether they conform to the fundamental principles of proper application of the police power. When, or if, any land-use regulation is challenged in court, the decision will be based on whether it is determined to be legal when weighed against the established and supportable principles of those basic tools previously mentioned. Another factor affecting the decision will be the ability to show the reasonableness and necessity of the local officials' actions taken in protecting the community and public interests. We have seen all too clearly that planning, without the adoption by elected officials of supportive policy and effectuating tools, will change nothing, achieve nothing, and one more plan will end up on a shelf gathering dust.

POLICE POWER AND EMINENT DOMAIN

While some who read this book will be well informed on legal matters, many may not have that advantage. Thus, a brief discussion of the theory of legal precepts applying to all local ordinances and codes relating to future land-use development seems appropriate. All governmental power to control the physical format of land development stems from two elements of constitutional law. These are the right of a governmental jurisdiction to exercise the authority of what is referred to as "police power" and "eminent domain."

Police power is the right of government to restrict and regulate private action, including the private use of land, without compensation paid to the individual for any presumed loss of a private right. This includes traffic regulations, health codes, building codes, sanitary codes, housing codes, law enforcement regulations and all other legally adopted provisions limiting what any of us may do that in any way would be harmful or damaging to ourselves or others. In the case of a zoning ordinance, not only does it tell a property owner what they cannot do with their land, but it also clearly states (or, at least, it should clearly state) just what can be done.

Police power has been a difficult principle to accept for those who speculate in buying land or for developers seeking to build, both of whom expect to be able to generate the greatest profit possible. Even more difficult for them to accept has been the growing concept that any development of any piece of land contains a community interest as well as a private interest. It is equally true that many of the conservative, free-enterprise landowners share this same viewpoint—those still believing that government and society have no right to interfere with whatever they may wish to do with land they own. Unfortunately, understanding and accepting this important concept of community interest in all land development remains just as imperceptible to many of those holding elected office and serving on planning commissions and zoning boards in our cities and towns.

The second constitutional authority granted to governments is eminent domain. This is an equally powerful tool that plays an important role in shaping urban form, especially the physical pattern of public capital improvements. Through its use government can acquire private land for a legitimate public purpose either by negotiation with the owner or, as a last resort, the power of condemnation. The main difference between eminent domain and police power is that the "taking" of land through the use of eminent domain, where in the public sector assumes ownership or total control, requires that "just compensation" be paid to the owner with no such compensation required under police power. No attempt will be made to explore the detailed process of the eminent domain function here as the procedure may vary from state to state and the purpose of this discussion is only to provide a basic understanding of the principle.

Since these two precepts are quite different in basic concept from each other, it is essential that care is exercised in making certain that any government action taken under the police power provision does not extend to limiting a reasonable use of land to the extent of inadvertently stepping across the very fine line separating it from eminent domain.

In developing a long-range plan, including the projection of future land use patterns, one of the most important elements is to identify the anticipated needs for public facilities, services, and infrastructure that will be necessary to serve existing development and projected growth. This includes public buildings, transportation facilities, water and sewer services, parks, recreation areas, and utility placement. The most efficient and economical plan will call for the location of these, including utility line placement, on privately owned land. Here is where the power of eminent domain and its use becomes essential in effectuating the plan since private property owners generally do not offer to donate their land or grant an easement to government or public utility companies; in fact, most are reluctant to sell, even with just compensation.

All planners and public officials need to keep clearly in mind several basic maxims when considering use of either police power or eminent domain in their planning. The use made of either one should always be based on, and supported by, thorough and detailed planning studies. Not only is this desirable for public explanation and to gain needed support, but courts are insisting more and more on the submission of tangible evidence provided by supportive documents when they review action taken by any governmental unit. Such documents are invaluable in convincing a judge of the reasonableness of the decision-making process used and the action taken by the elected officials—a prime consideration in any court review. In relationship to the zoning process, another fundamental to be remembered is recognition that the adoption of the initial ordinance or any subsequent revision has the potential of being challenged in court. Supportive documentation is vital and it must show how well the established principle mentioned earlier, but worthy of repetition, has been observed: a governing body taking zoning action must always be able to demonstrate that it is *necessary* for protection of the public health, safety, and general welfare. The charge that this is not the case will always be included in the complaint filed by the challenger's attorney, in addition to the broader charges of being unconstitutional, confiscatory, arbitrary, capricious, and the latest popular charge of taking of property without just compensation. More will be said later about this last contention of illegal action.

LAND USE ATTORNEYS AND EXPERT WITNESSES

Because it can be very lucrative, a number of attorneys have become land use experts. In addition, many persons trained in city and regional planning have continued their education and become lawyers as well as planners. Unfortunately, some attorneys representing a developer in land use cases charge a normal, or slightly reduced fee for their time, then tack on a contingency fee or "piece of the action" provided there is a favorable decision for the developer plaintiff. This piece of the action can be part ownership in the land, receipt of several lots in the subdivision, becoming a member of the firm developing the project or creating a special district for the developer, all of which are questionable ethical practices when done on a contingency basis.

From the standpoint of a local government having a suit filed against it, one of the most important considerations is to be sure that the municipal attorney is someone with excellent courtroom skills and broad experience dealing with the multitude of problems through which a city may find itself in court. Secondly, in view of the growing number of land use cases, it is most important that the attorney be thoroughly versed in land use law and the ramifications of planning, zoning, and subdivision policies as well as precedential court decisions. A good municipal attorney without these skills will be the first to recommend that a reputable land-use attorney be brought in to assist or even handle the case completely. Many very important land use cases have been lost by a local government whose attorney did not have the necessary qualifications and was therefore unable to advise them along the way or present a good argument for the defense.

A Case in Point

In an increasing number of states, the courts expect that a municipality sued about a land use action will present one or more expert witnesses, persons schooled and experienced in planning and zoning matters. The New Jersey Supreme Court insists on this for cases heard by lower courts. Following two far-reaching opinions by that court in landmark cases relating to fair-share distribution of low-income housing in New Jersey municipalities (*Mt. Laurel I* and *Mt. Laurel II*), that court also went so far as to exercise a very firm hand in affecting fair-share housing guidelines. In *Mt. Laurel I*[2] a number of exclusionary restrictions were included in the township's zoning ordinance, which prevented extensive low-density residential development. The court invalidated the ordinance on the grounds that Mt. Laurel had excluded lower- and moderate-income groups and proof of a discriminatory intent to accomplish this purpose was not necessary.

Tips on Testifying

Before moving to a discussion of a few important Supreme Court decisions, I would like to offer some suggestions for municipal elected officials, planning commissioners, zoning board of adjustment members, or planning staff persons called upon to testify in court. These are based upon my role as an expert witness in thirty-five cases in New Jersey, New York, Maryland, New Mexico, and Colorado.

1. Planners, municipal officials, and municipal employees should remember that when the decision depends on the opinion of the judge, he or she is the one you need to impress. You must show the thorough consideration that was the basis for either the action taken as a policymaker or the recommendation made to the elected officials as an employee. If testifying as a qualified outside expert witness, the judge needs to be convinced that you became involved not just because you are being paid to do so, but that in your professional opinion you believe sincerely that the decision made is reasonable and the only correct one for the public interest (or is unreasonable and wrong if you are representing a contesting private client).

2. All testimony must be thoroughly discussed in advance with the attorney handling the case. You must be honest with that attorney about any reservations you have about testifying.

3. The opposing attorney may subpoena you to give a deposition prior to the actual trial. Here the rules are quite different than in a courtroom and the primary purpose is a "fishing expedition" for the other side. The only people present are the plaintiff's attorney, the defending attorney, a qualified court stenographer and you. All kinds of questions may be asked, some relevant and some not. Your attorney can object, but only for the record being made by the court stenographer and all of this testimony can be introduced in the trial by either party's attorney. You can answer each question or refuse to do so, but the latter will undoubtedly be used against you in court. Here again, the skills of your lawyer become very important in protecting you and controlling the questions asked as well as providing you with the opportunity to correct any case-weakening answers you may have given. The reason for the deposition is to find a basis for attacking your credentials, if you are an expert witness, or to discover a weakness

in your testimony in general as a municipal official.

4. Therefore, it is most important that you are well informed, have studied all applicable material such as transcripts of hearings, and know the reasons for the action taken before the deposition as well as in preparation for the actual trial.

5. A cardinal rule for both expert witnesses and local officials is to *never, never* volunteer any information about which you have not been asked a specific question either at the deposition or in court. Answer the opposing attorney's questions truthfully and as briefly as possible. Under no circumstance should you try to be cute with your answers to an opposing attorney.

6. Equally important for local officials, both elected and appointed, is that you should not attempt to qualify your vote or your recommendation by stating you did not agree with this or that point in it, but you felt the overall proposal deserved the action you took or recommended. Legally, as a part of the responsibility contained in your oath of office or your professional ethics, as an elected or appointed official, if you disagree with any part of what has been proposed, you must vote or recommend without qualifications. Where you don't agree with any part of an ordinance or a resolution under consideration, as an elected official it is

your responsibility to vote against it.

7. If you are a professional planner and are asked to participate in any case in a community other than the one in which you work, whether you are employed by a private client or a local government, carefully investigate the case before making any commitment to testify. Make certain you can base your opinion on professional judgment, that you believe in it firmly, and that you can be accepted as a qualified expert witness. If this is not true or you are uncomfortable with any part of it, do not get involved.

8. For anyone testifying in a deposition and/or a court case, one caveat to remember is be on the lookout for opposing lawyers' trick questions. A good example of this is something I have experienced and concerns anything you may have written or where you have been directly quoted in print. Where this is applicable, you may find the opposing attorney surreptitiously reading something from your writing or quote and twisting it to represent a differing viewpoint than you gave in your testimony. The attorney will then ask if you agree or disagree with the statement, and should you fail to recognize it, you are a dead duck!

9. After direct and cross-examination have been concluded, the judge can ask questions of an

expert witness, usually for further clarification of something in your testimony that he or she may not understand completely. When this happens it can be jackpot time for a good witness! The lawyers on both sides dislike this situation, but they can do nothing about it. Any question a judge asks can only be objected to for the record with no argument or cross-examination permitted. A professional witness is then in the position of being able to enlarge on opinions already given, introduce additional information, and even philosophize, while all the opposing attorney can do is sit there and sweat. A final word of caution, however, is to beware of one of judges' favorite questions, especially in zoning cases: "In other words, Mr. Smith, it is a case of reasonable persons differing in their opinions, isn't it?" As an expert defending a municipal ordinance, if you give a "yes" answer to this it is the death knell for your side since that is exactly what a judge who is inclined to rule against your client is looking for.

In addition the justices established the doctrine that New Jersey communities must meet their fair share of the present and future regional need for low- and moderate-income housing. The township was given three months to correct the deficiencies found, and the court suggested that anyone dissatisfied with the revision could challenge it in court. The ordinance was then revised, permitting only twenty acres out of 22.4 square miles to be used for higher-density housing, and another challenge was instituted with the revision upheld by the trial court. The plaintiffs appealed and the state supreme court consolidated the appeal with five other cases regarding the fair-share housing rule.

This became known as *Mt. Laurel II* [3] and the decision confirmed and expanded the fair-share doctrine previously adopted. In it, the court held that the fair-share obligation was not limited to developing municipalities, but extended to all municipalities designated in a 1980 state development guide plan as growth areas. After *Mt. Laurel I* the New Jersey State Legislature adopted legislation authorizing the preparation and adoption of a State Development and Redevelopment Plan. [4] The growth designations in the plan indicate the municipalities subject to the fair-share allocation.

Also, in that far-reaching, oft-cited opinion the court asked for more specific legislative action on the fair-share obligation and the legislature responded by adopting a fair housing act in 1985,[5] which created the state Council on Affordable Housing to implement the *Mt. Laurel* doctrine. The supreme court then established three "Mt. Laurel" judicial districts in the state under its rules of the court and assigned a judge in each one to hear fair-share housing cases related to the *Mt. Laurel* doctrine. The judge could also hear challenges of the certification or denials of certification of the master plan's housing element submitted to the Council on Affordable Housing by each municipality.

Court-Appointed "Special Master"

All New Jersey municipalities are now required to have a master plan, which must be reviewed and updated every six years. Each of the three judges are authorized to appoint a "special master," usually a professional planner, when the trial court finds that a municipality's zoning ordinance does not satisfy its *Mt. Laurel* obligation and has ordered that it be revised. The rule of the court pertaining to special masters reads in part:

> To facilitate this revision, the trial court may appoint a special master to assist municipal officials in developing constitutional zoning and land use regulations. . . . While the appointment of a master is discretionary, we believe that such appointment is desirable in many cases where the court orders a revision of the land use regulations, especially if that revision is substantial. . . . At the end of the 90 day period, on notice to all the parties, the revised ordinance will be presented in open court and the master will inform the court under oath, and subject to cross-examination, whether, in his or her opinion, that ordinance conforms with the trial court's judgment. That opinion is not binding on the trial court. The master's powers are limited to rendering opinions, proposing findings, issuing recommendations, and assisting the court in other similar ways as it may direct."[6]

There could be no better example of how the outside force of the judicial arm of government has the authority to exert a far-reaching influence on local governments' development of urban form; this is the major point of this chapter.

Even if the state in which you live has not advanced to this point, it is still a good idea to make use of expert witnesses, since it is likely the plaintiff's attorney will use one or more in support of the opposition's case. For the municipality, the planning director or another member of the planning department staff probably will be used to present the factual information and supporting documentation showing the administrative procedures followed and the supportive planning information justifying the decision. That person however, is not permitted to testify as an impartial expert due to an obvious vested interest in being employed by the community.

THE APPEAL PROCESS

Most municipal and state court planning and zoning decisions, and even those filed in federal court, will not be heard by the U.S. Supreme Court—primarily because the Court could never fit them all into the calendar. Justices of the Supreme Court must approve the bringing of any case before them, even if the case involves an important legal question. After a review by one or more of its members, the Court may decide that the decision of the last appeal court that heard the case is appropriate and issue a statement indicating that they will not certify it for their calendar. When this occurs, the decision of the previous court of the highest jurisdiction is deemed to have been upheld.

Other reasons that many cases are not appealed to a higher level include the expense involved in the appeal process and the time it takes to move through the court system. Costs can be prohibitive, especially for a private individual disagreeing with a municipal decision. Another factor is that developers, as well as other individuals, are fearful that taking a case into court or appealing a lower court decision may end up with them winning the battle and losing the war. These people are aware of, or have experienced, the ways in which some local governments make it tough on those who have sued them, particularly if they have been successful in that suit. There are occasions where this is done by a bureaucratic slowdown of the application process, stricter interpretation of ordinances and codes by inspectors, and even adoption of a zoning ordinance amendment making just enough changes in the wording to say that the rules of the game have changed.

THE "BACK-ROOM" SCENARIO

An even more scurrilous action practiced by a few elected officials has a scenario like this: a very hot, controversial zoning matter is before the governing body and a large crowd of objectors has appeared and are energetically expressing their opinions. The council goes into executive session or declares a fifteen-minute recess before making any decision. With their municipal attorney and pertinent staff they reassemble in a back room. After a few minutes of discussion it is obvious that, for any one of a number of reasons, the majority would like to approve the applicant's request. These include vested interests of their own, a personal animosity toward zoning, economic pressure, or political considerations. The attorney tells them that if they turn the request down, he or she does not think that they can win a decision if the case goes to court, and the developer applicant already has indicated the intent to file suit if the application is denied. At this point some less-than-outstanding public servant on the council says, "Well, let's turn it down and let the developer take us to court, not spend too much on our case, and when the court throws our decision out, we can tell those people out there and other objectors that we did all we could, but the court would not support us." The sickening part is that I have witnessed such a scenario and that was exactly what the council did and exactly what happened!

This situation can also be reversed and it plays out the same way. Just assume that the veiled motives are strong enough among the council members that, for one reason or another, political futures need to be protected by openly supporting the development interests. Therefore, council approves the zoning change and leaves the burden of any court challenge to the citizen objectors. They know it will be difficult for a group of taxpayers to come up with enough money for lawyers, experts, and other court costs. The objectors, however, surprise them by successfully doing this and filing the suit.

The municipal attorney is now in the position of defending the council action at taxpayers' expense while the citizen objectors must pay the cost of pursuing what they feel are their best interests. The taxpayers must also bear a portion of the costs to have the case they are contesting defended by a public official. Council members have, on the surface, secured their position with the development interests and, should the objectors be successful in having a court overturn their decision, can individually state to their constituents that they really never were in favor of the project and are delighted that things turned out as they did.

Neither one of these scenarios present a very pretty picture and, fortunately, they are the exception rather than the rule, but there is no doubt that these political games are played. These situations re-emphasize the importance of all of us knowing our elected officials, observing their performances, and trying to ensure that high-quality leadership characterizes the kind of people we trust with shaping our future. Not enough of us invest sufficiently of ourselves in our own government to belie the rather pessimistic and frightening attitude prevalent in this country that all government is bad and just cannot be trusted.

Regardless of any implications otherwise over the years, the same thing cannot be said about those appointed to our courts. For the most part, the judicial system has maintained a high standard, both in the persons involved and the wisdom of their decisions. We have been most fortunate in the way that assuming a judicial robe seems to bring out the very best in people. This has been especially true with the Supreme Court. As previously indicated, the Constitution is a very complex, complicated, and yet flexible and malleable document. It provides the opportunity for personal opinion, philosophy, political conviction, as well as the type of legal training, background and experience to influence decision-making. The miracle of it all is the stability with which the Constitution has been maintained by persons appointed to the Supreme Court.

THE LANDMARK EUCLID V. AMBLER CASE

In spite of some who have tried to create another impression to serve their own interests, the Supreme Court's consistency has held true when the Court has reviewed cases relating to land development. The first case on the legality of comprehensive land use zoning was reviewed by the Court in 1926 (*Village of Euclid* v. *Ambler Realty Co.*). This case involved the constitutionality of the zoning ordinance of the village of Euclid, a suburb of Cleveland, Ohio.[7] So much has been written about this case, one of the most basic and famous zoning cases, that only a brief summary will be given here.

The village of Euclid had zoned a portion of village land adjacent to the corporate boundary between it and the city of Cleveland for residential use, excluding nonresidential buildings and apartments. Across the boundary, Cleveland had created a more intensive-use zone in which industrial development and other uses prohibited by Euclid had taken place. Ambler owned some of the land next to Cleveland's boundary with frontage on a boulevard running through its property in Euclid, which it wanted to market for apartments and commercial and industrial users. Ambler sought permission to have it zoned for these purposes and the village refused to allow it. Ambler then filed suit attacking the constitutionality of the village's action on the grounds that the residential zoning was a "taking of property without just compensation." The U. S. district court agreed with Ambler and ruled that Euclid's action was in violation of the Fourteenth Amendment of the Constitution. At this point the entire future of zoning in this country was in jeopardy.

The government of Euclid appealed to the Supreme Court, arguments were heard, and a skillfully prepared *amicus curiae* (friend of the court) brief was filed in support of Euclid by Alfred Bettman, a noted Cincinnati attorney and planner, on behalf of a number of organizations including the National Conference of City Planning and the Ohio State Conference on City Planning. The majority opinion, written by Justice George Sutherland preserved the right of the village, and local governments in general, to utilize the police power embodied in zoning to determine their own desired land use patterns as long as it stood the test of being reasonable for the public interest. A portion of that opinion—still the legal basis for zoning after sixty-plus years—provides support for my convictions regarding the presence of a community interest in the private use of land. See *The Citizen's Guide to Zoning,* [8] for a more detailed discussion and an excerpt from Justice Sutherland's opinion.

This decision once again justifies the argument that the judicial system is a force with a powerful influence on urban form. The entire zoning process, the right of American cities to determine future land-use patterns, and the repertoire of local government effectuation tools were on trial and at grave risk. Had the court interpreted the Constitutional provision for police power differently, the public would have no say about urban form development or government influence on private land use. The ownership of land would have carried with it the right to ignore community interests and exploitation of the public sector would have prevailed. Justice Sutherland's opinion was carefully drafted to insure that any such impression would be eradicated once and for all. Other related decisions since 1926 have fundamentally preserved this valuable concept, even though the limits to which government may go in the use of police power regarding private land have been adjusted or clarified.

THE "TAKING" ISSUE: FIRST ENGLISH EVANGELICAL LUTHERAN CHURCH V. LOS ANGELES COUNTY

The "taking" issue deserves a detailed discussion. The following case in which an opinion was rendered by the Supreme Court in 1987 deals specifically with taking. When the decision came out, pro-development lawyers were quick to seize on it and begin proclaiming in loud voices that the Court had either ruled that all zoning was a taking of property or, in a more modified tone, that it had greatly restricted what local governments could do under the zoning authority. These scare tactics not only were expressed by word of mouth and personal representation of developer interests before local governing bodies, boards and commissions, but also by articles appearing in newspapers and several national publications.

This sky-is-falling hoopla quickly diminished as more rational attorneys and other zoning experts analyzed the opinion calmly and realistically. The characterization of this as mere hoopla is supported by an article written by Dwight H. Merriam, a partner in the law firm of Robinson and Cole, Hartford, Connecticut, president of the American Institute of Certified Planners.[9] The truth of the matter is that the Court did nothing more than sustain what has been the law on zoning, eminent domain, and the taking issue since the beginning of zoning in this country. It said that no municipality can use its zoning powers in such a way that the line between police power and eminent domain is crossed over by zoning (police power) that denies all use of private property. Action doing so is considered to be a "taking" and the owner is entitled to compensation.

The case engendering this opinion was *First English Evangelical Lutheran Church of Glendale* v. *County of Los Angeles.* [10] In 1957 the plaintiff church purchased 21 acres in Mill Creek Canyon along the banks of the Middle Fork of Mill Creek in the Angeles National Forest. The canyon and the creek were a natural drainage channel for a watershed area in the forest. The church established a campground there known as "Lutherglen" which was used as a retreat center and recreational area for handicapped children. In July 1977, a fire destroyed the hills above the campground and some 3,800 acres in the forest, creating a potential hazard should a heavy rainfall occur. On February 9 and 10, 1978, a storm produced an eleven inch rainfall and the resultant runoff exceeded the capacity of Mill Creek and flooded a large area resulting in the loss of life for ten people. Lutherglen was flooded and a footbridge and the five existing buildings within the campground were destroyed; fortunately no lives were lost in the camp.

The county, in January 1979, adopted an interim ordinance prohibiting anyone owning land within defined boundaries of the interim flood protection area in Mill Creek Canyon to "construct, reconstruct, place or enlarge any building or structure, any portion of which is, or will be, located" in the designated area. The ordinance was made effective immediately as being "required for the immediate preservation of the public health and safety," but did not include a specified time limit for the interim period, a key provision in other interim ordinances that have been sustained. A little more than a month later the church filed a complaint of "taking of land" in the superior court of California, which, before the case came to trial, was amended to allege two other complaints against the county and the Los Angeles Flood Control District. The first was that the defendants were liable for dangerous conditions on the upstream properties left by the fire which contributed to the flooding and further, the church was denied all use of Lutherglen. The second complaint charged "inverse condemnation" and liability for cloud seeding just before the storm that contributed to the flooding of the campground. Monetary damages for First English Lutheran were sought under each count.

The California Supreme Court in another case (*Agins* v. *City of Tiburon*) [11] had rendered an opinion dismissing a taking charge in the city of Tiburon's placing of five acres of undeveloped land in a residential planned development and open space zone to implement an open-space element the state law required in comprehensive plans. Relying on this, the California lower court declared the complainants' charges in the First English Lutheran case "entirely immaterial and irrelevant, with no bearing upon any conceivable cause of action herein." The church appealed to the California court of appeals and, again based on the *Agins* case, that court affirmed the trial court's decision. A further appeal was filed with the California Supreme Court which denied review. Based on this ruling the complainant's (First English Church) attorneys appealed their case to the U.S. Supreme Court which "noted probable jurisdiction," certified acceptance of the case, and heard arguments.

A six to three decision was delivered by Chief Justice William Rehnquist, which if read less than carefully, could mistakenly be construed to close the door on flood-plain zoning and control of development within an area so designated. The Court did rule that even a temporary taking, where proven through the pursuit of appropriate administrative action, can justify the payment of damages to the owner of property. But, the opinion stopped short of clarifying completely the doctrine on the point at which any other stringent zoning limitations might be construed as entering the classification of a taking. The end result was that the Court reversed the judgement of the state court of appeals, and remanded the case to that court "for further proceedings not inconsistent with this opinion." In June of 1989, the appeals court reconsidered the case and rendered a rewritten opinion again finding that there had not been a taking. Lawyers for First English Lutheran can file another appeal to the Supreme Court and whether this will be done is still not known at this time, thus leaving the matter still unresolved.

Other Reassuring Comments

A number of views contrary to the immediate interpretation of the opinion by the development interests have been written by lawyers, including several by Merriam for "The Law and the Land," a publication of his firm,[12] that give a more careful analysis than the first shotgun blast salvos of those representing builder's and developer's wishful thinking. Two quotes from the majority opinion clarify the Court's interpretation of whether or not stepping over that line between police power and eminent domain had occurred. In the first, the Supreme Court distinguished between the California *Agins* case, which they had upheld, and *First English Lutheran* by stating:

> Thus in Agins, we concluded that the *preliminary* action did not work a taking. (Supreme Court opinion, p. 15, emphasis added)

The second defines some of the limits of their opinion in the *First English Lutheran* case:

> We also point out that the allegation of the complaint which we treat as true for purposes of our decision was that the ordinance in question denied appellant *all use of its property*. We limit our holding to the facts presented, and of course do not deal with the quite different questions that would arise in the case of normal delays in obtaining building permits, changes in zoning ordinances, variances, and the like which are not before us. (p. 16, emphasis added)

Two other cautionary views about accepting without question the attempts of development interests to try to convince us that the *First English Lutheran* case places normal zoning and local action in jeopardy came from the office of the general counsel for the National Trust for Historic Preservation (NTHP) and the associate general counsel of the Federal Emergency Management Agency (FEMA).

In the first of these, a cover letter notes that this decision had been misconstrued in the press as threatening historic preservation controls and assures members of NTHP that historic preservation ordinances still remain valid. The counsel indicated that the Supreme Court had addressed the narrow question of what remedy is available to a property owner, assuming that a governmental regulation has been invalidated as a "taking" of all use of his or her property, referring to the requirement of just compensation. Further, where this action is the result of an indefinite-term "interim ordinance," the owner has a right to be compensated for the temporary loss of "all use of property" between the time that the regulation results in a denial of all use and the time that the regulation is invalidated. Nonetheless, it is essential to recognize that the case does not in any manner change what types of actions constitute "takings" of private property.[13]

In the second opinion from FEMA, the associate general counsel expressed concern that the *First English Lutheran* case might be misinterpreted to affect the legitimacy of flood plain designation and the National Flood Insurance Program.[14] She summarized the opinion and indicated that the Court, even though it reversed the lower California court and remanded the matter to that court "for further proceedings not inconsistent with this opinion" had left the merits of the taking claim open for an additional decision by the appeals court. The Supreme Court had ruled only on the applicability of the just compensation clause to "temporary" regulatory takings. Thus the decision leaves open the question of what constitutes a taking. Further, she indicated that the minority opinion written by Justice John Paul Stevens, concurred in by Justice Harry A. Blackmun, and Justice Sandra Day O'Connor supported this conclusion and quoted from a statement made by Justice Stevens as follows:

> No matter whether the regulation is treated as one that deprives the appellant of its property on a permanent or temporary basis, this Court's precedents demonstrate that the type of regulatory program at issue here cannot constitute a taking. . . . Thus, in order to protect the health and safety of the community, government may condemn unsafe structures, and close unlawful business operations, may destroy infected trees, and surely may restrict access to hazardous areas—for example land on which radioactive materials have been discharged, land in the path of a lava flow from an erupting volcano, or land in the path of a potentially life threatening flood. When a governmental entity imposes these types of health and safety regulations, it may not be 'burdened with the condition that [it]

must compensate such individual owners for pecuniary losses they may sustain, by reason of their not being permitted, by a noxious use of their property, to inflict injury upon the community'.[15]

Thus we see that, while this is an important case and will undoubtedly increase litigative action against zoning regulation by local government, a definition of when an action under the guise of exercising the police power inherent in government constitutes a taking by the Supreme Court and requires compensation to the owner still remains unclear. To further obfuscate this question, between 1922 and 1987 nine cases adjudicated by that Court related generally to what is a taking and what is the proper remedy for a taking, yet none resulted in a clear legal doctrine which readily can be understood by elected policy-makers enacting land use regulations. The one thing that is evident and provides the safest guide for action is to make sure that zoning or land development regulations do not deny the owner of that land *all use* of the property even on an undefined temporary basis.

Nollan v. California Coastal Commission

The latest case relating to the taking question, following the 1987 decision of the Court in *First English Lutheran,* was another California case, *Nollan v. California Coastal Commission.* Here a state public agency was involved as a result of its responsibility to protect the beachfront and control access to the beaches along the coastal areas. Purchasers of a small bungalow and lot adjacent to the beach desired to replace the existing structure with a larger home. Approval for a building permit by the coastal commission was conditioned on the owners, the Nollans, allowing the public a lateral easement to cross that part of their property bounded by the high-tide line and the seawall.

Other aspects of this case, as well as comments on the above, are included in *Land Use Law, Second Edition,* by Daniel R. Mandelker:

> The Commission required the access dedication because the new house would contribute to a wall of residential structures that prevented the public from realizing psychologically they had a right to enjoy the coastline. The house would also increase private use of the beachfront and, with other development in the area, burden the public's ability to pass along the beach. The Commission imposed similar conditions on all but seventeen of the sixty development permits it had granted in the same tract of land.

The Court held that a taking clearly would have occurred if the Commission had required an easement across the Nollans' property and had not imposed an access requirement as a permit condition. The question was whether requiring access as a condition to a land use permit 'alters the outcome.' To answer this question, the Court reaffirmed the two-part taking test adopted in Keystone but elaborated the standard for determining when a regulation 'substantially advances' a 'legitimate state interest.'[16]

This is a reference to the case of *Keystone Bituminous Coal Assn.* v. *DeBenedictis* (55 U.S.L.W. 4326), another taking-related case decided in 1987. The part of the opinion referred to reads "We have held that land use regulation can effect a taking if it does not substantially advance legitimate state interests. . . or denies an owner economically viable use of his land."

The Nollan case seems to have contributed only to further muddying of the waters on the taking question and is sure to add to the possibility of any public agency facing increased court challenges in the future. This is supported in another article written by Merriam for a publication in which he also adds some worthwhile advice regarding how to better prepare for the years ahead.

There are far more unknowns as a result of the *Nollan* decision than with *First Lutheran Church*. The challenge for planners and developers alike will be to ensure that the most flexible regulatory techniques, such as floating zones and planned unit development ordinances, are preserved, even though they almost always use numerous conditions to tailor development to particular sites. There is a great need for more planning, both in the development of regulations and in the project review and approval process.[17]

A FINAL WORD

At this point it should be evident that conditions and special requirements in negotiating and bargaining in connection with adopted regulations must be scrutinized very, very carefully. Equally evident should be the vital outside role the courts, especially the Supreme Court, have played, and will continue to play in the future in local governments' shaping of urban form. This is another strong reason that land use regulations, decisions under those regulations, and all local philosophy related to the development of land should be based upon carefully conceived planning objectives and studies, not primarily on economic development, political expediency or because of a lack of courage to provide leadership. As has been said, it is true that all action taken in shaping land use within a city or town has some element of politics and is a political action, but it must not be the dominant factor in why a decision was made. A good adage to keep in mind is from Alexis de Tocqueville, included in a book, *The Wit & Wisdom of Politics:* [18] "There is hardly a political question in the United States which does not sooner or later turn into a judicial one."

NOTES

1. Herbert H. Smith, *The Citizen's Guide To Zoning* (Chicago: Planner's Press, American Planning Association, 1983).

2. New Jersey Supreme Court Opinion, *Southern Burlington County NAACP v. Township of Mount Laurel* (405 A.2d 381, N.J.), 1979.

3. New Jersey Supreme Court Opinion, *Southern Burlington County NAACP v. Township of Mount Laurel* (456 A.2d 390; 92 N.J. 158), 1983.

4. New Jersey State Legislature (N.J. Stat. Ann. 52:18A–196 to 52:18A–297, 1981).

5. New Jersey State Legislature (N.J. Stat. Ann. 52:27D–301 to 52:27D–334, 1985).

6. New Jersey Supreme Court, *Rule of the Court* (92 N.J. 281).

7. Supreme Court of the United States, *Village of Euclid v. Ambler Realty Co.* (272 U.S. 375, 47 Sup St. 114, 71 L.Ed. 303, 1985).

8. Smith, p. 25.

9. Dwight H. Merriam, "Land Use: The True Meaning of Nollan and First Lutheran Church" *The Connecticut Law Tribune* (14 CLT 2, January 1988), p. 13.

10. Supreme Court of the United States, *First English Evangelical Lutheran Church of Glendale v. County of Los Angeles* (55 U.S.L.W. 4781, 1987).

11. Supreme Court of the United States, *Agins v. City of Tiburon* (483 U.S. 104, 1980).

12. Dwight H. Merriam, "Taking Remedy Finally Confronted in First Lutheran Church," *The Law and the Land* (Hartford: Robinson and Cole, Vol. 2, No. 3, August 1987).

13. Letter To National Trust for Historic Preservation members from Catharine N. Gilliam, Director, Office of Preservation enclosing a Memorandum from the Office of General Counsel of N.T.H.P. (July 9, 1987).

14. Letter to Federal Emergency Management Agency Regional Directors from H. Joseph Coughlin, Jr., Special Assistant to the Administrator enclosing Memorandum from Susan Kantor Bank, Associate Counsel of F.E.M.A. (June 18, 1987).

15. Supreme Court of the United States, Dissenting Opinion (85-1199, June 9, 1987) p. 4,5.

16. Daniel R. Mandelker, *Land Use Law*, Second Edition (Charlottesville, VA: Michie Company, 1988), p. 43.

17. Merriam, "Conditions on Development Approvals Jeopardized by Nollan," *Land Use Law* (Hartford: Robinson and Cole, Vol. 2, No. 3, August 1987), p. 6,7.

18. Charles W. Henning, *The Wit & Wisdom of Politics* (Golden, CO: Fulcrum, Inc., 1989) p. 106.

4

Four Cities
That Have Made
Planning Work

The preceding chapters have provided some insight on the outside forces that have considerable influence on shaping our urban form, as well as those that are most directly responsible for the future development of our cities and towns—the local governments. Thus, it is appropriate now to examine the cities visited in more detail. Individual cities' planning processes are discussed in these next three chapters, while some additional aspects of the structural and political climates will be examined in chapter seven. The first step, however, is a more detailed analysis of some characteristics of each city, the policies they appear to be implementing, an overview of their successes and failures in making the planning process work, and most importantly, the effect on its people, now and in the future. The titles of chapters four, five, and six reflect my evaluation of the relative success of these cities in understanding and applying the planning process and the degree to which they have made it work to maintain quality in the composite urban form. The primary factors considered in establishing the categories of cities are:

1. The perceived planning attitude of both elected and appointed public officials.

2. The relative influence of the planning function on policymakers' decisions.

3. Methods of application of the word "planning" by elected officials, planning commission members and planners.

4. Involvement in and commitment by the neighborhoods and general public in insisting on good leadership and the building of quality urban form.

5. The maintenance or development of an atmosphere of pride and a sense of place and community by officials and the electorate.

THE CITY IS THE PEOPLE

Henry S. Churchill, a noted pioneer architect/planner once wrote a book entitled, *The City Is The People*.[1] This title represents exactly what I believe to be the most important aspect of any city, town or village; it says what has been emphasized several times within these pages regarding the need for leadership. In the final analysis, however, that leadership must be found among the people. There must be some form of common interest and motivation. There must also be a holistic viewpoint of the need for preserving the best of the present and, working together, building the best possible future. Recognizing the importance of these attributes, searching out effective leadership, and providing the support for it, is not present in many local communities or higher levels of our governmental structure today.

How extremely unfortunate that in general we have regressed into the kind of society, with a few exceptions, where the people have in some way or the other refused to be actively involved. When people are committed, where they elect good leaders and support them, planning and all other processes can and do work! The examples of the following four cities prove this, either by the way they are making it work now or by what they were able to accomplish in the past.

PORTLAND, OREGON

Portland deserves the Oscar for best planning policy performance— that is building a great city with outstanding urban form. All five of the requirements mentioned earlier are patently evident together with a sixth most desirable element, that of strong support of active and progressive media, especially the major local newspaper, the *Portland Oregonian*. The city has received national attention for its efforts in city development, transportation planning and action, and the dramatic rebirth of the downtown area. The fifteen-mile light-rail line which runs from the center city to the Cleveland Station in suburban Gresham and the excellent design aspects of the station areas are a model for other cities to follow. Actual ridership has been double that of the original projections made for the work week and, amazingly, the weekday average is exceeded on the weekends. Total ridership for the first year of operation was 7,230,000. The design standards established to guide major development, not only in the downtown area but throughout the city, are studied with envy by other cities which lack the leadership qualities and citizen commitment and support that are a hallmark of Portland.

The qualities that make Portland a place in which you would like to live and work have not come easily, nor have they just happened. They can be traced back to a heritage from the early settlers of pride in the environment, a determination to do things right in their town, and a belief in supporting a good government, which acts in the best interests of the total community, even if that means putting self-interest aside. There has been a stability in this tradition over the years, and newcomers to the city are quick to sense and adopt this Portland attitude as their own philosophy. This delightful and valuable characteristic is not confined to Portland, but extends throughout the state of Oregon. The city has had the help of the state legislature and the governor's office over the years with Governors Tom McCall and Neil Goldschmidt leading two shining examples of state administration. Oregon has some of the most progressive environmental as well as land use controls and local planning and zoning laws of any state in the country. A study of the pamphlet titled, *Oregon's Statewide Planning Goals, 1985*, published by the Land Conservation and Development Commission should be required reading for every legislator and every legislative candidate, in every state in this country.

A Sense of Community

One other important attribute of the Portland community that has contributed heavily to making it an attractive place is the leadership and support of the design community. The architects, landscape architects, engineers and art devotees doing work in the city have initiated, encouraged, prodded, and practiced an appreciation of quality of design and city fabric not found in many places. This may have been encouraged by the firm position taken by the city administration in adopting a strong planning policy and sticking to their guns in seeing that it is carried out. Regardless of whether it was engendered by some of the leading design firms or imposed and accepted, it is to be commended. The AIA members, especially the highly regarded firm of Zimmer, Gunzel, Frasca Partnership, which was responsible for the design of the light-rail line stations and a large percentage of the major buildings in Portland, have displayed a holistic space and community appreciation that one can only wish had prevailed in other cities. When a developer approaches a local design firm about a project, a large part of the city's work is already done for it by that firm's explanation of the quality expected by local government.

My first research trip to Portland was undertaken eight years ago on another type of project. At that time, Neil Goldschmidt was mayor and was in the midst of his project to renovate the downtown area. One of the things I still remember is that in the first five minutes of our conversations, all eight business and civic leaders I interviewed about Portland's downtown housing policy spontaneously talked about "our Mayor" and the things he was doing for the city. The impression created was that this man had raised the sights and commitment of the entire population about the future of their city. There can be no question that Goldschmidt is responsible for the planning attitude prevailing in the city today, although he certainly had help from the other city commissioners, as well as business and civic leaders. Those elected officials who have come after him have continued in this vein and it is a tribute to the Portland people that they have retained the ability to seek out, elect, and support good leadership. Interestingly, even in interviews eight years later, everyone still brought up the contribution to the city of Neil Goldschmidt.

Public Support of Planning

The most current interviews, without exception, verified and supplemented the previous summary comments I have made about Portland. Most people still indicated that while planning support comes more from the public officials than a massive outpouring of citizen demands, this doesn't minimize the overall public support for planning. There is public backing for aggressive projects such as the light-rail system, the central city plan, and the implementation of the downtown plan. The most important ingredient for the success of the city according to elected officials, the business community, and private citizens is that of leadership.

However, in the case of Pioneer Courthouse Square, a major open-space renovation project in the heart of downtown—that was opposed by the then mayor, the development commission and some of the business leaders—Portland citizen influence and leadership overcame the objections and succeeded in getting this project built. The square was partially paid for by individuals buying a total of between 50,000 and 60,000 bricks for its construction. It has been highly successful, used by people both during the day and early evening, and provides a sense of space and community pride. There was a lot of support for the square from the planners and the architectural community who worked to see that this project was completed. This is a good example of how the leadership in Portland works whether it comes from concerned people or the elected officials and the importance of the vision supplied by the planners and the architectural and design communities.

How Portland Makes it Work

Two staff members of the Portland Development Commission, Larry Dully and Chris Kopca, provided information on that organization's role as well as comments on the unique successes of the city in planning and implementation. The commission was created by a vote of the people in 1958 and is called the Urban Renewal and Economic Development Agency. In addition they also: manage a large housing loan program; try to retain and attract business through recruitment and business loan programs; and provide public improvements and develop land in and around the center city. One of their major functions is to carry out city policies that might not be brought to fruition through regulation and private initiatives without financial aid from the city. The agency does not get involved in construction of office buildings under the policy that this is a role for private enterprise. One of the interviewees indicated: "We view ourselves as negotiators in the process. We have the financing mechanism to do this." The Development Commission is really the action agency for the public sector and they consider themselves as the development arm of the city.

A further explanation of why Portland is what it is in terms of good urban development, one of the commission staff added, is Portland's unique topographical and natural features, which make it unique as compared to Pasadena or Oklahoma City. The topography is different in that the downtown area is confined by the Willamette River on the north and east and by hills that rise from 800 to 900 feet on the south and west. Since Portland was founded its economic and cultural center has been on the south side of the river. After the turn of the century a lot of the nicer residential development took place in the hills directly above downtown. These factors have contributed to the focus on the downtown area. Also, both Oregon and Portland are conservative financially, but progressive on a lot of social issues. The staff member indicated that another advantage Portland had was that, "the growth has not been as rapid as in other cities like Denver in the 70's and we have had time to think and plan. People here are patient and know that what they build today they and their children will have to live with tomorrow."

Other comments from these two interviews indicated that in Portland people seem to be more able to talk to each other and work out their differences, which appears not to be true in many other cities. There has been minority representation on the city commission for a number of years and the community is somewhat homogeneous. The entire county board of supervisors is comprised of women, while the city commission, as of this writing, is all men.

In the early 1970s the state initiated a statewide land use process. Through this program, goals and guidelines were established for the entire state and the incorporated municipalities requiring that each city have a plan and decide whether goals and findings relative to every development action are consistent with the plan. As one staff member added, "Having to adopt findings that go with an action has caused people to think before they make a decision."

Portland and Seattle Compared

Harriet Sherburne, Vice President-Development for Cornerstone Columbia Development Company, a major private development company in Portland, provided a detailed description of her own company's attitude and that of the local development community regarding the city's policies and programs pertaining to structuring its urban form. Having had previous experience in Seattle, she was able to compare the two cities' policies. One of the major differences contributing to Portland's accomplishments is that they have not just written the rules or made the plans. They actually have created a professional organization within the city structure with a strong commitment to assuring good urban design principles. The city has applied not just pure planning, but planning with a professional development approach and a recognition of how important an understanding of the philosophy of economics is to urban form development. They have encouraged what they want and helped to shape those things by writing clear policies that are recognized as valuable by the private property owners; this allows everyone to then work together toward implementation. Most private property owners have bought into the system. They have seen that it is better to go with the design principles than to fight them, and therefore, you have had the happy situation that things have gone forward. Ms. Sherburne stated, "In my estimation, we have had very sophisticated elected leadership that has been supportive of planning and it hasn't been just lip service. I think that it has shown remarkable teamwork."

When asked about the influence of neighborhoods, Sherburne indicated that Portland has an effective neighborhood activist group. People in neighborhoods ask political candidates what their attitude is and how they feel about planning. There is conservatism and yet there is also strong progressive and enlightened self-interested strength. A great number of people have a sense of community and a sense of pride in that community, therefore they are concerned about the future. Like the rules of the road, if the purpose is obvious and the rules are well written, so that they can be easily understood and will result in an effective system, then everybody can live with them. A lot of this philosophy is again credited to the fact that Portland's early settlers were second sons of patrician families from places like Boston, not like the wildcat speculators and get-rich-quick people who started Seattle. The early Portland settlers had a sense of dignity and order. They believed that they should chart an orderly future. They went about the planned layout of land instead of the Seattle method of flipping coins to see where streets would meet. Further, Seattle only paid lip service to planning because the federal government said you had to have some plans or you couldn't get any federal money. Sherburne concluded, "The question of leadership is critical and the important thing is to have personable people with a sense of organization and a willingness to come forward and bear some of the burden of responsibilities for dealing with ever-more-complex problems, instead of shying away."

Planning director, Norman A. Abbott, AICP, noted that in both Oregon and Portland the comprehensive plan has considerable weight and decisions are based on goals-policy analysis. The planners here do the goals-policy analysis and if they say that a project is not in keeping with that policy, in all probability it is not going to get done. If the decision is made to bypass this process, it will be challenged by the citizens through the State Board of Land Use Appeals and possibly be overturned. He compared Portland with other places he has worked and said, "It is just a whole different ballgame here when it comes to decision-making and setting out goals, policies and land use decisions. The city commissioner who is assigned the responsibility for the planning department is very supportive of planning. People in Portland know what planning is all about and why it is important."

Here is one example of Portland's advanced planning policy. A few years ago a parcel of land at the corner of 1st Avenue and Morrison Street, only a block from the McCall Riverside Park, was enticing enough to attract a developer with plans for building a major highrise structure. However, the proposal asked for a number of exceptions to the ordinances and standards upon which the developer was unwilling to compromise. As a consequence, in true Portland fashion, the city officials stood firm and refused to deviate from their adopted plan and policies and the proposer withdrew. Soon thereafter, the local developer whom I interviewed next, but who did not provide this information to me, approached the city and said, "Tell me what you want me to do and it will be done that way." As a result, One Financial Center was constructed and is one of the most attractive and valuable assets in that area of the city.

A Private-Sector Viewpoint

An interview with One Financial Center's developer Pat Prendergast, president of Prendergast & Associates, was enlightening and impressive. It is his opinion that Portland and Oregon are way out in front nationally in both their planning and the timing of planning actions taken. The city and state did good, complete planning before major growth occurred; Portland's comprehensive zoning downtown and central city plans were all in place either before or as the growth occurred. Plans and maps were followed as closely as possible. "To me that is the difference," he added. "My company has done work in Seattle and Denver and I have watched them, along with Dallas, Houston, and Los Angeles do it too late. Denver has no planning of any consequence. There is zoning, but nobody has really bought into the metropolitan concept—e.g., transportation and political jurisdictional problems."

Prendergast expressed an admiration for Oregonians, indicating that they love their state as much as they love their own principles and values. There is a reconciliation between their strong individual attitudes and pioneer spirit and governmental planning because they watched neighboring California's problems develop and became bound and determined they were not going to let that happen. Perhaps reluctantly at first, they have gone along with planning, both regional and statewide. There is a lot of natural beauty and a good environment that transcends some residents' personal beliefs. There have been some hard-fought land use battles, both state and local, but on the balance planning has served the state well and there is now evidence of it. He concluded, "The abuses that have occurred in some of the Sun Belt states such as California are now having a reverse impact on growth. Oregon is probably a better place to develop than some of those Sun Belt cities because we have planning that works. That adds value and confidence and protects what we have."

The "Portland attitude" is exemplified by William Naito, considered by many to be "Mr. Portland." He added further support for the things said previously, but the most impressive thing is the man himself and his support of the city demonstrated by his willingness to be involved in every conceivable worthwhile civic endeavor. These activities—in addition to his successful import business and the owner of considerable land—are largely in the Pioneer Historic District. Some of his civic activities include organizing the annual Portland Festival downtown, being a major player in the light-rail line project, and working with Neil Goldschmidt to get Nordstrom's Department Store to return to the downtown area. He also was involved with the development of the original central city plan and the new revised downtown plan. In May of 1988, he was awarded an honorary doctorate by Linnfield College in recognition of his contribution to the development in downtown Portland and his support of planning for the future of the city. He is an excellent example of the kind of people who have helped in making Portland a great city.

Planning Is A Process

Portland's revised central city plan was adopted in March of 1988. The plan's background and all its major points are well covered in APA's *Planning* magazine.[2] Four years in preparation, the plan's principal innovations are the inclusion of the Willamette River's east side as well as the west in the concept of the future central city and the resultant proposal for relocation of approximately one mile of a four-lane freeway, Interstate 5, now planned for along the east bank of the river. Those familiar with Portland over the years will recall that Neil Goldschmidt and community leaders succeeded in accomplishing the removal and relocation of a similar freeway on the west bank in order to build the McCall Riverside Park, now one of

Portland's most attractive amenities. The proposal for doing the same thing with this highway is gaining strong citizen support.

Newspaper reporter Gordon Oliver quotes former city commissioner Margaret Strachan, who initiated the project in 1984 as saying, "If the central city plan did nothing else at all but bring the term central city into use, then it was a success." Oliver continues:

> The new plan is actually a revision and expansion of the 17-year-old downtown plan; this time though, the city decided to look at a larger area and link existing policies for the districts into a cohesive whole. . . . The final product, approved unanimously by the city council after extended debate, has been widely praised by civic and political leaders as a means of refocusing the city on its riverfront while preserving the best of the downtown plan. . . . An overall plan goal is to make the Willamette River 'the binding element of the central city'. . . .
>
> Now that the bitter political struggles are fading into history, many observers say the plan remains a sentinel for the future. It already has wide public acceptance, adding to Portlanders' belief that theirs is a well-planned city prepared to handle growth without being overrun by it. Business leaders see the city's planning efforts as a powerful tool in drawing new firms into the area. In the end, even severe critics of the process think the city has come up with a winner. 'When you compare where we are to other cities,' one of them says, 'it's absolutely amazing.'

CHARLOTTE, NORTH CAROLINA

The second city that has demonstrated how planning and coordination can work was somewhat of a surprise to me, primarily because it had changed greatly from the last time I had been there eighteen years earlier. It was then a pleasant, medium-sized city, but displayed signs of needing improved planning and zoning and was in some danger of losing the vitality of its central business district to outlying areas. What a difference those years have made! Now, Charlotte is a booming, progressive city obviously well aware of where it is, where it wants to go, and how it is going to get there. Exploring the city one finds an organized physical form, attractive structures, a revitalizing central business district, impressive public buildings and facilities and pleasant residential areas. There is an aura of coordinated planning and policy implementation as well as an understanding of the importance of aesthetics and design.

Cooperation, Coordination, Plus Consolidation

In 1970 Charlotte's population was 241,420, and Mecklenburg County in which it is located had a population total of 354,656. The 1980 Census indicated 314,447 people in the city and 404,270 in the county. The estimates for 1987 were 375,000 and 460,260 respectively with a projection of approximately 485,000 and 573,000 for the year 2005. The recognition of this growth and the potential for the future prompted the city council of Charlotte and the board of commissioners of Mecklenburg County to merge all planning responsibility into one planning commission and department in 1955. This has proved to be quite advantageous in achieving coordinated planning and development for the entire area.

At the time of my visit this consolidation had been extended to most public services including the educational system, with the only exclusions being law enforcement, fire protection and parks development and management. Consideration is now being given to the possibility of including these latter three services. The epitome of the recognition of the value of working together is the recent construction of the well-designed Charlotte–Mecklenburg Government Center building in the center city where all city and county offices are now housed. What has been evidenced throughout the area is that this kind of interrelation of governmental operations can be effective and provides a model many other places would be wise to emulate.

The chairperson of the Mecklenburg Board of Commissioners, Carla E. DuPuy is a dedicated public official and a strong supporter of long-range coordinated planning. In fact, she is now working with a commissioner from a South Carolina county in an effort to form a regional planning discussion coalition among the seven counties from both states that surround Charlotte. Her comments indicated that Charlotte–Mecklenburg were fortunate in having people with a sense of community who are committed to keeping their area one of a desirable quality of life and development. There is an excellent relationship between governments and the business community and frequently representatives of the private sector will volunteer to help the elected representatives find a solution to a problem. Singled out for special mention was the commitment of the financial institutions: NCNB National Bank and First Union National Bank, two of the largest banks in North Carolina, are headquartered here as is Duke Power Company, along with other locally owned businesses and industries and national corporations that have located in Charlotte in recent years.

The consolidation and cooperation between the city and county has proved most beneficial in DuPuy's opinion. It has allowed comprehensive planning even though the county has to deal with larger parcels and bigger developments while Charlotte must concentrate on infill, renewal and rezoning. Sharing their goals and objectives with each other has helped to assure that as the county is creating new communities, appropriate standards are met which will allow them to be readily absorbed into the city when the time comes for annexation. "We work hard to make sure that all the standards are identical and, while we still have separate zoning ordinances, they are practically identical," she said. It is worthy to note that a revised, combined zoning ordinance is under study and is likely to be adopted, provided some changes to the state enabling act are approved. A combined subdivision ordinance and building standards code already are in force. Responsibility for administration and enforcement of the various joint endeavors is shared by the city and county governments with each assigned to manage specific functions.

A Community In Action

One of chairperson DuPuy's concerns is that Charlotte is growing because it is attracting many new industries and companies from the north as well as from foreign countries who may feel left out of the civic process: "This is bringing in new folks and there is a new crowd out there on the streets that feels disenfranchised. They don't feel a part of the process. We are in the middle of this Civic Index Program exercise where we have tried to pull in some of them and let them see what we are all about. For too long we have gotten along too well not to figure out how to bring these people into the system without becoming divisive."

Although not all of the following information was included in the commissioner's interview, she did comment on the creation of the Charlotte–Mecklenburg Citizen's Forum, organized five years ago, with which she is involved, and its benefit to the entire community. The fact that this organization was in existence is one reason the National Civic League offered to assist the area in undertaking the Civic Index Program. The forum was started in an attempt to overcome a developing polarization regarding growth versus no-growth viewpoints. The planning staff recognized this trend and addressed the issue head-on by creating a broad-based involvement process for development criteria and a revised comprehensive plan. One of the things the planners charged the community representatives with was that the planning function needed to have a forum of citizen leadership that could get people with differing views together to discuss difficult issues like growth and develop a consensus of what the policy should be.

As a result, elected officials got together with major developers to begin discussing differences, and to move this forward, they decided to schedule a retreat in which both civic leaders and those interested in development would be invited. After the retreat, a series of meetings continued with the overall result that the developers became convinced that the elected officials were not going to just roll over and let them do just what they wanted, so they needed to work something out to assure their survival. Consequently the building interests made a number of concessions and agreed to continue to work with officials and civic leaders. This process led to unanimous agreement to proceed with formation of the new plan containing clearly stated policies pertaining to land development. In addition, the Citizen's Forum was established to move from the land use problem into other community issues.

One of the forum's early activities was to commit assistance to a neighborhood action program called Project Catalyst. An historic and traditionally black school, Johnson C. Smith University, is located in the Biddle-Five Points neighborhood in northwest Charlotte. The university has a new president, Dr. Robert Albright, who came on the scene energetically determined to make the school a vital part of the community, as well as improving its educational programs. Before the new president arrived, the concern of the university had stopped at its boundaries, but Dr. Albright became a member of the Citizen's Forum and through his efforts the idea of Project Catalyst was endorsed by that organization and officially inaugurated. An experienced community-activist lawyer, Sharif Abdullah, was hired as director and a consulting firm engaged to prepare a plan for revitalization of the long-neglected neighborhood.

The plan prepared contained specific proposals for land use development, public improvements, and design suggestions for each section of the entire area. After submission to the planning commission the plan's concept was approved by city council. In addition, endorsement and support came from residents of the neighborhood, area business people, at least two interested developers, and the University of North Carolina at Charlotte. Through all of this, President Albright is given the credit for being the driving force that has kept the idea moving forward. The plan calls for revitalizing the neighborhood's central business district, new housing, improved access, creation of more pleasing aesthetic character, job creation, and major public improvements and, while it will be some time before all of this will be achieved, the impetus and enthusiasm necessary to make it happen seem to be present.

The ambitious proposal's implementation will cost $60 million according to Abdullah's estimate. He and President Albright believe that a way can be found to bring it to fruition. Abdullah believes "The best of all worlds is when the development ideas come from the neighborhoods themselves. Things can change when people say this is how we need to develop, this is the kind of housing we need and they go out and find a developer or encourage a developer to come in and build in keeping with their ideas. The key is exposing the positive aspects of the community to interest those with the dollars to invest here." One of the committed businessmen, Nasif Majeed, summed up the problem well. He said, "The bottom line in the combined effort is to put pride, purpose and power back in northwest Charlotte neighborhoods. If you don't have the economic power, you are like a blade of grass on the Atlantic coast in a hurricane."

The real catalyst that can make this challenging concept a probability, instead of a possibility, is the evident community pride and commitment present throughout Charlotte. These projects are making Charlotte–Mecklenburg even more of an area where it can be done.

The Planning Function Is Important

The planning director, Martin R. Cramton, Jr., was one of the more impressive directors encountered during my visits, primarily because of his demonstrated leadership capabilities. He is enthusiastic about the cooperation achieved through the combined planning function and the support afforded planning by both city and county elected officials. The funding for the department is divided on a fifty/fifty basis between the two governments. There are forty-seven persons on the staff in three operating sections—community planning, strategic planning, and annexation. Because of the progressive annexation law in North Carolina, annexation can occur simply by the passage of a resolution by the annexing city; this process is used frequently by

Charlotte. There are six small incorporated towns in the county around Charlotte and the city has an intergovernmental agreement with each on the "sphere of influence" in order to avoid competition for annexation.

Regarding the structure of the two governments, Charlotte has a weak mayor/council/manager form with a council of eleven. Seven of the council members are elected from districts and the rest, as well as the mayor, run at-large. Mecklenburg County has a seven member board of commissioners and four of these represent districts. After being in Charlotte for nine years, Cramton is of the opinion that once people are elected, even from the districts, they subscribe to a civic ethic encompassing the entire community. "People do look at their district's interests, but also take a broader view of the world and the total governmental jurisdiction of the city and county," he said.

A new comprehensive plan known as the Generalized Land Plan, 2005 was developed over a two-year period through a 2005 citizens advisory task force, numerous community meetings and more than thirty in-depth presentations of its strategies to elected officials, the planning commission, and the chamber of commerce. The plan was adopted at a joint meeting of the Charlotte city council and the Mecklenburg board of commissioners. While the plan is fundamentally a strategic one, it contains some excellent policy statements now being followed. Its contents are divided into context of change, growth assumptions, key issues, goals, objectives, tools, and land use strategies. This is one of the most informative, understandable, and effective long-range plans I have read.

The Power of the Neighborhoods

According to one of the neighborhood activists, Mary Ann Hammond, there are a large number of neighborhood organizations among the approximately two hundred neighborhoods in the city. Charlotte maintains a registry of neighborhood organizations and keeps them informed of action taking place that may be of interest to them. She believes that the planning commission's opinion carries a lot of weight with the council members. Her neighborhood was successful in obtaining a major down-zoning for a large part of their area with the council compromising only for one large property owner; the requested change was reduced slightly, but standards were still more strict than what was sought by that owner. It is her belief that candidates for council who are smart will run in support of planning and they will be asked by the voters when knocking on doors how they stand on this subject. She, too, is a member of the Citizen's Forum, believes in it and feels that it is doing a good job for the city.

A private planning consultant, Robert Young of Robert Young & Associates, added support for the increasing power of the neighborhoods and the community-planning attitude in the city. Even though he mentioned that the change from election entirely at-large to a combined district and at-large representation had taken place in the city during the 1970s and about two years ago in the county, there is no question that citizens and neighborhoods are part of the power structure in the community. He believes that the attitude of Charlotte people is that when there is a problem to be solved, citizens jump in and help provide the solution.

A Public/Private Partnership That Works

Charlotte has been blessed with a very diversified economy including banking, commerce, real estate, and insurance. As a result there is money here and business organizations and the people who run them have been very generous in both their personal involvement and in donating funds for worthwhile civic projects. An outstanding illustration of this is the First Union National Bank and Urbco'Lat Purser, Connecticut Mutual's real-estate arm who co-sponsored a $200,000 design study to update portions of the city's 1980 central area plan (see APA *Planning*, May 1988). Because so much was going on in the central business district, these two private firms took the initiative on this project by going to city officials and obtaining their approval to work together to update certain segments of the plan. Through this process the city can achieve a vision of what needs to be done to provide open space, pedestrian ways, and direction about where certain forms of land use need to locate in the area. According to a bank official the purpose of the study is to "raise developers' sights" from single-lot concerns to those that aid overall urban form development.

A good summary of Charlotte's planning attitude was provided by Young. He said, "I think we are all concerned about the image of Charlotte, the quality of life, and the quality of environment. We are going to grow and become more cosmopolitan, but I believe that we are still going to maintain the care for this city that we have had in the past."

Young provided further support for my contention that it is the cities who plan effectively and set high standards that are sought out by economically sound developers, not those misled by the fallacy of "all growth is good." He said:

> Good developers look at a city and when they see a sense of planning, a concern for quality, good requirements and standards to maintain that quality and what is being done to provide amenities for that city, they recognize it as a good place to invest. Those are the things that attract people, industry and jobs to a community.
>
> Because we have those things is the reason Charlotte continues to have growth and economic development when a lot of the country is in an economic slump. There is a real quality design commitment here and my out-of-town private clients tell me they are glad to find it. They understand that in order to be successful with their product they have to do just as well, if not better, with their proposal and its design than the last guy who came here.

That is an economic fact of life which, unfortunately, so many of our cities have not been able to understand.

Economic Development in Uptown

The Charlotte Uptown Development Corporation has played an important role in revitalizing that portion of the central city known as Uptown. It was created as a nonprofit corporation in 1979. Once again, the private business sector took the initiative, believing that something should be done in the area, not by government, but by the private sector. Through the chamber of commerce, a task force was formed to study ways to accomplish this goal. The conclusion was that something like an authority should be formed with some financial support provided by the business community, and also using state legislation permitting the establishment of municipal service districts with authority to levy a special tax within that district. The city passed the necessary local legislation in 1971 allowing it to contract for services with a nonprofit organization. "Thus the Uptown Development Corporation came about and we are, in one sense, a creature of the city," reported the executive director, Michael Schneiderman. Over the years, the top corporate people of the city have served on the board. It is through their influence and vision that the corporation has been successful. Their mission is economic development and they work with the banks and other parts of the private sector, as well as with the city. The board is comprised of sixteen people representing the corporate sector, residential areas, city council, county commission, chamber of commerce, planning director, city manager, and nonprofit representatives. "This allows a good melding of ideas that will get things done for the Uptown."

Schneiderman emphasized that their role is with small developers working on buildings in need of rehabilitation, facilities that need to be built and the integration of public and private money to make a partnership deal work. He emphasized a close working relationship with the planning department. "When major developers come to town with a project, we tell them to go see the planning department first. Even on small projects, we work very closely with that department. It is the planning commission here that handles negotiation and compromises that may be necessary to make that project work in accordance with community standards. They work out the nitty-gritty stuff."

This attitude is quite different than those found in San Diego and a few other cities, where economic development corporations seemed to be independently calling all of the shots for the elected officials. In this, and many other ways, I found Charlotte an exciting city that illustrates that planning can and does work.

MINNEAPOLIS, MINNESOTA

While Charlotte was a pleasant surprise, disillusion and disappointment best describe my reaction to Minneapolis. Even so, it is being included in this chapter because the city has made planning work extremely well until very recently. The changing situation regarding governmental structure and attitude clearly suggests that unless there is strong governmental leadership so the business community and the general population can be revived to the high level of participation experienced in former years, there are troubled times ahead. Just as had happened in a number of other cities, the problems stem from a positive goal that nevertheless offers the potential for divisiveness, lack of common goals, and loss of vision for the future of the total community. That is the changing of the governmental structure from a strong mayor and at-large election of council representation to a weak mayor system with the election of all council members by districts.

The Minneapolis Dilemma

For years Minneapolis has been acclaimed, and justifiably so, as a vision oriented, community spirited city with a planning attitude that achieved commendable results. The central city was vibrant, Nicollet Mall was highly successful and a model for other cities, the skywalks and the new development downtown were written about and pictured in books, magazines, and media across the country. Many of those projects and others are indeed great accomplishments and Minneapolis certainly is not being chastised or classified as a second-class city. Instead, I have a sincere concern and a belief that it is time once again for voices to be raised that proclaim, "We must preserve the concern for the *total community.*" This was borne out by several of the persons interviewed who expressed the concern that there not be loss of that which the people of Minneapolis have fought for. Now more than ever, the interested and committed people in the city have to seek out and elect those who will provide exemplary inspirational leadership, keeping their responsibility to the total community as well as serving their ward constituents. In many places where there are both district and at-large elections of council it is a district representative who has been reelected consistently and manifests leadership quality and city-wide concern who is then enabled to become mayor. Continuation of public service and political ambition are never stifled by maintaining a broad vision where true leadership capabilities have been made evident. Thus the dilemma is whether once again people will be concerned enough to regain the image of a city with a meaningful planning attitude or permit divisiveness, politics, and outside forces to cause a further decline in the quality city it has been.

On the Brighter Side

Robert A. Worthington, AICP, executive director of governmental affairs of the OPUS Corporation provided an excellent summary of Minneapolis's heritage. As in Portland, this has been an important influence on the recent planning accomplishments of the city. He felt that the planning process has been an effective shaper of the form and the distribution of land use activities, not only in the city, but also in the surrounding suburbs and the adjacent satellite towns. There seems to have been a tradition of planning that goes back to the late 1950s and early 1960s when a group of civic and political leaders encouraged the council of governments, predecessor to the Metropolitan Council, to develop a vision for the area permitting it to grow, but preserving the quality of life for its people.

The tradition of a planning philosophy actually goes back to the early Minnesota settlers and was institutionalized by a number of long-range planning studies over the years. These had a major influence on legislation passed by the state over the years including the mandate that every community have a zoning ordinance based on a comprehensive plan that gives consideration to more than just physical land use. The creation of the Metropolitan Council followed, with a purpose of adding substance to influence coordinated planning, encourage increased depth of plans in local communities, and provide assured continuity on a regional basis. In recent years, this broad area-wide comprehensive concept seems to be slipping away as community governmental structures have changed to individual district representation.

However, there are still some good things the people of Minneapolis have done and are still doing. There are elected officials who still have the city as a whole at heart and there are many high-quality city administrative staff members. A number of favorable comments were made about the planning department, the planning director and the mayor during my visit. In his interview Mayor Donald M. Frazer said "In the broadest sense I see planning as absolutely critical. I see planning as working two ways as a conscience for us. One is to look down the road and see what is coming and to anticipate the probable outcome. The other is providing an enabling activity once we know what our goals are. I value both aspects of planning."

The mayor indicated his interest and his concern for the neighborhoods, especially their children and youth, stating that the city needed to think of neighborhoods as places where people live, interact with one another, and where there are plenty of people problems. He has come to believe that the emphasis on housing and housing blight, while important, is not nearly as important as is what is happening to families. One of his ideas is to put a family-service center in every neighborhood. Along with this, a citizen's board would be created to allocate resources to families in need. He believes that there should be an effort to recreate small communities within the larger one to try to revitalize the sense of belonging and of place which he feels is essential in any major urban city.

He also indicated a conviction that the planning department should remain fairly strong, in spite of some of the frustrations it has experienced. In addition, he spoke highly of the Metro 2000 plan that focuses on the downtown area, but he referred to the center city "as everybody's neighborhood" and strongly believed that this is an important concept. Metro 2000, an update of the Metro 85 Plan (1970) and Metro 90 Plan (1978), resulted from a cooperative effort between the Downtown Council, primarily a business group, and the planning department. That type of past planning effort has played a very large role in the way that the city's development priorities have been established. "The fact that we had plans enabled the city to be involved with the development process and give support to the private sector," the mayor concluded. "They needed to know what was happening before they would invest or make public investment decisions." Shortly after my visit, Mayor Frazer was again reelected by Minneapolis voters.

Governmental Relationship and Cooperation

Planning director, Oliver E. Byrum, AICP, another capable and dedicated planning professional, pointed out a unique feature of Minnesota legislation that does not require the city to go to a vote of the people for approval of bond issues. Instead these are submitted to the legislature, including general obligation bonds, and upon their approval the bonds can be issued. Minneapolis has both general enabling authority as well as specific authority granted by the state on particular projects such as the convention center. He also commented on the cooperation between Minneapolis and Saint Paul, which occurs primarily through the Metro Council, although the planning functions of the two cities do keep in touch with each other and meet together periodically. There is a Minneapolis/Saint Paul Fund that established a joint project for building low- and moderate-income housing. This is financed by the two cities and a major foundation. The two mayors work well together politically and there is a good deal of combined political work with the legislature. His summary was, "The cooperation is fairly good and a lot of it is through the Metro Council; housing and political cooperation is very good."

A Current Evaluation

The comments of Robert C. Einsweiler, AICP, included a current analysis regarding the relationship of the planning commission and department with the city council. In his opinion, after examining their influence on the built environment and policy implementation, the relationship has not been very productive. Two reasons were given for this. The first is that the planning staff has long been integrated within city government while the commission sits at the side with only an advisory role. The result has been that the commission

became the unit used by the politicians for their "hot potatoes" and issues they would like sent up as trial balloons. Commission members
sometimes get very frustrated with this, but that is the way city council wants to use it. He believes this is a useful role even though it
means that their effectiveness is fairly indirect.

He does credit planning's role within the central city area as being
influential, particularly in providing the vision for downtown development. A tradition has existed for some twenty years of rather far-
out plans for downtown developed by the planning staff and the
business community. The planning commission then has the opportunity to revise the proposals. An example of how this works is a situation involving a proposed basketball arena along Hennepin Avenue
in an area where the city planned to replace a "sin strip" with retail enterprises through redevelopment. Using the plan the city convinced
the developers to move back a block where they were still able to get
their desired skyway connection to City Center. As a result, the developers of the arena got a good site, the city protected their plan for the
Hennepin frontage, and everybody was satisfied. This again proves
that good planning, well supported, can provide a win-win situation.

Citywide and Regional Planning

Peter Jarvis, AICP, further substantiated the effectiveness of the planning department in the downtown area, but added that this has not
been the same in other areas of the city. There is a lot of talk about
neighborhood preservation, but as Jarvis put it, "it is a far more difficult animal to get your arms around." So far as comprehensive plan
proposals are concerned, the attitude is entirely different outside of
the central city area. He continued with comments about the Twin
Cities mentioning that this two-city area has been pointed to as the
great experiment, the greatest success story in regional planning. In
his opinion there is a lot of truth to that. At the regional level, until a
few years ago, the ability of the Metropolitan Council, established by
the state legislature in 1967, to deal with major regional systems like
transportation, parks and open space, solid waste, sanitary sewage,
and airports has been very beneficial to the region. It provided a policy direction that had an extraordinary impact on the metropolitan
area. However, during the last six to eight years, as compared to their
first decade, that council has almost been like an entity searching for a
mission. He credits this to their broadened scope of activity and feels
that they have attempted to take on everything from criminal justice

to health planning. The quality of their effectiveness, therefore, has decreased.

The Choice Ahead

These interviews confirmed the concern expressed about the future of this city with a proud past and a powerful potential. The voters of Minneapolis have made one choice in response to what they perceived to be a problem. Now they are faced with what, in my opinion, is an even more important choice. They can choose to permit the governmental system to which they have changed to become the sole prerogative of professional politicians and stand by and witness the development of pork-barrel struggles, trade-offs, and a constant competition for power which only requires that they do nothing. The other choice, far more difficult, but essential for survival as an outstanding city, is to band together, determined to act collectively if any sign of danger of the abuses mentioned above appear to be likely or become evident. They must insist on the election of strong leaders with broad vision for the total city, and that a planning attitude and a sense of community be preserved. Failure to choose the latter option and provide business, financial and private citizen support to make it work will only result in validating the predictions of troubled times ahead.

PITTSBURGH, PENNSYLVANIA

In the 1920s and 1930s Pittsburgh was a steel town with a reputation for being a polluted, dirty, unfit-to-live-in place. Through the leadership and the support of some of its wealthy pioneer families, Pittsburgh began an exciting transformation in the 1940s. Aided by the later election of David Lawrence as mayor, the city's business leadership came to the forefront and began to express itself. The business community and the financial institutions awoke and joined with the political powers to rebuild, renovate, and revitalize the city. This, in a sense, culminated during the eleven years of Mayor Richard Caliguiri's term, until his death in 1988. The remarkable success once again gained Pittsburgh a national reputation, one totally opposite of the earlier one.

Pittsburgh, in my opinion, now again faces a major Y intersection on the road to its future. As is the case in Minneapolis, the choice the people of the city must make today is just as important, if not more so, than that of the earlier period. The people of the city met the challenge in the 1970s of choosing which direction to take; the political, business, and civic leadership rallied, made the right choices and worked together for an outstanding rebirth of a vibrant city from a depressed steel town. Here, the entire structure of government has been changed with the mandated council election entirely from nine districts and a weak mayor system. It is almost certain that this situation is going to test the ability of both citizens and leadership as to whether they can again pull together and see that the right choice is made and diligently pursued; that is, insistence on total community commitment with elected officials not just serving a political fiefdom or political ambition. However, based on the outstanding rebirth, the results achieved and the leadership provided in the 1970s and 1980s, there can be no doubt that Pittsburgh deserves to be included among the list of those cities which, during a period in their history, made planning an effective tool of government. The quandary the city now faces is what it will become in the future.

Community Concern Expressed

Of the seven persons interviewed it is interesting to note that all were highly complimentary about the turnaround and the accomplishments during the 1970s and 1980s. However, five of the seven expressed serious concerns about what the future may hold. The opinions clearly indicated the basis of concern about what can be done to assure a continuing sense of the total community and overcome the ward system's tendency to divide people and encourage petty politics.

One council person interviewed, while commenting on the changed system, was more optimistic than others as to what would happen, although he did state that, in his opinion, only the neighborhoods working together might provide the means of maintaining a citywide view. He felt the next five years would see the population comprised of younger and less conservative people and that there would be a broader and more service-oriented economic base. He believes that the city will continue to lose population. The major responsibility for this was assigned to the differential in the levy of the wage tax between city and non-city residents. Those living and working in Pittsburgh are taxed 4 percent on wages and those from the suburbs who work there only 1 percent. Further, he is convinced that the only way to achieve a better balance between the city and the suburbs is for the state legislature to intervene and take action as was done in the Minneapolis/Saint Paul area. The lack of depth in these comments and the absence of any concern for planning for the future leaves one in doubt about the political leadership potential for Pittsburgh.

Some more meaningful encouragement was provided by the executive director of the Allegheny Conference, David Bergholz. The conference, established in the 1940s, is privately supported, has 150 sponsors and a large number of influential people as members and on its board. His opinion was that Pittsburgh had the decided advantage of having the support of money from foundations and many large corporations with headquarters there. At present, the agency has convened a group to devise and hopefully establish a special assessment district similar to what New Orleans has done in its downtown area. The conference could continue to be a very important influence on where the city will go in the future.

Community/Neighborhood Planning Concerns

The community planner's concern centers on what the ward system will do to the effective neighborhood organizations encouraged and fostered during the administration of Mayor Richard Caliguiri. Pittsburgh's topography does not lend itself either to neighborhood or citywide initiative and certainly not to being cut up into whatever arbitrary districts are determined and put into effect. The ward system also may adversely affect the coordination of the allocation of capital improvement funds now being distributed on a citywide basis should the usual in-fighting occur over funding of projects in individual districts. The one hope expressed was that there may be a recognition of the importance of neighborhoods pulling together in a district overlapping several of their boundaries and that residents will work together in a comprehensive way, at least in that district. However, the new system could lead to planners being considered even more as buffers or negotiators, and planning could then play only a supportive role. Too, it may become even more difficult for the comprehensive planning section by increasing their focus on regulatory measures and zoning changes that have far-reaching implications. This would move the city in the direction of program or pragmatic planning rather than visionary, long-range planning.

The neighborhood planner, Thomas Cox, director of the Northside Civic Development Corporation, agreed that what lies ahead is a most important question. It appears that until the district boundaries were set the incumbent council members interested in being retained were running on an at-large basis just to be sure they kept their names in front of the people who might be in their district. He was convinced that after the first election under the new system had taken place "you will see ad-hoc alliances in the neighborhoods for the purpose of gaining access to that councilperson." He does feel that the neighborhoods are going to have to form a citywide alliance of some kind and figure out what issues they have in common and how they want these things dealt with. A great deal depends, of course, on who gets elected to those council positions.

The Importance of Leadership Revisited

As further evidence of the planning and accomplishments of Pittsburgh in the past and the kind of things perhaps jeopardized under the new system, especially a "weak mayor" who is almost isolated from the council, David Matter, director of development, Oxford Development Company, enlarged on some specific actions of the Caliguiri administration. When first elected mayor in 1977, Caliguiri created an informal body in his office known as the Mayor's Development Council. Matter, who was the mayor's executive secretary, a position similar to that of city manager, was designated chairman of the council. It was comprised of all agency heads who had some responsibility for physical development and redevelopment together with some outside agency people such as the development director of the Port Authority and the president of the Regional Industrial Development Corporation.

This council was created primarily to respond to outside development interests and to provide a coordinating mechanism within city government so that they could stimulate new development. Their first major endeavor was to work with PPG Industries in selecting and developing the best site for their new headquarters building in the downtown area. After extended discussion, it was decided that the Market Square location was preferred by both the city and PPG. A large portion of this land was in separate private ownership and acquisition would involve the use of governmental powers. A task force was then formed by the Mayor's Development Council to implement the project. This group and PPG met once a week for over a year to get everything worked out; PPG went so far as to include the planning director and the redevelopment director on their architectural selection team. This was an example of working planning and urban design into a project at the earliest possible moment. The loss of this kind of cooperative and coordinated approach is Matter's major concern about Pittsburgh's future. Nevertheless, he still expressed a confident belief that the business community and civic leaders will continue to be influential in what lies ahead. "I think that there are a lot of opportunities," he concluded. "We have to be selective. We can make the city grow and we can do it in a planned fashion that will respond to Pittsburgh's new economic life as a financial services and educational, bio-medical, robotics center."

Comprehensive Planning in a Democratic Capitalistic Society

Most of the problems now facing Minneapolis and Pittsburgh are symbolic of the difficulty of accomplishing long-range comprehensive planning in a democratic, capitalistic society. David Lewis, AICP, AIA, a noted urban designer, in his provocative and erudite manner, provided a good analysis of this dilemma for Pittsburgh and other American cities.

> Economic development is clearly something that every city has to keep in order to stay alive. On the other hand democracy means the exercise of policy that is reflective of the public interest, the public will and public aspirations. Good leadership, therefore, is that leadership which sees the future of the community in metaphorical terms: how can I affect it through my leadership and metaphorically, where is it going? That means the development of strong policy whether it is in comprehensive plans, economic factors, budgeting or whatever it is.
>
> All of these are metaphors of direction of any community. All of this must carry with it the keeping of that democratic place properly and responsibly informed of policy recommendations and decision making process. There is a wonderful quote from Thomas Jefferson which goes like this: 'The most effectual means of preventing the perversion of power into tyranny are to illuminate the minds of the people. If once the people become inattentive to the public affairs, Congress, Judges and Governors shall all become wolves. This seems to be the law of our general nature.'[3]

Even in the eighteenth and early nineteenth century, the elitist Thomas Jefferson recognized the importance of working with people, educating them to what you were trying to accomplish and why, and making them feel a part of the process. This need is far greater in today's society.

AN EDITORIAL SUMMARY

My sincere concern has been expressed several times regarding the trend toward city charter changes that result in the election of all city council or county commission members by districts; what I have referred to as a return to the ward system. In no way does this imply that I advocate exclusionary representation in government or do not believe in equitable representation of minorities, women, or even various geographic sectors and economic areas of a city. However, I have yet to experience or observe a return to the ward system where the entire elected leadership was able to maintain a meaningful, effective, community-wide future vision. Perhaps there may be one somewhere, but I have observed closely what has happened in Albuquerque, even with a supposedly strong mayor and seven members of council all elected from districts, as well as other cities with which I am familiar. Invariably the ward representatives develop only two major concerns: getting things accomplished immediately for their constituents in order to guarantee reelection, and seeking the limelight and press coverage, constructively or destructively, in order to lay a base to run for mayor; it usually pays more and certainly is considered a higher political status symbol and a springboard.

It is my personal belief that understanding the dangers of what has long been an outmoded system of government is important enough to have deserved some mention in chapter one about the power of the petition and referendum force. In the next chapter, we'll examine how we have gotten on such a deteriorating slide in our cities. A better way must be found to insure fair and equitable representation of all our people and still maintain that all-important sense of community. I believe that the answer lies in the grass-roots heart of our political system, the neighborhood political precinct. If this means partisan elections and politics, so be it. At least then the political parties can be forced by an aroused public to take a stand on providing that equitable representation without having to revert to the ward system. Perhaps it might be time for the creation of an Equitable Representation Party working to achieve this at the local, state, and national levels.

The cities where planning is working or has worked, regardless of the potential problems resulting from changes in governmental structure, have recognized the importance of leadership, keeping people informed and involved, and planning *with* their citizens, not *for* them. Two vital facts emerge from this chapter. The first is that given the right circumstances and a concerned citizenry, local government planning can work and does build a better urban form and a better community. The other is that it must always be remembered that continuing an efficient, future-oriented management and operation in any city requires vigilance and, like everything else, it is subject to change. In fact, it is always in a tenuous position and can be threatened or lost from failure of leadership to respond to the needs and wants of people, complacency on the part of the general public, or changes in either internal or external economic or social forces. Put simply, continued enjoyment of good government is just like the maintenance of a good marriage. It takes constant dedication and hard work on the part of all parties.

NOTES

1. Henry S. Churchill, *The City is The People* (New York: W. W. Norton, Inc., 1962).

2. Gordon Oliver, "Portland Goes For Broke," *Planning*, Vol. 55, No. 2 (February 1989), pp. 10–15.

3. Thomas Jefferson letter to the Reverend Samuel Miller (1808).

5

Some Have Tried

From my visits to the various cities, a second category has emerged of those cities which, at some time or the other in recent years, have tried to make planning work with varying degrees of success. This should be recognized as strictly a judgment call on my part based on conversations during the interviews, physical inspection, and review of printed materials. Undoubtedly the categorizing of some of the cities in this and the next chapter will not meet with wholesale approval by all of the officials or residents in these places. However, the original intent of this book was to present an analytical evaluation by one planner of some years' experience who is seriously concerned about what has happened, and is happening, to our cities and their metropolitan areas.

BALTIMORE, MARYLAND

Baltimore, often heralded as an outstanding city because of what it has done in downtown development, seemed a paradox to me. It is obvious that some great things have been done, especially downtown near the harbor. As a city it appears to be enjoying a booming economy, yet on the fringes of the central city signs of decay and neglect are quickly evident. In spite of redevelopment activity and its "homestead" program that makes empty houses in need of repair available for as little as one dollar (provided recipients agreed to renovate and live in them for a stated period), the housing and people needs have not been met in a way to make a city great. Even in the downtown area the attempt at creating a mall is questionable in design, aesthetics, maintenance, and its contribution to city quality. There are a number of empty stores and those occupied, with the exception of two department stores, are mainly T-shirt shops, novelty shops, cut-rate drug stores, eateries, service businesses and the usual Woolworth's-type variety stores.

The Inner Harbor Area

By comparison, the Inner Harbor Area is an exciting place. Most of the buildings are well designed with plazas and plentiful landscaped areas. Skyways have been strategically located to provide access and reduce pedestrian street-crossing at ground level. Harbor Place is a delightful plethora of all types of shops, restaurants, specialty foods, and fish markets. It attracts people, frequently large crowds, both during the day and evening. Excellent use is made of the harbor and of flowing water in the pedestrian ways and the buildings' design. Special events take place frequently and there are sidewalk musicians and entertainers to provide additional variety. In spite of all of this, however, it is easy to gain the impression that overall urban design co-ordination is lacking. Several somewhat obtrusive high-rise buildings are spotted at locations that seem to be incongruous with the immediate nearby development. The World Trade Center, although not excessively tall, dominates and overpowers the harbor area around it. There is considerable pressure for additional intensive development along the waterfront and the planning department is now doing a study of proposals extending over the area of the downtown section known as Fells Point. Conversely, Charles Center, the civic and convention center, are well integrated in relationship and design.

Baltimore's Planning Background

Baltimore, incorporated in 1797, has had a planning function for many years and some excellent planning work has been done. The first plan was for streets and roads in a new annexation of 1816. A planning committee was created in 1918 following another annexation and in 1939 was given the responsibility for maintaining a master plan. A charter revision in 1947 established the planning commission and the department of planning and the present form of both was part of a further revision in 1964. There is a comprehensive plan that has served as a general guide and the foundation for a number of major projects for which the city is noted. All private and public projects are technically required to be certified as complying with that plan.

The paradox lies not in the efforts of the planning department's staff to provide the tools for an effective process, but in the limited role the department has been permitted to play in achieving coordinated comprehensive planning by the various governmental administrations. The basis for this statement will be explained further in the report on the interviews conducted in the city. These make it quite clear, especially when combined with an analysis of the governmental structure, that the paradox comes from the things that have been accomplished in spite of the lack of a planning attitude on the part of the city administration over the last twenty or so years. The only exception seems to have been one mayor, Theodore R. McKeldin, who understood the need to plan for the future as well as the present and who at one time supported a study of how to make the planning department more meaningful. His efforts were unsuccessful.

Governmental Structure

Baltimore's charter has created an unusual structure in the strong mayor/council form of government. In addition to the mayor and council there is a Board of Estimate consisting of the mayor, president of council, the city solicitor, and the director of the Department of Public Works. They must approve the budget and, according to the opinions expressed, they really run city government. "Nothing happens unless it is approved by the Board of Estimate" was the statement made several times. The city's internal structure is further complicated by a system of financing private development projects referred to by some critics as Baltimore's "shadow government."

This unusual arrangement, together with the seeming lack of overall urban form coordination, attracted the attention of some of the local architects and led to their requesting the American Institute of Architects to send one of their Quality Urban Environment Study Teams (QUEST) to Baltimore. This resulted in a thorough study of the city's development history and governmental structure by a team of ten architects and planners. A report summarizing the investigations and findings after a concentrated two-and-a-half-day study was written by Simpson Lawson of Calvin Kytle Associates, later published in the *AIA Journal* from which much of this information has been taken.[1] The team interviewed several persons involved in the development of the city including Mayor Donald Schaefer, former mayor Theodore McKeldin, James Rouse, William Boucher, David Wallace and others covering a broad range of topics.

The existence of the "shadow government," referred to by city officials as "creative financing," attracted a great deal of attention from the QUEST team. Its composition and responsibilities were explained by Martin Millspaugh, president and chief executive officer of Charles Center–Inner Harbor Management. The city finance director and a retired chairman of the board of an insurance company have been named trustees for the city and act as the "lender of last resort." Although one is a city official, they act as private individuals running a bank comprised of some $150 million in city funds and urban development action grant funds entrusted to them. Their purpose is to back the loans that probably would be considered too risky for financing by private sources. City representatives defended this arrangement by indicating the projects for which financing can be arranged through this procedure are essential in making the city's development strategy work and the trustees have greater flexibility in putting deals together in a number of ways. The team queried Millspaugh about the arguments for and against the trustee system. He indicated that they are the same in this very telling response. "It works because the trustees, being private individuals, *can bypass all city charter requirements for competitive bidding and selection of consultants and architects. They can make deals like a private business would. The argument against it is that they are doing that outside the city government, outside the charter provisions and therefore avoiding the system of checks and balances that have been built up over the years"* (emphasis added). The question still remains of whether this is an appropriate and ingenious way for representative government to perform or whether it is another example of abdication of elected responsibility leading to how we got where we are in local government.

The current planning director, Larry Reich, is a veteran professional planner with over forty years of experience. He has held that position in Baltimore for twenty-three years and survived through five mayors. Reich deserves a great deal of credit for the ability he has displayed in adapting to the unusual governmental structure, the vagaries of various mayors and councils and the job he has done for the city in spite of all this.

Among all the questions that could be raised about the logic of Baltimore's city charter there is at least one good and wise provision in it charging the planning commission to annually prepare a six-year recommended Capital Improvement Program (CIP). The Board of Estimate has broadly defined the CIP as "any physical betterment or improvement and any preliminary studies and surveys relative thereto, including, but not limited to, any property of a permanent nature, and equipment needed in connection with . . . such . . . improvements when first erected or acquired." Excepted from this are "projects or improvements costing less than $5,000, vehicular equipment, items of a repair or maintenance nature costing less than $100,000 or which are of an emergency nature, salaries other than those which are properly capitalized as a part of the project cost."

Reich quickly saw the opportunity this presented for the planning commission and the department to define an effective role for themselves in having some clout in shaping the city's future. Consequently he has developed the most thorough and complete CIP process I have ever seen. The entire program is now completely computerized and every project approved in the current year's Capital Improvement Budget (CIB) is followed step by step from approval to completion. Each year the department and the planning commission publish an attractive document titled "Baltimore's Development Program" showing clearly the status of previous years' projects not yet completed, those approved for the current fiscal year, and those recommended for the next five years. Any municipal official, elected or appointed, can tell where his or her favorite project stands and, most importantly, nothing approved for which money has been allocated or bonds sold has any possibility of "falling through the cracks." Also, this system provides an excellent opportunity for civic organizations and an interested public to make sure that bond money is spent on projects for which the money was intended and not shifted around without being made public.

The Views of Others

While all of this makes planning look very good in Baltimore, there is another side to the story. Part of that is revealed by a booklet entitled, "Baltimore City Planning Commission/Department of Planning Guide." In this publication, all of the sections of the department are listed and while there is a current planning section, there is no long-range or comprehensive planning section. More concern for comprehensive planning was revealed in an interview with Mark H. Beck, AIA, president of Beck, Powell & Parsons, Inc. and one of the architects involved in bringing in the QUEST team. Speaking of the Inner Harbor area, he feels that its development has had considerable influence on the present downtown urban form and nearby areas of the city, especially along the waterfront. At the present time there are proposals for some very tall condominium buildings to be located on the south side of the Inner Harbor that already have received zoning approval. In his opinion, these are totally out of scale with the surrounding neighborhoods, but probably have been approved in the belief they will be of economic benefit. On the east side of the harbor, a good mile and a half from the Inner Harbor, a fourteen-story condominium has been built after considerable controversy. However, it was approved by the planning commission with the blessing of the mayor. Undoubtedly this will cause increased pressure for further intensive development in that area.

The loss in this situation is the potential of blocking the harbor view from existing homes behind the condominiums, in spite of them being located on a hillside. He felt that had there been longer-range planning, there probably would have been some control criteria established. Baltimore has no height limitation other than some height control along the water's edge and a requirement for stepping back for the higher portion of a structure. An encouraging comment from Beck was that the new mayor "is feeling his way as to what the right directions are and is greatly involved in this particular community." It is essentially an older, residential blue–collar community with some "yuppie" gentrification and the residents want to preserve the present scale of the area's development.

Other Influences on Development

On the eastern side of the harbor, economic forces seem to have become the most important factor in future development, as well as elsewhere in the city. Backers of anything appearing to offer increased economic development seem to be saying, "build a lot, build it high, build it dense." Construction on the harbor's eastern side also has increased demand and sparked redevelopment and rehabilitation of some existing structures used for warehouse purposes. There may be some question if this is the right kind of form for that area as they are all four- or five-storied and block the view of everything behind them.

Beck had high praise for downtown planning and revitalization, but pointed out that this had to be credited mostly to the business community, especially James Rouse and the early Greater Baltimore Committee (GBC) which Rouse is largely responsible for organizing. The GBC established the Charles Center Development Group and ultimately was able to exercise a private-sector planning initiative, create a specific plan and see its successful implementation.

As a verification of my impression of a lack of coordination and refusal of elected officials to support the planning department, Beck indicated that within the city government there is a division of responsibility, as well as a number of other separate quasi-independent agencies with planning and development authority. While the planning department is confined to providing the overall principles of planning, the housing and community development department is the implementing authority and is very much a factor in planning for the city. In addition he mentioned the Charles Center–Inner Harbor Group, a Charles Street Corridor Group and the Market Street Development Area organization; all have authority to do planning activity, meet and negotiate with developers and condemn land with city council's approval. Also, there is a Regional Planning Council covering a five-county area that comprises the Greater Baltimore Metropolitan Area.

Another architect/planner, Charles A. Kubat, AIA, AICP, associate principal of RTKL Associates, Inc., is very much involved in AIA activity in Baltimore and was also instrumental in securing the QUEST team study. He agreed that the initiative of the private sector was largely responsible for planning and accomplishing the major inner-city development, particularly around the Inner Harbor. In addition, he and his firm were involved in the successful effort to prevent the state highway department from carrying out their plans for running an expressway near the water's edge of the Inner Harbor that would have blocked the availability of the land now being put to such good use as a major attraction for Baltimore. If the state highway department would have had its way, in his opinion, all of present-day downtown would have been ruined. The only design standards applied in the city are the review and design recommendations of another AIA group in which Kubat has been involved known as the Design Advisory Panel. Although the city refers major projects to them for review, their recommendations are only advisory.

Economic Development

The Economic Development Corporation president, Bernard Berkowitz, AICP, worked for the planning department in 1966 when Larry Reich came on as director. Reich brought with him a strong belief in policy planning, and soon after the new director's arrival, they began working on the components of a comprehensive policies plan with one area being that of economic development. Based upon Reich's experience in Philadelphia, they began to tie the CIP more closely to the comprehensive plan. Berkowitz stayed with the department as head of its economic development function and the CIP, rising to assistant director and then deputy director before leaving in 1974 to join Mayor Schaefer's staff as physical developer coordinator. Schaefer had established a number of coordinator positions on various issues, but the track record showed that the physical development coordinator was always the most significant one.

The idea of creating an economic development commission was first put forward in 1968 and was part of a bond referendum that year with proposed funding of $3 million. While Schaefer's predecessor as mayor put it on the ballot, he did not get behind it fully and as a result it was not approved. Three years later when Schaefer first ran for mayor it was put on the ballot again with Schaefer's strong support; he rounded up additional backing from the newspapers and others which aided in the referendum's approval. In 1972 the Baltimore Economic Development Corporation (BEDCO) was created and in 1980 Berkowitz left Schaefer's staff to become its director. When BEDCO was first organized, its purpose was to begin a land banking program and industrial parks operation. Three and a half years later it was decided to merge the city's economic development function and action was taken to dissolve this city department and transfer all its responsibilities to the Department of Housing and Community Development. This department then contracted with BEDCO to perform all economic development functions for the city.

BEDCO, therefore, really is a city entity, funded operationally from the city's budget with a board of directors appointed by the mayor. Also there are a number of advisory committees for special areas of their operation. Certain of their programs operate under policy direction from the private sector such as the venture capital program, even though it is funded with city money. One example of the subgroups created is the Downtown Office Task Force comprised of realtors and building owners. Berkowitz felt that the public/private partnership is a reality in Baltimore, although responsibility for policy determination rests predominantly with the city and the mayor's office.

Coordination of Economic Development and Planning

Berkowitz pointed out that the concept of the programs and structure of BEDCO and its funding was first proposed in the economic portion of the planning department's comprehensive plan. However, it is interesting to note that he did not comment on the fact that in city government the planning department is being bypassed currently and the coordinating agency with which BEDCO works directly is the Department of Housing and Community Development. When I expressed a feeling that there were a large number of separate agencies charged or concerned with action programs affecting planning and city development which gave an impression that there was no centralized coordinating agency, Berkowitz disagreed. He explained that there is an ombudsman-type agency in the Housing and Community Development Department and that agency has the legal responsibility for economic development which is contracted to BEDCO. The various development corporations such as the Charles Center–Inner Harbor Management are all under contract to the city through that department. It was also his opinion that when Schaefer was mayor he and his staff did a lot of the day-to-day coordinating. He felt that it was too early to tell just what the direction would be under the new mayor. Because of his past association with planning, it was obvious that Berkowitz operates differently than some other economic development directors and maintains a close working relationship with Reich and the city's planning department.

The Role of the Greater Baltimore Committee

The development consultant interviewed, William Boucher III, president of Boucher & Associates, has been involved in Baltimore civic affairs for many, many years, and had first-hand knowledge of the decline and rebirth of the central business area as well as the development of the current situation. For twenty-six years he was the executive director of the Greater Baltimore Committee (GBC) and thus involved with the creation of the Charles Center and the Inner Harbor renewal projects. He said that the slogan of this group, comprised of one hundred of the chief executive officers of the region (never publicly printed) was, "What's best for the city is best for business." The GBC was organized in 1955 by a group of younger private-sector executives led by James Rouse who had become convinced that the city was in deep trouble. This had been brought into sharp focus with the closing of one of the last major department stores in the downtown.

Wisely the GBC began to look for some projects which they felt would be easy to accomplish quickly in order to create the feeling of dramatic success from their efforts. The identified projects were the development of a new convention center for the downtown, the implementation of the proposed Jones Falls Expressway to provide much needed access to the center city, and the establishment of a Port Authority. The expressway was approved by the voters within a month of the GBC's start-up, certainly not just due to their efforts, but they could take some credit for its passage. Within an eighteen-month period the civic center was authorized and the Port Authority created.

From there, this group of private-sector leaders moved on to concentrate on the central city and some one thousand acres around it and soon decided that a comprehensive development plan for that area should be their next project. They approached the mayor and planning commission about this idea, but the response was that it couldn't be done. Consequently, the private-sector group decided among themselves that they would put up $350,000 to do the plan. With this kind of demonstrated commitment, the city then agreed to cooperate with them. Their first step was to hire David Wallace and his firm Wallace, Roberts & Todd from Philadelphia to organize and prepare the plan. In the meantime, members of the GBC began to contact heads of corporations and businesses whom they knew had been considering moving out of downtown and successfully convinced them to take a "wait and see" attitude or to make a definite commitment for space in the new office buildings to be built. There had been no new major construction in the downtown area in almost thirty years, but the support of the president of the First National Bank and others was obtained and a spirit of optimism had been created.

The Beginning of the Inner Harbor Development

Again, instead of trying to develop the entire one thousand acres all at once, the decision was wisely made to start with a smaller area where accomplishment could produce evidence of success. A thirty-three acre area outside the center of the city that would connect the financial district and retail district to an area of deteriorated, vacant stores was selected as the first site for planning and development. Credit should be given to David Wallace for his strategic method in interviewing 264 business people about their own plans for the next five or ten years and getting the city's support through use of its redevelopment authority. However, it was indicated to me that "irrelevant" would not be too strong a word to use as to the role played by the city planning commission and department in all of this. On the other hand, it is probably true that, if this had been proposed by the planners at this time, they would have been run out of town. Nevertheless, the result was the start of the Charles Center and the rebirth of downtown, all planned by the private sector in partnership with the city. A nonprofit corporation, the Charles Center Management Corporation was formed, later becoming the Charles Center–Inner Harbor Management Corporation, which had one client—the city of Baltimore.

After Charles Center was well underway, then Mayor McKeldin contacted the GBC executive director and said he was interested in getting another large project started during the term to which he had just been elected and the mayor brought up the Inner Harbor idea. The private-sector group was pleased with the mayor's support and thus the Inner Harbor Committee was formed with GBC's director serving as chairman. It was proposed that the private sector, instead of putting up all the money as they did with the other plan, would be responsible for two-thirds and the city would supply one-third. The mayor agreed but, interestingly, Schaefer who was then a member of the city council opposed this idea, as did Jeff Miller, the dollar-a-year man the GBC had obtained as director of the Charles Center project.

Attempts to Strengthen Role of Planning Rebuffed

In fairness to the private sector, it should be pointed out that they tried several times to get the city administration to strengthen the role of the planning department in the city structure and to designate it as the responsible city agency in these projects. The suggestion was made to the mayor at the time of the Charles Center development that this would be a good time to do so. Previously GBC had suggested restructuring the Board of Estimate by taking the public works director off and using the planning director. This idea of increasing the power of the planning department in this way was considered heresy and too radical, and was, of course, turned down in connection with Charles Center and later, when another attempt was made to strengthen the department with the Inner Harbor project.

Nevertheless, the Inner Harbor project proceeded with the city using its power of urban renewal again and the private sector bringing David Wallace back to do the planning. This was in the early 1960s, at the same time that the state highway department was planning to cram its freeway along the waterfront down Baltimore's throat. Fortunately, in that period the planning commission had a strong chairman and planning did play an important role, along with GBC and private- and public-sector interests, in preventing the throughway from happening. Larry Reich arrived on the scene to assume the role of planning director as all this activity was occurring. In summary, the Inner Harbor development would not have happened without the Charles Center and the Charles Center could not have happened without the private sector.

An Important New Challenge

There is one final illustration of the challenge now facing the city administration and the people of Baltimore. It has been mentioned several times that there is a newly elected mayor. He is Kurt L. Schmoke, Baltimore's first full-term black mayor. A challenge exists for both him and the people of Baltimore. He has a great opportunity to pull the people of the city together and build a stronger city with a stronger sense of community. The question is will he set this as his major objective or will a feeling of obligation to the black community, his major constituency, contribute to divisiveness and the possibility of losing the effective support of the private sector? The hope for the city is that he will choose the former.

SAN DIEGO, CALIFORNIA

At the time of my visit to San Diego, I would classify that city as having reached the apex of an urban form resulting from the belief that all growth is good regardless of the problems it may cause. Beyond that, there appears to be a lack of preparedness and financial capability to deal with this growth. Highway engineers and automobiles and other combustion-engine vehicles have become the dominant force in shaping the city's physical character. Even so, in the past, and still in existence, there have been and are people and agencies that have tried to achieve effective planning and, while it has been difficult and is limited, there has been some success.

According to Michael Stepner, AIA, AICP, assistant planning director, growth has always been a major topic in Southern California.

Certainly it has been a pressing item of discussion in San Diego for over sixty years. People have been concerned about how fast the city is growing and the quality of that growth since the days of John Nolan, an early pioneer in planning consulting, and his comprehensive plan of 1927. In fact the city has prepared or had prepared for it a number of plans. The problem has been that necessary implementation actions have fallen through the cracks, as a result of the recently changing economic conditions, or were rejected by a vote of the people as was the case in 1967. Still another plan was prepared and adopted in 1979, this time in support of the plan proposal to restrict growth in "urban reserve areas," but was quietly disregarded after another vote of the people overturned an action taken by the council. Like Denver, the city went from a boom period of the 1970s to a recessionary period in the early 1980s. Where normal housing growth had been about nine thousand units per year, in the first three years of the 1980s this number fell as low as two thousand. Unlike in Denver, this recession quickly ended and between 1985 and 1987 San Diego saw fifteen to eighteen thousand housing starts a year.

Growth Pressure Results and Reaction

The pressure for growth was there and the private economic situation was right during the last half of the 1980s (and still is), but the city has not been able to organize and coordinate overall planning or keep up with public facilities and services. Because of Proposition 13, the city financing mechanism for new subdivisions calls for hitting the developer at the front-end for as much of the servicing costs as possible and this eventually ends up being passed on to homebuyers as increased sales prices. The process and legal mechanisms in California do not allow cities to spend money for the needed services until it is all in hand, but they do not get to this point until the housing is completed. By then there already are people occupying the units screaming and yelling because they don't have the services they expect. This places the cities in a next to impossible situation and as a consequence there is a sense of turmoil and panic emanating from the San Diego administrative and planning operations.

In the meantime there has been an increasing interest on the part of the general public in the institution of growth management controls in the San Diego region. This interest resulted in four proposals for limiting growth and providing growth management controls, one by the city council, one by the county and two citizen initiatives being placed on the ballot in November 1988. Due to confusion over the wording of these proposals, the lack of unity on the part of supporters and, primarily, the $2 million spent and the pressures generated by the development community, all were defeated. The usual argument of the developers that any limitation would destroy the economy and increase housing costs was again used to good effect. This left the city scurrying around passing stop-gap emergency, piecemeal measures to try to maintain some degree of control and protect environmentally sensitive lands from growth intrusion.

Lack of Coordination

The conclusion was easily drawn from other interviews that San Diego has a more disjointed, uncoordinated approach to shaping its urban form than Baltimore. Unfortunately, it also has not had the direct private financial involvement in downtown projects from which Baltimore greatly benefited. Stepner listed for me the various agencies involved, one way or another, with planning and development for the city. Included were San Diegans, Inc., a private, nonprofit business group; Center City Development Corporation (CCDC), the urban renewal authority for the central part of the city; Central City Association (CCA), composed mainly of retail business people; Downtown Marketing Consortium (DMC), a marketing super agency in the mayor's office; and the Center City Planning Committee (CCPC), created by the mayor. This last committee is chaired by Ernie Hahn, a major nationwide developer who is responsible for the development of the city's Horton Plaza shopping center, and is comprised of some twenty people from various governmental agencies that own or control the use of large parcels of downtown land, including the port commission, transit district, and the U.S. Navy. In addition there is representation from the chamber of commerce, visitor's bureau and residential and environmental groups.

The charge to the CCPC is to update and revise the Center City Community Plan of ten years ago and determine the next stage of where the city's downtown is going. Although the planning commission does have representation on this committee, the role of the planning agency in this is unclear and, again, there is no indication of any relevant relationship that this revised plan will have with the comprehensive urban development of the total community, if the plan is ever developed. Putting all the information obtained together, it appears that there are at least eight separate organizations, four of these created by the city, charged with or assuming some responsibility for downtown development.

Community and Neighborhood Planning

San Diego does have an organized neighborhood planning program in the planning department. The city has been divided into planning districts and Stepner indicated there are forty Community Planning Groups, some of which are organizations with other than neighborhood concerns such as environmental and business development interests. However, the planning groups exist primarily in the neighborhoods with each of these having its own elected council which has no authority other than that of representing the neighborhood in making recommendations to city council. These planning groups have been given the responsibility of developing a suggested "community plan" for their area. Other than the department community planners working with the groups—and, hopefully, pulling them together toward a citywide plan—there is no centralized coordination of the rest of the separate organizations.

The effectiveness of the neighborhood planning groups and the value of the planning agency representatives assigned to work with them was questioned by Kathy Giles, a very highly involved neighborhood activist, who said:

> One of the big problems is that the developers know that if a planner is going to recommend against their project all they have to do is go around the planning department and directly approach one or two council members. Pressure is then exerted on the neighborhood planner to either modify or change the recommendation. What leadership there is in San Diego looks at land solely as a commodity where the owner is entitled to maximize his or her benefit even if it results in subsidization by the public sector. Any other concept about land ownership is considered communistic.

The Real Power in Downtown Planning

There was no question that the most powerful organization as far as the central city is concerned is the Center City Development Corporation (CCDC). This was established by the city after officials and civic leaders visited Baltimore and is patterned on the operation of the Charles Center–Inner Harbor Management Corporation there. Theoretically it is a nonprofit corporation operating under contract to the city as a redevelopment agency as well as the primary control agency for all development in three large center-city sectors. These are three of the four sectors of the 1,200 acre portion of the city designated in the 1970s general plan as center-city redevelopment areas. They are referred to as Columbia, Marina, and Horton Plaza, for which the CCDC has the responsibility for renewal and guiding development, and the Gas Lamp Quarter for which the responsibility for administration, except for redevelopment, rests with the planning department.

In essence the final control of what happens in these areas still remains with the mayor and council as they must approve all action of the CCDC and the planning department. Each of the areas has been assigned a predominant land use characteristic by the adopted plan with that for Columbia being office development, housing in Marina, a mix of retail and offices in Horton Plaza, and historic preservation and restoration in the Gas Lamp Quarter. Again, the city council can (and during my visit, did) change the predominant designation for an area when they passed an ordinance specifying that eighty percent of the Marina area would be residential and twenty percent commercial, based upon a recommendation of the CCDC, not the planning commission or planning department.

This ordinance amendment says a great deal about San Diego's elected officials' commitment to long-range planning. Like most other cities San Diego wanted to build a new convention center and the prevailing plan called for it to be located in the Columbia area. The San Diego Port Authority, another separate organization affecting downtown development, just happened to own some land in the Marina area and agreed to build the convention center on that site with its funds and lease the building to the city. Thus the reason for the ordinance changing the plan designation from "predominantly residential" for Marina to a specific percentage designation. Accordingly, it would appear that any hotels needed to serve the convention center, unless they are considered "residential," might have to be built in the Columbia area or the Horton Plaza area, that is until the CCDC convinces the council to again change the planning designations.

What about the relationship between these many agencies, especially the CCDC, planning commission and planning department? According to San Diegans, Inc. executive vice president, Roy Potter, he and his organization work very closely with the planners. The same cannot be said for the chamber of commerce, the Central City Association, the Port Authority, the Navy, also a large land owner in the center city, and certainly not the CCDC. The words of the CCDC representative explaining the process a developer would have to follow in gaining approval for a project in one of the three designated areas under CCDC control best place this in perspective:

> If a developer proposes a project in one of our designated areas he or she comes to us with that first. The proposal then goes before a Residents' Advisory Committee of people living in that area, then to a subcommittee of the CCDC board or to the board itself, then to the planning commission to get their input, and finally to the city council acting as the Local Public Agency (LPA) for renewal. About the time it is going to the CCDC board the planning department comes over and gets copies of the plan and they write a staff report that goes to the planning commission.

When asked the hypothetical question supposing that the CCDC recommends approval to city council and the planning staff report recommending against it was approved by the planning commission, who is going to win with the council, the reply was:

> I think the CCDC would win. That is because I don't think that the city council respects planners as people who influence implementation of what they think. The developers and the city council give more credence to the people on our board of directors because of their interaction and who they are socially. It almost has nothing to do with planning, but it has a lot to do with politics and egos. I don't think that the planners have been very aggressive nor have they presented their cases as strongly as other people have. They have not been effective in their presentations in overcoming the strong, well presented arguments of the developers. It is the dynamics of what is going on rather than listening to what are the best things for the city.

How San Diego Adds Up

There is no doubt from an overview of long-range planning and urban form development coordination that the future of San Diego could be headed in a much better direction than it presently is. Part of this can be credited to some of the outside forces discussed such as the state taxing policy, mandated regulations enforced half-heartedly by reluctant local officials, and the tendency of citizens for government by petition and referendum. Some of the difficulty arises from the diversity of philosophy, interests, and cultural backgrounds of its people.

However, I must say that from the people on the planning staff I met, talked to, and watched in action, my opinion differs widely from that of the CCDC representative. I found them to be capable, seriously dedicated professionals, spread too thinly from lack of staff, and somewhat frustrated by the absence of a widespread planning attitude throughout the city. During my visit I attended a work session of some members of the city council and a meeting of the planning commission where planning staff presented reports, answered questions and expressed their views. In both cases these were well done, laced with facts and information, clearly indicated alternatives and well thought out recommendations. What I saw, however, was an absence of even the faintest indication of a real understanding of the planning process or a planning attitude from any council member present at the work session or planning commissioner present at that public meeting. Instead, it was economic development at any cost and politics carrying the day on every issue.

Perhaps the situation is as neighborhood activist Giles said to me after the planning commission meeting:

> I don't believe that there is a planning ethic here. In many respects, I think that it is a smokescreen. I think that it is a bunch of hype. It is something that is used as opiate of the masses—we'll make everybody feel good because of planning. The reality is that the plans are thrown out of the window as soon as there is political pressure for a change. It is the city council that does this and a very small power clique controls what is happening in San Diego.

Even more dramatic were the comments of the taxi cab driver who took me to the airport when I left. He was not your usual cab driver in that he spends two months a year in Paris, France and gave me quite a lecture about how much smarter Europeans are regarding cities than we Americans are. Just before I left him, in talking about San Diego he summed it up this way: "I wish they thought more about the future. All we do is keep building highways so we can keep the maximum use of our cars—and now we already have gridlock. Nobody thinks about the future!"

DENVER, COLORADO

Denver is included here, as previously mentioned, because of earlier planning efforts in making it an attractive, livable city and the attempts of the mayor and the planning department to instill a planning attitude in the city since 1983. The interviews conducted provided a good cross-section of representative involvement. Since much of the evaluation, as well as specific examples of factors affecting Denver's development have already been covered in chapter two, only a few additional highlights and a summary of the present situation will be included here.

Like a number of other cities, Denver suffers from an overbalanced council district election system. There are thirteen council members with eleven elected by district vote and only two by citywide vote. As is the case in cities operating under a predominant ward system, a sense of the future of the total community has been very difficult to achieve. Frequently actions taken by individual members of council have been solely based upon what their district constituents, even if expressed by only a few, appear to want. All council members and the mayor are elected for four-year terms at the same election and it would be possible for an entire turnover to occur in any one election. Several districts are heavily populated by ethnic minorities, others are classified as "working class" neighborhoods, a few have wealthy enclaves, and only one or two have a reasonable ethnic and economic mix.

During the writing of this book, the Denver Housing Authority proposed to acquire dispersed foreclosed single-family HUD houses and relocate lower-income families from older, concentrated, large-scale public housing projects into some of the blue-collar neighborhoods to achieve better integration, as well as to provide improved housing for these people. The immediate reaction of the present residents of those neighborhoods—who produced overflow crowds of protestors at several public hearings, and, therefore, gained the support of a majority of the council members—was that we can't allow this to happen or, at least, "NIMBY" (Not In My Backyard). Consequently, the proposal was placed in limbo, and we have another example of how influence from a special interest of affected neighborhoods can foreshadow any consideration of a citywide problem. It should be said that the public relations of the authority's staff prior to springing this on the general public was very badly handled and indeed almost nonexistent. As a result of this and the hearings, a management study of the housing authority administrator's general performance was instituted and he has now resigned.

The inner ring of development around the central business district has unfortunately been permitted to develop as a hodgepodge of indiscriminate commercial uses and mixed residential density of apartment structures of varying heights, four-plexes, duplexes with a wide variety of quality together with older single family housing units also varying in quality and condition. Denver's zoning ordinance is a confused mess of legalese, so complicated that it is unclear and impossible for the average property owner to know what can and cannot be done. It also is antiquated to the point that the council regularly approves amendments to previously enacted amendments and it has been said that variances are now being granted to vary older variances. The city is desperately in need of preparing and adopting a totally revised, updated zoning ordinance, but the politicians and the pressure groups have successfully prevented this from happening. Until this occurs Denver will continue to have zoning interpretation and action controlled by the whims of administrative bureaucrats and politicians.

Some Optimistic Signs

All of these factors, together with the total absence of any interest in planning over a long period, has made it difficult to stimulate and develop a community and citywide planning attitude in Denver. In the election of 1983 the successful candidate for mayor, Federico Pena, won on a campaign committed to planning for the future of Denver and he effectively used the slogan, "Imagine A Great City." Since that time, in spite of a number of problems and some fumbling by the administration, though still playing catch-up, the city has moved ahead—however, not without criticism from some of the mayor's enemies. The strengthening of the planning department and the hiring of William Lamont, AICP, as planning director together with the fact that appointments were made of a number of known civic leaders to the planning board have instilled the rebirth of a planning attitude, at least in some people in the city.

At the same time, much needed physical developments that will generate sound economic development have been undertaken, but not just because of that. Some of these developments are in keeping with the administration and planning department proposals, although a few were adjusted in proposed size or location without deviation from the basic concept by a vote of the people or numerous community and neighborhood discussion meetings. These include a new downtown convention center, a new Cherry Creek Mall Shopping Center, a revitalizing physical improvement and beautification project for the North Cherry Creek Shopping District, a plan beginning to become a reality for the Lower Platte River Valley, (the only remaining, large open-space in the center city), and a giant step toward the construction of a new international airport on the eastern edge of Denver.

One of the most promising things of all is the completion of a draft of an excellent revised comprehensive plan formulated by the planning department with extensive citizen involvement. Fortunately, thanks to action taken by the council during this writing, it can be said that an even brighter spot can be noted. I am pleased to be able to report that while writing this chapter the plan became an actuality when a strong turnout of citizens involved in the plan's development and other supporters made their voices heard at the public hearing conducted by the council that resulted in a unanimous vote to approve the plan. Now it is to be hoped that the council will maintain a commitment for the plan's implementation and the involved citizens will fulfill their stated intention of a continuing pressure to see that this is done. The next election of both the mayor and city council is an extremely important one and could turn on the issue of support for the plan. All neighborhood organizations should realize the importance of this, get together to support candidates who offer leadership capabilities and every voter should follow the aforementioned Boulder example and ask each candidate whether they support planning before they decide for whom to vote.

SAINT PAUL, MINNESOTA

Saint Paul was not the subject of as much in-depth investigation as some of the other cities, but my visit there did provide some insight on its planning approach. I must honestly say that the present apparent philosophy of urban-renewal-type, pragmatic-oriented action is not that which I feel is the most important to the long-range future of this city and certainly is not the kind of comprehensive planning from which the city has benefited in past years. Saint Paul is included in this chapter because the city has some impressive specific development accomplishments, an active neighborhood program and including Saint Paul allowed a comparison with Minneapolis and other cities. Saint Paul's policy and strategy-oriented planning approach is somewhat similar to that of Baltimore and appears to be slightly more effective than those of San Antonio and Corpus Christi as discussed in chapter six. Nonetheless, it would appear that many decisions concerning the urban form follow the same pattern of being based upon economic development rather than on the principles of coordinated planning and urban design. The city has an action-oriented mayor who obviously has gained the respect of many for his leadership qualities, including some with whom I spoke in Minneapolis. Their strong-mayor system gives people the opportunity to know who is responsible for the administration as compared with the handicap of the system under which Minneapolis has chosen to govern itself. All Saint Paul council members are elected from wards.

Material obtained on the city provided a general overview of the focus for the planning division, a subdivision of the Department of Planning and Economic Development and the Planning Commission. In its 1987 annual report the commission is shown as being divided into five committees. These are economic development, neighborhood and housing, steering, zoning, and urban revitalization action, but as in Baltimore, a comprehensive planning committee is conspicuous by its absence. All of these are active, working committees and their major accomplishments during the year are itemized in the report including such things as the review of ninety-two applications for zoning changes (and recommending twenty-one of them to city council), an "adult entertainment" study, the Highway 280/University Avenue Redevelopment Plan and a review of plans of the Watershed Management Organization with recommendations to city council. Saint Paul has a somewhat out-of-date comprehensive plan and the commission proposes to update and replace major elements of it in keeping with a recent report titled, "Saint Paul Tomorrow," which is a study of present conditions and a general indication of future directions for the city. For example, one of these elements is an update of the ten-year-old land use plan for which the commission, working with community participation, will prepare recommendations for any necessary changes making it more current. Also on the 1988 agenda was a new Economic Development Strategy to focus community efforts toward greater economic opportunity for city residents.

Neighborhood Planning

Saint Paul is to be commended for its obvious community and neighborhood involvement in shaping the future of its neighborhoods. One of the better aspects of the planning process in the city is this extensive work with the neighborhood areas. Planning districts have been established throughout the city and an effective program of working with people has been devised and implemented. This includes a Neighborhood Partnership Program and more recently the development of an Urban Revitalization Action Program with URAP program guidelines prepared by the commission and adopted by the city council. Each district has a planning council with which the planning division works in preparing district plans in keeping with the overall goals for the city. Again missing is any discussion of how the opportunity will be provided for developing a sense of the future for the entire city among the individual neighborhoods or how educating the residents on the importance of this can be used to an advantage.

The transmittal letter with the 1987 annual report indicates the high degree of importance given to the neighborhoods with the following opening comments:

> . . . The year saw new initiatives suggested by the Saint Paul Tomorrow study, including support for Better Neighborhoods and initiation of an Urban Revitalization Action Program with a high level of neighborhood initiative. And the Commission has been hard at work on many individual issues of importance to neighborhoods: community residential facilities, adult entertainment, college zoning and Shepard Road to name a few. In 1988 we look forward to working closely with you to meet the major planning goals established by the Council[2]

The neighborhood involvement program in Saint Paul is unquestionably a priority item for Saint Paul's planning and has much of the kind of action and initiative generation that other cities would do well to emulate, provided the need for carrying it one step further is understood. It could be an excellent way to develop a community spirit and a feeling of city pride if the need for all neighborhoods to care for the future of the overall development of the city were included along with a work program for the planning division to work effectively in uniting the neighborhoods for this purpose.

NOTES

1. Simpson Lawson, "Baltimore Re-Examined," *AIA Journal* (November 1982).

2. Saint Paul Planning Commission, *Annual Report 1987*, Department of Planning and Economic Development, Planning Division.

6

Then There Are Others

Using the criteria set forth in chapter seven, especially that of evidence of the presence or absence of a planning attitude on the part of elected officials and the citizenry, the remaining cities studied were placed in this final category. Considerable similarity was found among them in their attitudes toward growth and economic development. These factors together with a highly politicized climate appear to be the prime factors motivating the policymakers. It is an interesting coincidence that all of them are located in the southern part of the country with four of them classified as Sun Belt cities.

THE MASON-DIXON LINE AND
PLANNING ATTITUDES

A philosophical analysis provided by Roy Potter of San Diego appears even more accurate after a review of the information obtained in these cities than it did when I first heard it. In discussing the attitude differential present in the people of San Diego and other more northern California cities such as San Francisco, his premise is that if the Mason-Dixon Line were wavingly extended across the country you would find on each side two differing mindsets regarding the role government should play in peoples' lives. The reason for this is due to three factors. The first is the prevailing attitude in the southern section that reveres private enterprise and private individual effort more than in the northern section where you find more group efforts, more planning, and more public concern. Secondly, the cooler climates of the north contribute to making it a necessity for people to work

together more on reducing energy costs, snow removal, street sand-
ing, etc. to survive through the winter. Thirdly, the people in the
southern section descended from settlers dedicated to escaping tyr-
anny of both government and religion; they continue to be more indi-
vidualistic while there is greater respect for the interest of the
community in the north. With the major exception of Charlotte, this
thesis is supported by the findings in my research.

In the five cities included in this chapter the search for a real sense
of total community, an overall planning attitude and a concern for the
future was totally unsuccessful. Disesteem for government regulations that express a community interest in the development of private
land was evident in each one. Certainly, there was evidence of a common interest in anything proffering economic development, but it almost always was based upon personal economic or short-sighted
political benefit.

There is nothing wrong with this attitude when it results, either directly or indirectly, in some type of common community good. Indi-
vidualistic self-interest becomes harmful, however, when it leads to a
lack of unity, group involvement, or policies that contribute to social
ills, deteriorating air quality, environment, and quality of life. Draw
this imaginary line extending up and around the northern border of
Colorado and you have another perfect example of the problems emanating from an overabundance of individualism and how it can adversely affect an entire state.

NEW ORLEANS, LOUISIANA

New Orleans is an example of a city where geographic location and
history provided an excellent opportunity for people to come together
over the years and, capitalizing on those two components, build and
maintain true greatness. Had historic preservation been a paramount
concern in the past instead of only recently, the appeal for tourists
alone could have been almost sufficient to provide a sustaining economic base for the city as is the case in Charleston, South Carolina.
The importance of future-oriented leadership in charting the direction of government is emphasized by the negative example of New
Orleans today. While there is some evidence that in political administrations of the past this spark of leadership existed, it has been totally
absent in recent years.

New Orleans' Planning Attitude

As the interviews disclosed, a lot of people talk about planning and the high regard they have for the planning staff, but the action taken belies any sincerity of intent. Funding for the planning function, already drastically reduced, continues to be considered an intangible item that can always be ignored, or cut even further. The city's comprehensive master plan is woefully out of date and in need of revision, but promised funds for doing so continue not to be appropriated. Several people spoke of the increasing growth of neighborhood organizations and their influence on the elected officials, but no one is raising any hue and cry for stronger citywide planning and goal setting. The lack of a current comprehensive plan supported by policymakers leaves the neighborhood groups and interested individuals without any sense of the larger picture for the entire city. As a result the neighborhoods feel that the only things they have to be concerned about are the individual projects that affect their own area. Robert Becker, AICP, planning director stated that he couldn't remember the city ever having developed overall community goals and a statement of policies for their implementation. This should be a major issue in this city, but it is not.

Five of the eight persons interviewed, commenting on the more than forty zoning moratoriums in existence in different neighborhoods, agreed that this is a mistaken concept of the use of a zoning ordinance. These moratoriums have resulted from neighborhood objections to proposals for specific types of use, such as liquor stores, T-shirt shops, fast-food restaurants, or buildings of excessive height. Storming city hall in protest results in the adoption of a moratorium on further development of that particular problem in a small section of the concerned neighborhood, but it is not applicable to the rest of the zoning district. Council members like this approach because it enhances their political power. The council member interviewed called the moratoria idea "an effective zoning tool." According to him, several people have challenged the council's authority to do this and, so far "we have been successful and have won every time there has been a court challenge." Others, however, completely disagreed and indicated there was doubt that any of the challenges had been properly presented with strongly researched arguments and facts. Had they been, the action of council would surely have been overturned. Where the fundamental zoning law principle—that all like users must be treated alike throughout a zoning district—went in New Orleans, no one seems to know.

The French Quarter

The French Quarter (Vieux Carre is preferred by the natives), certainly one of New Orleans' greatest assets, has suffered the greatest abuse of any area from the lack of long-range vision and comprehensive planning by city officials. Anyone with eyes and a sensitivity for historic urban-design quality who has visited it in recent years can see readily the degradation permitted to occur under the guise of commercial economic development. Here is an area established in 1718 as the first settlement in La Nouvelle Orleans. It was recognized as an historic district in 1924, officially chartered in 1938, placed on the national register by the Department of Interior in 1967, and its boundaries—corresponding to those of the original city—established by state constitutional amendment in 1973. Yet, through numerous zoning mistakes, and as a result of an overzealous, myopic quest for so-called economic development, it has been debased beyond belief by its own government, which continues to do so today.

How To Destroy A Valuable Asset.   There is an official city Vieux Carre Commission comprised of nine members appointed by the mayor from a list of names submitted by the New Orleans AIA chapter, chamber of commerce, and Louisiana Historic Society with the mayor retaining the power to appoint three at-large members. The ordinance creating the commission was originally passed in 1925 and has been amended several times in attempts to clarify its jurisdictional powers; however, the constitutional amendment, the city ordinances and the existence of the commission and its executive director have not been enough to protect the district. According to Ray Boudreaux, past president of the Vieux Carre Property Owners, Residents and Associates, Inc., there have never been public officials in the city with sufficient understanding and sensitivity about the value of the historic and cultural perspective of the district. Instead it has been treated merely as something to exploit for additional shoddy commercial development and even federal, state and city proposals destructive to its character have been proposed, or, in some cases, actually constructed. Zoning by the city supercedes the district's own requirements and restrictions; however district residents have continually fought with council in an attempt to keep zoning as compatible with the Vieux Carre's standards as possible. Seven of the city's zoning moratoria are in effect in different areas of this district as a result of neighborhood protests against the proliferation of character-destructive uses allowed by the city.

The potentially most damaging threat to the character of Vieux Carre began in 1946. At that time the Louisiana Highway Department hired Robert Moses, the controversial power broker from New York to prepare a report and recommendations for improving the muddled traffic pattern in New Orleans. As he had done in New York and elsewhere, Moses's report, "Arterial Plan for New Orleans," proposed an elevated expressway along the Mississippi River through the entire Vieux Carre riverfront. In spite of initial objections, the city's "Major Street Report, 1951" advocated construction of a six-lane surface street through the area or, if that was not feasible, the proposed elevated expressway.

Support for the expressway came from the downtown business community, especially the very powerful central area committee of the chamber of commerce, along with other advocates of "progress." There was so much support for this project that in the years between the Moses proposal and 1969 the city planning commission placed the expressway on its Major Street Plan of 1958, and then-mayor Victor H. Schiro succeeded in getting the city council to approve his 1963 capital improvement budget with $2.1 million for right-of-way acquisition. Further, the Federal Highway Commissioner officially approved the route of the riverfront expressway in 1966 and the possibility arose that the ultimate location of a new bridge over the river connecting to the expressway, proposed by the Mississippi River Bridge Authority, could add to the potential impact on the Vieux Carre.

Fortunately A Few Cared.   Opposition forces continued to grow in numbers and in 1967 a suit known as the Pontalba case was filed in the federal district court seeking to prevent the construction of the expressway. This began continued delays through court proceedings, changes in federal legislation pertaining to environmental protection in President Lyndon Johnson's era, and growing local and national support of the Vieux Carre's plight, plus any number of additional reports and hearings. Finally, on July 1, 1969, Secretary of Transportation John A. Volpe canceled the riverfront expressway project because it "would have seriously impaired the historic quality of New Orleans' famed French Quarter."[1] (*The Second Battle of New Orleans*, by Richard O. Baumbach, Jr. and William E. Borah, is recommended reading for those interested in this important illustration of the potential for adverse effects caused by a lack of organized comprehensive planning in New Orleans—as well as the power of aroused, aggressive citizen action when enough people become concerned.)

Another Blow to The Vieux Carre. The French Quarter's problems did not end with Volpe's cancellation of the expressway. The latest battering has come from the Urban Park Commission and its proposal to build the New Orleans Aquarium, which—in spite of neighborhood opposition—is already under construction. The site is on the riverfront between the southwestern boundary of the district and the river. A portion of the open view of the river as well as access is being blocked. Both representatives of the Vieux Carre and the Preservation Resource Center expressed strong objections to the selection of this location with no real basis from a comprehensive plan as to why it should be built there. This, together with the private development along the riverfront, emphasizes even more the lack of a public planning attitude in the city. Private developers such as the Hilton Hotels Corporation, builders of the Hilton Riverside and Towers and the Riverwalk bring in their own architects and planners, tell the city what they want to do, and get approval with no direction provided by a specific riverfront development plan.

The Downtown Development District

Although still an example of piecemeal planning and development, a somewhat more positive note is the commendable work done by the planning department with the help of the Wallace, Roberts and Todd firm from Philadelphia in the Growth Management Plan for the downtown district. The result of a joint public/private decision made some fifteen years ago was the creation of the Downtown Development District with its own taxing authority on businesses and land owners within the district. Consequently, some good things have happened in the downtown area that have received national notice. The fact remains, however, that this is another independent body, a group of different individuals and interests, and their planning work, again, is not related to an overall city plan for the future. The comment was made that the Development District leaders have addressed themselves to raising money and increasing profits for businesses located within the district more than they have concerned themselves with city planning.

The chamber of commerce—primarily representing the attitude of this business community—has historically been an advocate of more commercialization of the Vieux Carre. This has been done under the expressed mistaken idea that this would lead to more tourists who stay in the hotels and shop downtown. The chamber was the prime agitator supporting the imposition of the freeway along the river through the area. Obviously, this adverse attitude to Vieux Carre preservation primarily has been motivated either by the desire to get more business for the stores and shops in the downtown district or a desire to degrade the quality of the French Quarter sufficiently to prevent competition by quality commercial enterprise in the area.

In summary, the theme running generally throughout the New Orleans interviews and research center around three basic problems. These are:

1. The lack of an informed planning attitude on the part of the elected officials, civic leaders, the business community and the general public.

2. The need for effective, current, comprehensive long-range planning supported by adopted goals, policies, and action programs by elected officials.

3. The threat to the future urban form, both from a physical and economic standpoint, as well as to the vital historic character that means so much to the attractive uniqueness of the city.

SAN ANTONIO, TEXAS

It was an audacious act to place San Antonio in this last group of cities, in view of the favorable national attention it has received. However, I will state that from my general observations, the interview comments, and the way some of the city's problems have, or have not, been dealt with, I was forced to conclude that the city is not an example of a place really knowing where it is or what it wants to be. The obvious evidence does not place it into the category of a well-planned city with an effective community interest, nor is the urban form that has resulted commendable from a long-range point of view.

San Antonio is famous because of its history, its cultural heritage, the Alamo, the HemisFair World's Fair of 1968, the delightful and commendable Riverwalk or Paseo del Rio, and for having laid claim to being the place where chili was invented. It is true that the early Spanish settlers wisely selected a location along the San Antonio River which later allowed the city to make the best use of a water asset of any community in the country. The start of the famed Riverwalk was provided by funds from the Works Progress Administration (WPA) during President Roosevelt's Depression recovery period. It has been expanded over the years and recently extended by rechanneling the river adjacent to the relatively new Rivercenter commercial and hotel development. This has provided increases both in business development and tourism. Interested readers are referred to an excellent account of the Riverwalk's history in an article written by Ann Breen and Dick Rigby in *Planning*.[2]

The construction of the attractive convention center complex on a part of the HemisFair land provides another major asset to the downtown, even though the city took twenty-five years to locate an acceptable project for this site. Because of strong objection on the part of the existing businesses and some citizen opposition, among others, the city rejected a proposal for development by James Rouse's Enterprise Foundation on this land some time after the fair closed.

The Question of Comprehensive Vision for the Future

The major question remains, however, of whether or not all of this development reflects a sense of vision for the future fully expressed and understood by the people of the community or have these things happened as pragmatic, individual projects? Another equally important issue is whether the people have been pulled together and given a sense of community pride and involvement that goes beyond political expediency? The information obtained indicates that neither of these things are present in the minds of those with whom I spoke. For example, in an interview with community activist and planning educator, Cathy Powell, AICP, the opinion was volunteered that in spite of the HemisFair providing a space for the present convention center, "the planning of it was done as a one-shot deal by a community that had no experience and little or no confidence in its ability to do something on that scale. Therefore, the approach was simply to get it done and not to think beyond the fair itself."

San Antonio had Henry G. Cisneros as mayor from 1981–1989. He decided not to seek re-election after the completion of four two-year terms. Cisneros is an individual with a strong and convincing personality who has excellent educational credentials including a masters degree in city and regional planning and a doctorate from Harvard. During his tenure he established a reputation for himself as a dynamic leader both locally and nationally. There is no question that his personality and speaking ability provided the tools to galvanize and electrify people into support for his ideas and policies for building San Antonio's future. Unfortunately, he also left no doubt that he did not believe that the best way to guide the development of urban form was the traditional comprehensive planning approach.

This was made quite clear in his keynote speech to some 2,700 attendees at the 1988 APA National Conference held in San Antonio. In this speech he stated that planning in his city would not be the type planners expect to find since his administration had been too busy getting things done to do the typical land use-type of planning. To me, it was ironic that he quoted the four "critical junctures" from an article by Dr. Michael P. Brooks,[3] indicated his support for them, and then neglected to explain anything about how Brooks had used these headings and what his comments about them were. Reading the article, one gets an entirely different interpretation of Brooks's concern and intent than what Cisneros intimated. In concluding remarks he reiterated that his "central theme" was economic development and his "order of the day" was the recognition of bargaining and negotiating. Additional portions of his speech further expressing his views about planning and planners appeared in the Viewpoint column of *Planning* magazine.[4] Whether the standing ovation provided him after his speech indicated support for his thesis or was the result of his persuasive presentation ability is a matter for conjecture.

San Antonio After Mayor Cisneros

After Cisneros's retirement, what are some of the problems re-elected mayor Lila Cockrell (the highly respected mayor before Cisneros), will have to face? It appears there are several major issues, all related to the future coordinated development of the urban form. Therefore, the fundamental decision will have to be made whether to continue the current disjointed approach to planning and reactive responses to major proposals and land development or try to reorganize the city structure so that preactive planning can take place. At present it is almost impossible to determine who is responsible for any of the planning and development functions, with bits and pieces of what might be called the planning process scattered between the mayor's office, the city manager, the public works department, and various special task forces established by Cisneros and Central 21, a group of twenty-one people appointed by the city council to guide downtown development.

The only clear thing about the city's planning process is that the planning department plays only a minor reactive support-service role with an inadequate staff. To further complicate matters, the planning commission and the zoning commission each operate separately. It is interesting that this separation occurred during Mayor Cockrell's earlier term when she attempted to have what was then a single planning and zoning commission undertake long-range planning. The chairman of the commission at that time, the president of the Home Builders Association, refused to do so, and it was then that Cockrell and the council decided to divide planning and zoning functions, things that should always be closely related, into two separate commissions, both of which have obviously been ineffective in creating any sense of coordinated urban form. To further contribute to the lack of co-relation, the Zoning Board of Adjustment, responsible for hearing variance appeals is another completely separate agency which further affects coordinated land use in the city.

Diversity Has Its Pluses and Minuses

In addition to the Riverwalk, one of the things that makes San Antonio unique is its long history of a diverse population, something that also adds to the problem of developing a common community interest. In an article in *Planning*, Robert Cullick estimated the city's population to be 936,000 of which 52.4 percent were Hispanic, 41 percent Anglo, and 7.8 percent Black.[5] Undoubtedly this engendered the move to council elections by districts instead of at-large in 1977, thereby further contributing to the potential for divisive application of government policy. Cullick believes that San Antonio "is staggering through the Texas recession. It's high on new ideas, but stumbling on the reality of streets that need paving and people who need jobs."

Planning consultant, William L. Telford, AICP, of Hallenberger/ Telford, Inc. agreed, adding, "The profile of San Antonio shows that it is a city of very low income level, and a very low educational level. We do not have an abundance of upper income people nor do we have the sophistication in the marketplace to support new development." Thus we find a city with major social problems, major infrastructure deficiencies, haphazard land use development, stifling traffic congestion, and a projected $27 million shortfall in revenue for the next fiscal year spending its time and energy seeking support to build a domed stadium so that it might be able to attract a professional football team.

Other Major Issues

Two additional, very important problematic forces are affecting land use development, not only in San Antonio, but also throughout the entire metropolitan area.[6] The first is the capacity limitation on potable water supply. The single source of water for over one million persons in the region is the Edwards Aquifer, an underground storage reservoir of 2,000 square miles lying north of the city's boundary. The importance of the acquifer to present and future populations has been recognized by the federal Environmental Protection Agency by its designation of the reservoir as the first "sole source" acquifer in the country. This action resulted from insistent pressure generated by a local conservation group, including one of the persons I interviewed. Protection and conservation of this valuable water resource has long been a controversial and complicated problem in San Antonio and Bexar County, within which the city is located, and yet it remains insufficiently resolved to completely assure there will not be a day in the future when the metropolitan area will suffer a serious water shortage.

In spite of a bad drought year in the 1950s that created a problem of water availability for San Antonio—which then had only approximately half its current population—the city did little to insure the protection of the recharge area, even firing a planning director who had advocated a moratorium on building on this critical land. This near-disastrous drought did result in the state legislature passing a special act creating the Edwards Underground Water District and giving it the responsibility for monitoring water level and quality in a five-county area around San Antonio. However, it was not until a few years ago that the city and the district became sufficiently concerned to hire consultants to undertake a more detailed study of the problem. The report entitled "San Antonio Regional Water Resource Study," projected that by the year 2040, demand could reach 896,000 acre-feet per year, almost 300,000 more than the average acre-feet demand over the last forty-seven years. Unless stringent measures are instituted to regulate usage and guide land development carefully, this could result in a catastrophic experience for the entire populace of the metropolitan area.

Developing such needed measures is easier said than done in what is an extremely complicated matter of jurisdiction. Involved are the Texas Water Commission, the Edwards Underground Water District,

San Antonio, Bexar County, the upstream and downstream counties, and the Environmental Protection Agency. Some progress has been made with the city and the district agreeing on an overall withdrawal limit of 450,000 acre-feet per year given an average rainfall. Higher limits are permissible when rainfall is abundant and some conservation programs designed to reduce the total usage by ten percent are in place. No resolution of the problem of the cost for building proposed reservoirs and implementing a total program, or establishing an appropriate regional agency for administration has been achieved. Nor has San Antonio's zoning ordinance been amended to strengthen land use controls or limit development in a way sufficient to protect the recharge area; indeed only a revision of the subdivision ordinance pertaining to sewer pipe installation has taken place to date. This is yet another example of the total community interest being subordinated to private development interests with a serious adverse potential for the entire community.

Highway Engineers at Work Again

Another major problem with a decisive influence on the city's land use pattern and its overall urban form is that of highways and transportation. It would appear that in Texas, the state highway department rules supreme, just as in some other states. In San Antonio it can be said that this department has been the greatest shaper of urban form, with several interviewees agreeing that the general rule is the state highway department leads and the cities follow. There apparently has not been any outcry in San Antonio that this is irresponsible or that the city is missing opportunities to shape its own future.

The full extent of how the city council accepts this as the proper procedure is best illustrated by the words of community activist, Cathy Powell, who said,

> I have sat in on council meetings where the head of the Transportation Department brought to the council the current plan of the highway district office. It was not on the agenda. Nevertheless, it was introduced and passed in a three-minute period with no discussion whatsoever. This was something where a decision was made that would affect the form of the city with no one saying, "Hey! wait a minute. Is this what we really want?" The attitude here is to just accept that the thing to do is let the State Highway Department lay out what it thinks makes sense and simply send it to the city which then says "O.K."

The latest example of what the highway planners may do to San Antonio is a proposal to make a major loop around the city into a fourteen-lane roadway by double-decking it. Should this occur the resultant effect on urban form and environmental quality as well as the potential danger to human lives is obvious. Perhaps the results of the latest earthquake in the San Francisco Bay area may cool the highway planners ardor for such impractical ideas and even heighten the San Antonio policymakers' understanding that they have a responsibility to protect the health, safety and general welfare of their citizens and other people as well.

Public Education in San Antonio

The final problem facing the reelected mayor and the people at large is one of long standing that continues to have serious social, economic, and to some extent, land use-development consequences. San Antonio's incorporated area is overlapped by twenty-one separate, independent school districts. Each of them is a political entity over which the city has no control. The center city is comprised of the old San Antonio school district and has a majority of the ethnic minority students. The result is that this district has a greater educational load than elsewhere and a tax base insufficient to support provision of needed programs or facilities. According to private planning consultant William Telford, "No professional people would think of allowing their children to attend school in this district. Instead, if necessary, they move out of the inner city to suburban areas where better educational opportunities exist." No evidence was forthcoming from any of those interviewed or any others to whom I spoke of any great public outcry about this inequitable, disjointed system nor was any proposed corrective action mentioned.

A Few Positive Actions

On the plus side, while even the planners admit that the city does not have a comprehensive plan or anything resembling a detailed land use plan, a policies plan was adopted by council in 1983 providing general guidance about land use decisions through statements on utilities, annexation, and other planning issues. In addition, what is called the Target 90 document sets forth goals and objectives for the city. This was a project initiated by former mayor Cisneros who takes great pride in the document and the fact that some five-hundred citizens were involved in helping to formulate it. There are also signs of increased neighborhood interest and involvement in the sixty organized neighborhoods. Although the city planning staff provides some technical assistance to these groups, there is no organized effort to promote neighborhood planning on a citywide basis.

One powerful force, primarily from the northern portion of the city, is the Community Organized for Public Service (COPS), a coalition initiated by twenty-six inner-city churches some fifteen years ago as an affiliate of the Industrial Areas Foundation of Chicago's Saul Alinsky and his school of political insurgency. On some issues such as the proposal to set spending limits for the city government, which Cisneros strongly opposed, COPS supported the former mayor and helped in defeating the proposition. However, on projects requiring the expenditure of public money on private-sector activity, COPS will lead the opposition, as was the case in the proposal for building the "Alamodome," a covered stadium and convention complex.

However, there are far more examples indicating lack of understanding of and support for long-range comprehensive thinking by the political leadership, the business community and the general public in San Antonio. The planning process in existence does not play any kind of visionary or leadership role; instead it is reactive with decisions made on a pragmatic, piece-meal basis. Perhaps all of this is best summed up by Cullick in his article, when he wrote that "The absence of strong planning mandates in San Antonio makes for quick work at public meetings. The nine-member planning commission, responsible only for approval of subdivision applications, the number of which has been down recently, usually finishes its weekly meetings in 10 minutes."[7] It is upon this kind of piece-meal, uncoordinated policy pertaining to planning and building of urban form that the future of the people of San Antonio rests.

MEMPHIS, TENNESSEE

Another city representing something of a paradox is Memphis. Referred to as "The Gateway to the South," Memphis is an older city, first laid out in 1819 by three owners of the land upon which it was located; one of these owners was Andrew Jackson, who in 1829 was elected U.S. president. Another of the three, General James Winchester, named it Memphis after the Egyptian city on the Nile, probably because of the advantageous location of the new settlement on the Mississippi River. Local tradition says that Memphis means "a place of good abode." It has been this over the years in spite of capture by the Union army during the Civil War, a severe yellow-fever epidemic in the 1870s, and numerous ups and downs in its economic health since its incorporation in 1826. The most devastating of its "downs" was going bankrupt in 1878 with a $6 million debt and having its charter revoked by the state, which then turned its government over to Shelby County. It was not until the beginning of the twentieth century that the city began once again to revive itself.

Memphis lays claim to fame for several notable individuals and their efforts. These include the founding of the Plough Chemical Company, now Schering-Plough corporation; the birthplace and the home of the world's largest hotel chain, Holiday Inn, and the creation of the world's largest overnight air-express delivery service, Federal Express, with its hub and headquarters contributing significantly to the Memphis economy. There are several other "firsts" about which it boasts, but two other circumstances have achieved even more worldwide recognition for the city. One is the renovation of the old, but magnificent Peabody Hotel together with its twice-daily "March of the Ducks." From their rooftop penthouse five ducks from the flock are brought to the lobby by elevator, march on a red carpet to the ornate lobby fountain and its surrounding pool with the King Cotton March playing. They swim for six hours until their return march back to the elevator. The duck march attracts dozens of adults and children as observers and it remains an attraction for parents and children during the time they swim in the pool around the fountain. It almost goes without saying that duck never appears on the menus of any of the hotel restaurants.

The Peabody Hotel in many ways mirrors the cycles Memphis has experienced over the years. The original hotel was built in 1869 for a total cost of $60,000. It flourished until the yellow-fever epidemic and the hotel closed in 1920. Not long thereafter a replacement, with the same classic tone, was constructed and enjoyed a boom period during the 1930s and 1940s. During the post-war period the Peabody again fell upon hard times eventually going into bankruptcy in 1975. However, like a cat with nine lives—and thanks to the Belz family of Memphis and some financial tax incentives from government organizations—the restoration of "the grand old lady" to its present splendor took place in 1981 at a cost of around $25 million and there is a plan for additional development in the future.

The final claim to world-wide fame for the city is having its most famous inhabitant grow up, go to school, and live there in Graceland mansion—the "King" Elvis Presley. Thousands of visitors are attracted to Graceland and Presley's resting place each year.

The Other Memphis

The above section gives the impression that Memphis deserves to be at the top of the list in chapter four. These beneficial efforts can be credited to the enterprising initiative of individuals with only the Peabody restoration receiving governmental assistance. On the opposite side of the coin, Memphis is another city obviously lacking in long-range comprehensive vision and overall community involvement in shaping its future. Several easily observed conditions support this conclusion. The first and most evident is the rather sorry state of most of the downtown. In fairness, it should be noted that efforts are underway to improve the situation through organizations such as the Center City Commission (CCC), a public/private partnership entity formed in 1977 by both the mayor of the city and Shelby County (an unusual title for county government) and its affiliates; Center City Development Corporation (CCDC), and Center City Revenue Finance Corporation.

However, during the post-war economic slump and before the creation of the CCC and a Central Business Improvement District (CBID), a goodly portion of the major commercial and office operations chose to desert the center city. As a result it is an open secret that the bulk of the population seldom, if ever, visits the downtown area unless they work there, or want to attend a function at the Peabody, visit the Beale Street restoration, or take in a performance at the beautifully renovated, downtown theater or some other special event. Out of a 1985 estimated population for the city of about 650,000, only 2,000 persons are considered to be residents of the downtown.

The Mid-America Mall and its Contrasts

A walk along the Mid-America Mall, reputed to be the longest pedestrian mall in the country, results in a feeling of frustration and disappointment. Traveling the Mall reveals a dichotomy in the quality and character of what has occurred. From Beale Street and Elvis Presley Plaza northward there is a mix of older buildings and empty stores, signs of neglect of mall maintenance and very little renovation or new construction for several blocks. Entire buildings remain empty, some dilapidated, many with boarded-up windows. As you go further north the work of the Center City Development Commission in promoting downtown revitalization becomes evident by some renovations and new high-rise office construction, but it is equally obvious that much remains to be done.

At the mall's northern end the story is completely different. Here are found a huge plaza and attractive fountains surrounded by the new Shelby County Court House and Jail, the Memphis Cook Convention Center Complex, Holiday Inn's flagship hotel Crowne Plaza, Mud Island Parking Garage and the Claridge Hotel (now converted into apartments) and the River Place Hotel. The entire area is an exciting and pleasing change and further emphasizes the problems involved in bringing the rest of the mall up to this standard of design. Several exciting new projects for the central city area are in the planning stages including the two-and-a-half-block development of Peabody Place around the existing hotel that will be expanded, further modernized and provide a direct connection to the mall which does not exist at present. Additionally, the attractive renovation of the famous old Beale Street and its restoration as a jazz center is almost complete.

In the meantime the city is experiencing rapid economic growth with an abundance of large and prospering suburban shopping malls and centers as well as several outer-city activity centers including hotels, office buildings, industrial parks and research centers, which create an additional pull from the downtown area. These projects reflect the lack of a meaningful comprehensive planning attitude and strong, well supported land use controls, as well as the eagerness for "economic development" prevalent in many of our cities today.

Downtown Planning

The CCDC has its own planning staff which maintains much closer coordination with the Memphis and Shelby County Office of Planning and Development (OPD) than was found in some of the other cities between development commissions and the public planners. The fact that the executive director, Michael Hagge, is a planning professional and a member of AICP undoubtedly has contributed to this communication and interface. However, responsibility for the preparation and implementation of physical and economic development plans as well as the coordination of public improvements within the center city area lies with the planning staff of CCDC. The development services staff of CCDC also is responsible for the coordination, site assembly, financing and physical development of both public and private downtown projects. This department acts as the liaison with developers and the general public, as well as with the Center City Revenue Finance Corporation, the Center City Development Corporation and the Design Review Board. The CCDC has recently completed a Center City Development Plan (CCDP) and is developing a related implementation plan and public presentation document.

In 1924 the Harland Bartholomew firm did a traditional master plan for Memphis and also updated it in the 1930s. These were the years of Mayor E. H. "Boss" Crump who was the power broker in Memphis from 1910 until his death in 1954. As one of those interviewed stated, "Crump was big on plans, but not much for seeing that policy was adopted to carry them out." When Crump was mayor, the city operated under the commission form of government with commissioners elected at large, each of whom was assigned the responsibility for one of five broad categories of city services. In a 1966 referendum, voters approved a change to an elected mayor and thirteen council members, six elected at large and seven from geographic districts. Since that time, apparently, those elected have not been strong supporters of comprehensive planning preferring, as do many other elected officials of the cities, not to be bound by preconceived and adopted plans.

The Policy Plan and An Expressed Attitude

The city does have a Memphis 2000 Policy Plan that was adopted by both the city council and the county commissioners in 1981.[8] This document contains a series of concise goals statements, 106 recommended policies, and assignments for strategies and implementation responsibility. The major categories included are the economy, land use, housing, transportation and public facilities. A citizen advisory committee helped with the formulation of recommendations in each category and public hearings were conducted by both the planning office and the legislative bodies before adoption.

A plan map sets forth an urban service boundary for the city, some designation of urban service centers, commercial and industrial areas, transitways, and flood-plain mapping, but remains very general in nature and lacks specific relationship to comprehensive land use planning. Like so many of the policy plans that have been adopted, it is replete with laudable goals as American as apple pie and motherhood, and is easy for public officials to support, but is just as easy to ignore when necessary for political expediency.

The planning attitude of the policymakers in Memphis remains as expressed by one of those interviewed: "All the time I hear the statement that governmental planning is an obstacle to any kind of reasonable development. The economics of the marketplace dictate what will happen and no planner alive can prepare a plan that is better than the one created by the dollar."

CORPUS CHRISTI, TEXAS

As Portland, Oregon was singled out as my Oscar winner for planning effectiveness, followed closely by Charlotte, I will have to nominate Corpus Christi, Texas as worthy of former U.S. Senator William Proxmire's Golden Fleece award for its lack of support of comprehensive planning for the development of an urban form. Those who disagree with this will, no doubt, point to economic forces, ethnic diversity and a governmental organizational structure that are the real causes of an almost total lack of a planning attitude in the city. To do so, however, is begging the issue of what societal collective planning is supposed to be all about: bringing issues to the forefront and pulling people together to deal with them intelligently in order to create a better urban form. Granted, the two-year term for elected officials works heavily against long-range thinking on the part of those officials, but in no way does it prohibit the exercise of enlightened and inspiring political leadership if that desirable quality can be found. It was not evident that such has been present or sought out in Corpus Christi during the last few years.

The Planning Attitude

Like several other cities in the South, Corpus Christi engaged the Bartholomew consulting firm to prepare a comprehensive plan in 1953. The firm was asked to do an update in 1966, but after three years of effort, the planning report contained several recommendations considered to be "controversial" by city council and, therefore, was never approved by the planning commission or council. Subsequently, as did San Antonio, Memphis, and other cities, Corpus Christi resorted to a policies plan for the designated period 1987–89. This consisted of a mission statement, a strategic action agenda setting forth goals and objectives on quality of life, economic development, relationships, service delivery, cultural heritage, and maximizing resources.

Some of the objectives have been achieved, primarily in the tourist area along the downtown waterfront, but a review of the plan merits the same comments made about such plans in Memphis. It is more obvious that Corpus Christi has followed the Cisneros philosophy of reactive pragmatic planning and, since the oil and gas industry hit bottom, the prevailing attitude has been that economic development is all that counts. This was substantiated by an interview with one of the assistant city managers, Tom Utter, who expressed the conviction that "the political system and the development system are nothing but the reflection of the economic system . . . the city council's major goal is jobs, jobs, jobs, and economic development calls the shots."

Apparently forgotten or overlooked is the inescapable fact that behind the glamour of the few lovely hotels, even fewer new office buildings, and a well preserved and protected beach front lies a city that is predominantly static. It is largely comprised of low-income families, many of whom live in substandard housing, and testifies to the lack of comprehensive planning and effective action. In spite of its "all growth is good" credo over the last several years, the city remains economically weak and, as even a sidewalk inspection will quickly confirm, the central downtown area has continued to decline.

Some Encouraging Signs

All of this is evident in spite of the few encouraging signs that have begun to appear from three sources. The first is the creation by the city council (at the encouragement of then councilwoman, and now mayor, Betty Turner), of a citizen group with which the University of Corpus Christi worked to develop a report called, "Corpus Christi 90." The group created task forces each of which worked on assigned topics such as culture, parks, economics, infrastructure, tourism, and the like. The most important task force was the one studying possible charter revisions. Their report included an insistence on the development of a comprehensive plan by 1986. Regrettably, the task force proposed the creation of a special comprehensive plan committee to undertake the preparation of the plan rather than the planning commission. Fortunately the city council did not agree and stuck with the position that this should be the prerogative of the planning commission and staff. With the meager staff provided in the planning department and the planners' conviction that this should be a thorough and comprehensive plan, the 1986 date originally recommended was not possible. However, sufficient support for the idea of having such a plan had developed so that in order to insure that it would be accomplished, an amendment to the city charter was approved in 1987 mandating continuous comprehensive planning by the city as a governmental function. The wording of the amendment gave the responsibility to the planning commission, and included the development of a master and general plan. It further requires cooperation by the other city departments, and all city improvements, ordinances and regulations are to be consistent with that plan. Although it may take as long as three years for the master plan to be completed, the planning commission and the staff already have it well on the way, using the approach that it should ultimately result from individual neighborhood plans in which residents participate.

The second bright spot on the horizon is the emergence of a stronger interest in the city's future and increased action by organized neighborhood groups. These organizations have become stronger over the last several years and the planning commission and city council are beginning to listen and respond to them. As a result they are gaining additional power and influence regarding what happens and where the city is going. The danger, as is always the case, is that instead of maintaining a broad citywide viewpoint, the interest and involvement can become confined to the special concerns and interests of the individual neighborhoods.

The third encouraging sign comes from the obvious support of planning by the city's major newspaper, *The Caller-Times*. Just before my visit to the city Jerry Norman, editorial page editor, wrote an article that sums up the situation in Corpus Christi so well that it provides an excellent concluding summary about the city and its planning. After a trip to San Angelo, Texas where he had formerly worked, Norman pointed out that the city is located in West Texas, which is thought of as a bleak place of rocks, cactus and scrub pines. Part of what he wrote under the headline of "There's No Substitute For Planning—But We Try" is included here.

> But San Angelo itself, well-watered as West Texas goes, is an exception. It is an attractive town, with lots of big old trees. A couple of rivers converge there, and a trio of lakes is nearby, one of them within the city.
>
> It is a bigger place now than when I lived there, maybe a third bigger, at least. Growth has been handled well. Downtown is no great shakes (sound familiar?) but there are a couple of new malls plus some other nice

shopping centers, and lots of well-planned neighborhoods that were new to me. Driving around, you get a very favorable impression of the city.

I couldn't help but think how someone new to both places might view it in contrast with Corpus Christi. This is a lot bigger city, of course—maybe three times as big. But San Angelo has the edge, if you're looking for a place that seems to have some thought behind what's taken place in it.

Neighborhoods there have an integrity lacking in Corpus Christi. There are blocks and blocks of houses into which business or industry or whatever doesn't intrude. Streets are wide in residential areas; none of this barely room to park cars on each side business (Corpus Christi has to be the champion worst in this category). Shopping areas are well-situated and easily reached. They look as though they belong where they are, and didn't come about as an after-thought, having once been residential.

And there's none of the leapfrog growth in little unconnected patches that seems to take place here. In short it looks like good zoning is being practiced.

Here in Corpus Christi, with the exception of a few older neighborhoods and some brand-new developments on the fringes of the city, there's just not that same sense of orderliness and purpose, that feeling of everything being in its place. It's not for lack of zoning; there are plenty of ordinances here. But planning has been piecemeal—and we have violated our rules over and over. Call it spot zoning, or strip zoning, or natural evolution—or special permits, the particular bane of planning in Corpus Christi. It still is a mighty high price to pay for the overall land use planning we're just starting to put in place.

Growth doesn't have to be uncontrolled, no matter how much you argue that market forces will determine where things are located—stores, houses, apartments and the like. That's only true to a point—maybe only as true as you let it be.

When a little old city in the middle of the brush country can put Corpus Christi to shame, as far as quality of life appearances go, we ought to think a little harder about what we're doing—or not doing, maybe.[9]

ALBUQUERQUE, NEW MEXICO

As indicated before, Albuquerque is one of the cities being included based upon my personal experience there, continued observation and a visit for interviews. I would have to say that it is a close contender to Corpus Christi for the Golden Fleece award when it comes to effective planning and a community-wide planning attitude. In 1940, Albuquerque was a placid, dusty little city with 35,449 residents. During the 1940s the U.S. Department of Defense—discovering that New Mexico was in the United States and that Los Alamos would be a great place for building the atom bomb—expanded the air base and built Sandia Laboratories in Albuquerque.

The Problems of Rapid Growth

Development quickly occurred in the city and the population increased to 96,815 by 1950 and 201,189 in 1960. The city has continued to grow, reaching 332,336 in the 1980 census, with a 1986 estimate of 366,750. Unfortunately the leadership and the people have failed to recognize the opportunity for building an outstanding example of city urban form and instead chose to make the mistake of allowing the permeation of the familiar attitude that "all growth is good, never mind what it is or what problems it creates." The vested-interest powers saw this growth only as an opportunity to enrich themselves and did so with relish, at the expense, regrettably, of the city's future. Consequently, Albuquerque today—like Corpus Christi and San Antonio—is a city where the present population should be asking, "How did we get where we are?"

What Could Have Been

When I went there as planning director for the combined Albuquerque/Bernalillo County Planning Department in 1971, Albuquerque still had the potential of turning undirected growth around and building a great city. Many of the things that could have done this—updating an outmoded master plan, saving the western face of the Sandia Mountains and the West Mesa extinct-volcano area from destructive development—were started during my time with the planning department.

These efforts continued and other programs were undertaken during my tenure as city manager to provide the base for strong planning, even though that sometimes was not easy with the attitude of some of the city commissioners and the control the development community had exercised for years in elections and city policies. A capital improvement program was initiated for the first time, the role of the planning department was strengthened, cooperation among city departments was developed, and the organization of the city manager's office was changed, with more direct responsibility placed on the city manager. Efforts were made to secure cooperation from the development community with city programs and neighborhood activism was encouraged.

I suppose that I was very naive in thinking that anyone could change a city where the powerful development interests had entrenched themselves with politicians and the political structure. They had profited by having everything their way for so many years; indeed, the city had even subsidized private development with bond issues for installation of infrastructure and utility lines that should have been provided by the developers. The mere suggestion that all this should be changed and zoning and subdivision regulations should be strengthened was enough to create a united assault from the power structure determined to get rid of such an upstart. This they did.

What Has Happened Since

Over the years things have not changed very much for the better. Today the physical shape of the city can be classified as a horizontally sprawled urban form, inefficient to service, expensive in terms of providing services, catering to private interests and the automobile with effective mass transportation totally unworkable and impractical. These comments have been substantiated recently by another former planning director. He said "City government basically accommodated private pressures exerted consistently for more than two decades. Private vested interests motivated the public response and was accommodated by public agencies and planning practices (primarily the public works department) not under control of the local planning authorities."

A former member of the planning commission and a highly respected civic activist added:

> Generally, my personal opinion is that no one entity has held sway, at least for long periods of time. We seem to go through phases where one viewpoint is upheld for a while, then the pendulum swings. Planners have been negotiators and buffers, but have put forth innovative ideas which have sometimes helped greatly and sometimes muddled things up. Our present crop are not great communicators, even with those who would support them. The planning department has gone through a period recently of having several different directors, none of them strong enough to 'lead the charge,' see future problems, or control the different factions within the department.

The Change in the Form of Government

In 1975, Albuquerque underwent a change in its form of government from commission/manager to strong mayor/council as a result of strong pressure from a disgruntled public. This resulted from the disputatious firing of the city manager by the then-city commission in spite of spirited opposition expressed by some 1,500 people attending the meeting that had been called to "dump the city manager." Here is another illustration of the power of an aroused citizenry using the potential of just even a threat of the petition-and-referendum prerogative available to them to effect a major change based upon action taken by an elected governing body. In the face of such strong opposition and the threat of a petition for referendum the city commission created a charter commission to study whether there should be a change in the form of government. The charter commission surprised the city commission by recommending a change to the strong mayor/council system and this was approved by the voters at a special election. In this case, not only a change in elected officials, but also a new city charter and a completely different governmental structure resulted.

Unfortunately all of this has not proved to be as advantageous for providing government responsive to citizen reaction or to the future of the city as had been the hope of the people organizing and effectuating the adoption of the new charter. Instead, it has made it easier for the get-all-you-can grabbers and takers to pursue their selfish interests and continue their exploitation of the public. Since the governmental changes there have been four mayoral terms and three different mayors. The first elected served two terms, but not consecutively. Only one of the three people holding this office has exhibited any vision and concern for the future and had some supportive understanding of the importance of the planning process in the building of the urban form. Regrettably, even he did not have the ability to meld the people into a responsive community and support his ideas—nor to get reelected. The other two have been totally lacking in this regard, believers in the all-growth-is-good philosophy, and more inclined to dance to the tune played by the private-developer interests and the business community exploiters than to provide the leadership necessary to see the importance of the city's future and to plan comprehensively for it.

A Good Illustration of the Importance of Strong Leadership

Many of the problems found in the city governance can be credited to the fact that though the charter adopted called for a "strong" mayor,

Albuquerque has not had one during the time it has been in effect. This stems from the first officeholder under the new system failing to exercise to the fullest the provisions set forth for performing as a strong mayor. The first council was permitted to usurp authority and power intended to allow an effective leadership role for the mayor. The other two mayors have not been able, or perhaps willing, to restore the mayor's position as originally intended. This lack of strong leadership together with the establishment of nine districts with all council members representing one of the districts and no at-large representation are the prime reasons for the justification of the additional statement made by the former planning commissioner summarizing the general condition of government in Albuquerque as follows:

> With mayors having vision/no vision and no organized community support, the council fractious with the mayor, and the planning commission almost ineffective, there has been no unified political force. There was, however, a continuing persistent development community. Politicians certainly have made compromises and decisions based both on their own philosophy and, unfortunately, at times for their own benefit economically or politically. Some developer entrepreneurs are greedy, others seem to have a sense of community and responsibility. In other words, there is no one answer. No one operates in a vacuum, but each player modifies the others.

In 1989, the incumbent mayor was again swept out of office and another was elected. The new mayor is Louis E. Saavadra who has the intelligence, the organizational ability, and the political experience to even now turn the city around so that it understands where it is, where it should be, and what has to be done for it to get there. The question remains, however, whether he will have the determination to do that or choose the easy way out by just trying to please everybody and be another four-year term, one-term mayor. Should this happen, Albuquerque will have suffered through nineteen years of mayors lacking in a sense of vision and leadership capabilities, disjointed, feuding councils, continued wild-fire, haphazard urban sprawl and continued enrichment of the greedy local private sector exploiters.

Illustrative of the interest in improving the city by the residents and their hunger for effective, inspiring leadership is that, amazingly, some excellent public improvements have been accomplished during the last fifteen years. The airport has been enlarged and the older section of it almost completely rebuilt and modernized. Enough people were interested in art and culture to see that a new art museum, in a beautifully designed structure, was constructed and to succeed in getting the state government to construct a state museum across the street from it. The Albuquerque Convention Center is being doubled in size and a new 600-room plus hotel is under construction next to a towering 22-storied office structure in the central city. The new governmental center combined with the formerly separate city hall and county office buildings and now houses both governmental units. To satisfy the city residents' love of the automobile, numerous arterial streets have been widened and Tramway Boulevard at the western foot of the Sandia Mountains is being extended and widened to true boulevard status. All of this appears to give the impression of dynamic leadership and a community that has it all together.

However, detailed examination indicates these projects are merely the result of pressure from isolated special interests rather than from a unified, inspiring city government. In the meantime, residential development has been allowed to continue a leap-frog, disconnected pattern demanding additional expensive public-service facilities; air pollution is approaching, if not surpassing, that of Los Angeles and Denver; and urban sprawl still reigns supreme. Albuquerque residents, instead of congratulating themselves on flashy, scattered pragmatic projects, should seriously consider what a much greater city it could have been with elected officials more concerned about the future. If they had elected people with vision and leadership characteristics who had instituted and supported a meaningful comprehensive plan with a strong zoning ordinance to guide and coordinate land use distribution, and pulled the people together in a sense of total community spirit Albuquerque today could be an outstanding example of how to build a great city.

With these five cities we have seen specific illustrations of lost opportunities resulting from the lack of community involvement and strong leadership, the absence of people's concern for the future, a nonexistent planning attitude and the permitting of economic development pressure, entrepreneurship, greed and political expediency to be the prime determinants of the future.

NOTES

1. Richard O. Baumbach, Jr., and William E. Borah, *The Second Battle of New Orleans* (Tuscaloosa, AL: The University of Alabama Press, 1981).

2. Ann Breen and Dick Rigby, "Sons of Riverwalk," *Planning*, Vol. 54, No. 3 (March 1988).

3. Michael P. Brooks, "Four Critical Junctures in the History of the Urban Planning Profession," *The Journal*, American Planning Association, (Spring 1988).

4. Henry Cisneros, "Viewpoint," *Planning*, Vol. 54, No. 6 (June 1988) p. 46.

5. Robert Cullick, "San Antonio Hangs Tight to Its Dream," *Planning*, Vol. 54, No. 3 (March 1988) pp. 4–10.

6. For additional information about San Antonio's water situation see Thomas F. Brereton's "Liquid Gold," *Planning*, March 1988.

7. Cullick, p. 10.

8. Memphis and Shelby County Office of Planning and Development, *Memphis 2000 Policy Plan*, 1981.

9. Jerry Norman, "There's No Substitute For Planning—But We Try," *The Caller Times*, Corpus Christi, Texas, March 19, 1988.

7

How We Got
to Where We Are

Much emphasis in this book has been placed on the outside forces of which all those interested in building a better community should be aware. We have seen the many ways these forces have established parameters limiting how local governments can function and what the planning process can and cannot do. Some of these have created physical patterns for our environment, others have provided the impetus and the financial means for rebuilding and planning urban development, and set the economic and legal boundaries in which we must operate. Not all have been as beneficial or helpful as originally hoped, but the fact of life is that we must learn to live with them and make the best of existing situations. It is vital for local officials and the general public to understand the influence of these forces, not only on the action elected and appointed officials can take, but also how their planning departments and planners are constrained in what they can propose and do. In turn, they may understand better some of the problems with which the profession must deal.

The primary purpose of the research trips around the country was to explore first hand the question of how local governments are doing in using the planning function to prepare for the future. These site visits and the one-on-one discussions with those involved in the various communities provided an excellent opportunity to obtain the community flavor, evaluate the attitude, philosophy and action of elected policymakers and assess the general public's mood. While it is essential to fully grasp the importance of the outside forces with which local governments must contend in planning and development of urban form, the bottom line remains that of how we are doing in local areas where we have the greatest opportunities for meaningful involvement which has the most direct effect on our lives, our investments, our environment, and our quality of life.

This chapter will review some evolving societal changes that are contributing to shifts in philosophy and the composition of our villages, towns and cities and affecting the way we live. A summary is included of the ways in which a sample of local officials and other key players view the composite elements of their cities and how they, and other residents, are dealing with their problems and facing their futures. Evaluative opinions on the survey results I later express will be founded on my belief that the only hope of finding an answer to the myriad of problems facing us today, wherever we live, is to rebuild a true sense of community at the local level, a sense of place and pride in ourselves and what this town or city in which we live is and what it can become.

HORIZONTAL v. VERTICAL PATTERN: THE NEW CORPORATION

In years gone by we had the advantage of the automatic development of a sense of community, as Roland L. Warren points out in his book, *The Community In America.*[1] Warren thoroughly developed the theory that communities in the past were made vibrant by a structure of a "horizontal pattern" instead of the "vertical pattern" that has evolved over the past several decades. By this Warren means that in earlier America residence, enterprise, social contact, and entertainment were based upon horizontal relationships within the community in both small and large cities. Factories, warehouses and businesses were locally owned with economic survival depending upon local involvement and good will. The grocery store, the furniture store, the hardware store and the variety store were owned and run by hometown people who had investments in that town or city and knew the future of their investments depended on both the product and service quality offered the customer and the quality of the community's future. Even the nearby farm families felt that town was their community also.

This vestige of horizontal relationship remained even after the first invasion of the chain-store and national corporations. The insurance person's product might be New York Life, Metropolitan, or Prudential, but ownership and operation of the business remained local. The same was true, at least for a while, in the grocery business. The name on the front of the store might be Piggly Wiggly, Kroger, or A&P, but the management lived there and had an investment in the community.

Conversely, however, as Warren stated "a barrier to effective community action is the loss of community autonomy over specific institutions or organizations located within it and closely intermeshed with the community's welfare. The decision of the absentee-owned company to discontinue its branch plant, the decision of the state highway department to build the new road on the east side of the river rather than the west, the decision of the national health agency that its locals may no longer participate in the united fund—all these represent decisions by community based units over which the community exercises little control."[2]

In our economic system this was an inevitable evolution even though it has contributed heavily to the loss of an intangible quintessential through which came a richness of community. Today the local plant manager may belong to the Rotary Club or the Lions Club and the country club, but his or her first sense of duty, responsibility and lifeline is through the district manager, the regional manager and up to the top management in New York, Chicago, Los Angeles, or perhaps Tokyo, London, or Calgary.

Some Things We Can Do

This vertical pattern must be recognized as a fact of life which we can ignore, accept with resignation, or learn how to make work for us. It was encouraging to note some of the cities studied are fortunate enough to continue to have locally controlled enterprises or else they have been managed to maintain a sense of local commitment in spite of increased absentee ownership. Baltimore, Charlotte, Minneapolis, Pittsburgh, and Portland are good examples of this. It is refreshing to learn that the business community of New Orleans has pledged to raise a $10 million support fund for the local symphony and other arts organizations. Equally commendable is the vibrant sense of community present in the Vieux Carre in New Orleans among residents in spite of some of the things the city has permitted to occur or imposed on the area and which the chamber of commerce has supported.

What this leads to is the belief that if we can get more people concerned about why we are where we are, then by working together, we can make the vertical pattern work for us and our cities. To do so it is essential that we understand and work to overcome the problem Warren defined well when he said "apathy turns out to be a lack of interest in community-wide projects which cut across the various specialized interests, thus becoming nobody's business."[3] All of us, especially those in the planning profession and those elected to public office, have a duty and responsibility to make planning for the future everybody's business.

One action we can take to revive or strengthen our sense of community is to capitalize on an encouraging trend in major national corporations and exert local pressure to further it. More and more reputable firms, the kind we want to locate in our area, are beginning to recognize they have a greater responsibility than they have shown in the past to each community in which they have a facility. Key to this is a practical business recognition of the fact that the stability of their sizeable investment and their employee morale are both related to the corporation helping to preserve and enhance the quality of life in the place they are located.

Examples of Corporate Roles In Community Involvement

There are some excellent examples of this in the cities previously mentioned and in Colorado. Martin Marietta, Manville Corporation, and Kodak in the Denver area as well as Hewlett Packard in Colorado Springs, are all major national firms exhibiting increasing community involvement. Credit for encouraging this trend must be given to the leadership exhibited by the locally owned Gates Corporation in Denver and the Adolph Coors Company of Golden. Both of these firms have a history of donating large sums of money as well as encouraging employee participation in worthwhile community endeavors. In addition, the founding families of each have established separate foundations for the purpose of giving back to the communities and the state from which they have benefited.

It is interesting to see the obvious influence of this acceptance of involvement by local corporations and companies on newly arrived corporations, especially if they are competitors of the longtime resident companies. This has been illustrated by the recent opening of a new Anheuser-Busch Company brewery near Fort Collins, Colorado, which places them in direct competition with the Coors Company as they both fight for improved positions in the beer market. Even before the plant was completed, the executives who were to be located in the area had begun a campaign to show evidence of how committed they were to the welfare of the community nearest to their plant as well as to the entire state. Heavy competition has developed between the two companies for the coveted sponsorship of major events in the areas of sporting, charitable fund-raising, culture, arts, and other community endeavors. At present the smartest thing a not-for-profit agency planning a fund-raising event can do is to be able to tell one brewery that the other one is interested in sponsoring their event. This healthy competition has already been beneficial to the entire state and illustrates one of the ways to combat and overcome Warren's vertical pattern that is so destructive to our sense of community.

Leadership of Elected Officials

The second area where there is hope for revival of a beneficial horizontal pattern of commitment lies in successfully developing concerned individuals into a force dedicated to rebuilding community interest through the quality of people elected to office. No community is totally devoid of those with leadership potential, but the ones who can provide it frequently must be sought out and encouraged. While it is true that strong leaders, a few of whom may step forward on their own, can inspire individual and collective involvement, they must be encouraged to run and get elected before they can implement their programs. The reality is that we as a society are not electing enough outstanding leaders. Instead, our society seems bent on making certain that honest, committed people will choose *not* to run. We have neglected to seek out those individuals, to organize groups in support of them, and convince them to sacrifice personally in time commitment and family relationships, as well as endure the ever-present critics.

The Power of the Media.   Regrettably the force that some hold as most responsible for those with a leadership potential being unwilling to put themselves in the public eye are the members of today's media. It is easy to draw the conclusion that the policy of some news media has become that of crucifixion and vilification of anyone daring to seek public office. Have we reached the point where the moment any novice steps forward to run for elective office, city-desk editors of papers or news directors of television stations call in their best hatchet people and say, "Get on this person's trail and see what dirt you can uncover, there is bound to be a skeleton in the closet somewhere"? Granted that this tactic, unfortunately, seems to be the way to sell more papers and more advertising than noncontroversial or good news, but this too is a sad testimony to the level a lot of us have sunk. It represents either what appeals to us or what we will tolerate without raising a voice in opposition.

These statements are not intended to include the honestly objective, factually investigative local newspapers and other media forms still existing today since this type of "watchdogging" can provide a much-needed community service. However, there is a very fine line between being a constructive public watchdog and being a destructive yellow-rag journalist. Regardless of the type of reaction, all media are sensitive to what its readers, viewers or listeners want or will accept and recognize their survival depends upon the economic well-being and the quality of life in the communities they serve and, in the case of the national media, the entire nation. In short, it is like most everything else in a community: change can be achieved through cooperating collective effort, whether the community be a local or national one. The power of people united in an objective can exceed even the power of the press or other media.

FORM AND STRUCTURE
OF GOVERNMENT

The cities selected for study here represent a broad and accurate picture of local representative government today in our country. Further confirmation of this was provided by the comments contained in the numerous taped interviews.

Having examined some of the more general aspects of the difficulties in maintaining vibrant broad community concern about where we are and where we are going in our increasingly evolving societal structure, we now need to consider the more specific findings in the cities selected to provide information for this book. The primary source of data for this examination comes from comments and opinions expressed and information gathered during my stay in each city supplemented by additional research of articles pertaining to several of the cities appearing in national publications. Four major areas were examined: (1) governmental structure; (2) political and community leadership; (3) public officials' planning attitudes; and (4) the major influences on policymakers.

The cities selected provided a good sampling of geographic location, economy, and population mix; in addition they also illustrate how city charters can differ greatly in the establishment of such structures. Within the fourteen cities where interviews were conducted, plus the other one about which evaluative comments were made from familiarity, there are examples of the commission, strong mayor/ council, weak mayor/council, and council/city manager forms of government. The number of differing techniques used by the cities in structuring their governing and administrative approaches demonstrated additional adaptations possible in city charters. It must be remembered that city charters have to be adopted by a vote of the people to be governed under a general state enabling act or approved by the state legislature; therefore, it can be assumed that, notwithstanding some deviations from the accepted political science norm for each type, these techniques have been considered the best approach for the individual cities in which they apply.

The one city still operating with the city commission method is Portland, Oregon. The commission system was initiated at the behest of President Woodrow Wilson when he was at Princeton University as a reform movement to overcome the political corruption of the old ward system and was widely adopted after 1920. Usually the commission is comprised of five or six persons elected at-large with each one assigned responsibility for the supervision of one or more departments. Commission members typically determine which of them will assume the title of mayor. Portland has chosen to vary this since its charter establishes that the mayor shall be elected directly by the voters, but also serve as a member of the five-person commission. Here the mayor assigns the responsibility for the departments to the commissioners. It is interesting that Neil Goldschmidt chose for himself the departments related to planning, community development, urban renewal and housing and used them wisely in building his reputation and influence and increasing the recognition of his leadership qualities. The commission form of government continues to serve the people of Portland well and fortunately reflects the concern of each commissioner for the entire community.

Five cities operate with the strong mayor/council system, but again differences are found in just how strong the charters have made the position of mayor. For years Denver's mayor was regarded as having the greatest amount of assigned authority of any mayor in the country. Recently the city council has been seeking a greater say in the day-to-day running of the government and through their initiative have succeeded in securing voter approval in slightly reducing the mayor's power. Others using the strong mayor/council system among the subject cities are Baltimore, New Orleans, Saint Paul, and Albuquerque, with each exhibiting some differences in application. New Orleans, for example, limits its mayor to two consecutive four-year terms. Both Minneapolis and Pittsburgh until recent years had been operating with a strong mayor/council format, but have now changed to the weak mayor form along with a change to election of council members from districts (wards).

The city council/city manager system reached its peak of popularity, especially for smaller cities, following the Great Depression. More recently, to some extent due to a demand by the voters to have the mayor more directly responsible to them for the way the city is managed, several of the cities have abandoned this form for the strong mayor/council form of government. Among the study cities San Antonio, Corpus Christi, San Diego, and Charlotte still operate with the city council/city manager form, but, again, there are differences in application. Normally the city manager is responsible for all departmental supervision, prepares the yearly budget for submission to the council, and has authority over all employees. San Diego's charter specifically assigns the responsibility for the planning, audit and finance departments to the city council. This leads to a loss of opportunity for overall coordination by the manager and prevents that office from having sufficient authority to assure cooperation with the comprehensive planning function from the other departments, a situation that, in my opinion, has contributed greatly to the lack of coordinated building of the urban form in San Diego.

During the last several years Mayor Henry Cisneros with his strong personality made San Antonio appear to have a strong mayor format even though it does not. Another example of a personality transcending government structure is Neil Goldschmidt who did exactly the same thing in Portland when he was mayor and before he went on to be President Jimmy Carter's secretary of transportation and, later, governor of Oregon. Baltimore's William Schaefer also represented this kind of strong personality well enough to become Maryland's governor. These people make the point obvious that given good leadership capabilities, the system becomes less important than who is providing this quality. An individual within this milieu and with determination can rise to great heights and operate effectively within any governmental system.

Analyzing the Districting Trend

As a result of the demand by minority groups for more equitable, direct representation, there is a growing trend to switch back to the old ward form of council member elections, either with a strong or weak mayor, only now it is called a district system. While agreeing with the need for an increase in equitable representation, my concern is that a ward system under any other name still offers the greatest possibility of all forms of government for isolated separatism, the building of political fiefdoms, pork-barreling, and the loss of broader community interest and concern. Hopefully, this danger will be recognized by the people of the communities choosing to use a ward format and they will be sufficiently vigilant not to allow the worst potentials inherent in this system to occur. However, Minneapolis, long noted for its community interest, shows evidence, after only a few years of the district system, of the loss of a citywide viewpoint, less cooperation among council members, less support for comprehensive planning and as one interviewee put it, "is drifting back into neighborhood and ward parochialism where the prime concern is how an issue relates to my district."

All of the above cities, with the exception of Portland, now have some form of council representation from districts. In seven, all members of city council are chosen by the voters of the district in which they live. Included are Albuquerque, Baltimore, Minneapolis, Pittsburgh, Saint Paul, San Antonio, and San Diego with the total number of council members ranging from seven in Saint Paul to seventeen in Baltimore. San Diego has a method not found in any of the others in which there is a primary election held in each district and the two top vote-getters then run in an at-large, citywide run-off election. This, at least, provides the opportunity for involvement of the total electorate in the final decision. Most of the other cities confine the determination of representation to run-offs within the districts unless one candidate exceeds a set percentage of the total vote cast in the first election, in which case no run-off is required.

The Terms-of-Office Complication

One other aspect offering less than an ideal atmosphere conducive to long-range thinking and planning relates to the length of terms of elected officials. It is difficult enough to get a politician—who is something less than a leader or statesperson—to think long-range within four-year terms. It is next to impossible when they must run every two years. This seems to be an affliction in Texas cities as both Corpus Christi and San Antonio suffer from two-year terms for both the mayor and members of city council. Pittsburgh had a variation of four council members elected for four years and five for two years prior to their recent change to an all-district election and this same arrangement of different length of terms was carried forward in the revised system now in effect.

While it has been said that good leadership can work under any system of government, it is obvious that where it is lacking, any of the different systems can offer impediments to comprehensive long-range planning and the maintenance and development of economically sound, quality urban form. In support of the importance of elected leadership with a planning attitude over the type of system are the two cities that, in my opinion, are doing the best job in effective planning: Portland with its commission form and Charlotte-Mecklenburg County. In the latter case, both city and county elect their officials using a combination of district and at-large representation, yet, working together they have one outstanding planning department and professional staff serving both governmental units. However, two quotes from interviews illustrate how either terms for two or four years—especially when combined with district elections, if not influenced heavily by a concerned, involved public—can, and do, work against vision and long-range thinking. A council member in New Orleans when questioned about some details of a major controversial project there, responded; "I am not sure of much about that project as it is not in my district." Another comment from a former city manager in Corpus Christi now in private development is also symptomatic of this problem: "Why in the hell should council members spend all their time in big-picture planning when they may well not be around to see the results?"

POLITICAL AND COMMUNITY LEADERSHIP

As far back as 1910, it was obvious that Denver's Mayor Robert Speer believed that building great cities with quality urban form is largely dependent on strong, vibrant leadership from elected officials. The recognition of this fact, while not necessarily related to the City Beautiful Movement, takes nothing away from the validity of the fundamental precept that cities are for the people and that workable plans must be built with the understanding and support of those people.

Strong aggressive leaders are the first to recognize this, and they set about involving people and taking advantage of the innate desire of the voters for inspired and inspiring leadership.

The most exemplary proof of this in the country is the revitalization of Portland, Oregon during Mayor Neil Goldschmidt's tenure there. His ability to impart an increased recognition of the importance of the future and a stronger sense of community pride left a lasting impact and continues today—dramatically underscoring his understanding that no elected official can do the job of building a great city by himself or herself. Looking back in time, even mayors who became the most successful benevolent despots—Hague in Jersey City, Curley in Boston, Crump in Memphis, and Daley in Chicago—knew the importance of building a constituency of supportive people, although their methods of achieving this certainly is subject to question.

If one explores the worth of vision as illustrated by the organizers and planners of the 1893 Exposition in Chicago and considers the essential quality of effective leadership, an appropriate question arises. If these two things, a fair and dynamic leadership, can have so evident an effect on the building of America's urban form why have so many of our cities not only permitted, but encouraged the condition that can best be characterized as Paradise Lost? A companion question to this one is why have we allowed our metropolitan areas to become the epitome of generic man's inhumanity to the environment and mankind or (in O'Harrow's words) to become a "messopolis"? Both of these are important questions relating to the quality of life, and most importantly of all, to the inheritance we will pass on to our children, and therefore they merit further examination.

If we really believe in sensible governmental planning as the only way to achieve planned change instead of allowing cancer-like, exploitive growth to throw nearly the entire country into a Paradise Lost condition—as we seem to be doing now—there are several components of our present system to which we must give careful attention. First and foremost in our consideration should be a careful look at what has happened, in a general way, to the quality of the people we elect to run our cities, prepare a budget, spend our tax dollars, and shape our future urban form. Have we paid sufficient attention to their capabilities, their viewpoints, their positions, and particularly their attitudes about and understanding of the planning process? When they campaign through the neighborhoods or make election speeches at local meetings, have we questioned them about where they stand and what they will do about planning when and if they are elected? Have enough of us made it known in our city that no one will get elected mayor or a member of a governing body who is not a strong proponent of effective long-range planning and coordination?

Certainly there are some outstanding contemporary elected officials who have served and are serving communities and states like Goldschmidt in Portland, Lugar in Indianapolis, Caliguiri in Pittsburgh, and former governors McCall in Oregon and Lamm in Colorado. What is the overall average performance, however, of those to whom we have given the responsibility for determining the future urban form of cities in this country? Unfortunately, under careful scrutiny the evidence overwhelmingly indicates we have allowed the average performance of our local officials to be that which leaves a great deal to be desired for any of us who genuinely care about that future. All too frequently the people we are electing to office have either a misconceived notion or absolutely no idea about what planning is, what a good planning process entails, or what kind of policy action it takes to make it work. Even worse are those who are in politics for their own vested interests such as real estate development, commercial enterprises, or those representing only the narrow viewpoint of a district or ward and not giving a hoot in hell about the bigger picture and what happens to the community-at-large.

Where The Buck Stops

Assuming there is only a smidgen of truth in the above, the frightening point that needs to be understood is a principle of our governmental system—the Harry S. Truman concept that The Buck Stops Here! It is the elected governing body of any community that has the final responsibility for each and every action taken and decision made on anything for which the city, town or village has the authority to act. Those elected officials are the ones who are or are not going to enact policies necessary to carry out any planning proposal made, to make a comprehensive plan work or fail, and ultimately to shape the urban form. Many well-conceived, workable and comprehensive plans have ended up gathering dust on shelves as a result of the lack of a planning attitude on the part of those elected and/or the lack of courage to take a stand and support the plan on a matter made controversial by those with vested interests or the emotional motivation of a few objectors. If questioned about their failure to support any plan, the usual answer given by that type of official is that the planners preparing it were too "far out," dreamers, impractical in their approach, and lacking in any understanding of politics. They say that it was all the fault of planning and those planners, but don't believe it!

The truth of the matter is in 99.5 percent of those cases it is not the plan or the planners' fault, but rather the failure of the elected governing body to have sufficient understanding, conviction, courage and commitment to the total community to take a strong position supportive of the planning process. In our system of government the axiom is that those elected to office must be the ones making *all* policy decisions. The results of whether or not a municipality will have a workable comprehensive plan—one that is consistently used—are based on the characteristics of the accumulative political character prevailing at any given time in the jurisdiction for which planning and the development of the urban form is taking place. Elected officials should not be permitted to escape from their responsibility by blaming the plan and the planners. To be completely fair, however, it was pointed out to me during my visits that not all of the above is *totally* inapplicable to some planning programs and planners either.

Just as the government system varied in the different cities, so does the effectiveness of leadership in the political sector and the community. The fact that the systems in existence operate well in Charlotte and Portland already has been indicated, but interviews in the other cities reflected that the leadership factor in the political and community sectors varied from about 1 to 7 on a rating scale of 1 through 10, with 10 representing the highest score. Certainly there are those who approve of Cisneros's brand of leadership in San Antonio and who sing his praises as a leader; however all but one of those interviewed in that city criticized him, particularly with regard to the lack of comprehensive planning and coordination of the various forces involved in urban form development.

As is to be expected, the mayor of Charlotte, Harvey B. Gantt and the chairperson of the Mecklenburg County Commission, Carla DuPuy are highly regarded by their peers and the general public. In fact, all five members of the county commission were reelected in 1988. Mayor Bud Clark of Portland was not a veteran politician when first elected and he also had the difficult situation of being compared to Neil Goldschmidt and other high-calibre mayors before him. He has definitely grown with the job and developed into a leader; he too was reelected in 1988. Several plaudits were provided Mayor George Latimer in Saint Paul for his strong, dynamic personality and direction of that city, but he has decided not to seek another term. Mayor Donald M. Frazer of Minneapolis is highly respected as an individual, an excellent public servant, but is completely hand-tied by the weakness of the mayor's position in that city's unfortunate charter. Some admiration for the leadership ability of former mayors such as San Diego's Pete Wilson (now a U.S. Senator), Pittsburgh's Richard Caliguiri, and long-ago mayor Robert Speer was expressed, but current elected officials in most of the subject cities were not widely praised in their communities.

In Portland, Commissioner Earl Blumenauer was recognized for his leadership ability by several interviewees there. He is the person charged with responsibility for the city's planning and development programs and he led the effort to complete the city's exciting new central city development plan. Looking at the other elected leadership among commission and council members, again with the exceptions of Portland and Charlotte, not one of the persons interviewed were sufficiently impressed by the membership of the councils to single anyone out as either doing an outstanding job or offering leadership potential. Councils indicated by most to be totally lacking in leadership or any sense of vision included Albuquerque, Baltimore, Corpus Christi, Memphis, Minneapolis, New Orleans, San Antonio, and San Diego.

One of the greatest surprises to me was to find that no one described Baltimore's former mayor, William Schaefer, as an exemplary leader. Instead he was identified as lacking in vision, having little regard for planners and planning, and running the city with an iron hand as he saw fit with little ability to listen to people and pull them together. As a member of council prior to becoming mayor, he strongly opposed the famous Harbor Place project, although, after it was built, he never refused to take credit for it.

Baltimore's administration and leadership picture is further clouded by charter and administrative actions that have created what is referred to as a "shadow government" about which detailed discussion was included in chapter five. A slightly better situation exists in Pittsburgh and Saint Paul and the city council in Denver was given improved marks on its planning attitude, due largely to four new council members; the entire council still has a long way to go to be considered as people with vision and a concern for the entire city's future.

The Relative Influence of Neighborhood Organizations

The leadership influence of neighborhood organizations also differed widely. From the cities studied it can be concluded that the neighborhood movement is gaining strength and power and should be recognized as a force to be reckoned with in the future of our cities. General community leadership is strong in Portland and Charlotte. Portland has some very involved neighborhood groups, a large number of outstanding civic leaders among the business community, and excellent interest and participation in city development, especially its urban design, from the architectural, landscape-architectural, and general-design professionals. The community interest and spirit is high among almost all sectors of the Charlotte population, where, largely as a result of the efforts of the planning department, a new comprehensive master plan has been adopted by the city council and county commission.

As an outgrowth of this citizen group on planning, the Charlotte/Mecklenburg Citizens Forum was established to move into broader areas affecting the city's future. One of the first things they undertook was to start Project Catalyst, an excellent example of a neighborhood revitalization effort. The forum also has been responsible for involving the Charlotte community in the Charlotte Civic Index Project. (See chapters four and nine). One of the most impressive verifications of my conclusions about these two cities, their leadership, acceptance and support of planning, community spirit and commitment is that not only has Charlotte completed this Civic Index Project, but a steering committee of civic leaders in Portland has been meeting to develop a plan for doing so there as well. It is equally telling that none of the other cities has felt such a project would be valuable and could be made to work in their community, with the exceptions of New Orleans and Minneapolis, which have indicated an interest. This is gratifying to me as I had suggested pursuing this useful tool to the planning directors in these two cities during my visits with them.

PUBLIC OFFICIALS' PLANNING ATTITUDES

The importance of what I have termed a "planning attitude" and what the planning director in Charlotte, Martin Cramton—who also deserves commendation for his contribution to the city during his nine years there—calls a "planning ethic" has been implied throughout this book. Because of its importance, specific evaluation of this attitude in the subject cities is merited. By whatever term it is identified, the most important element necessary for the planning function to work in American society is an infusion of concern about the future of the city along with an understanding of and support for the community's role in guiding and directing building for the future; that is "a planning attitude." Without this the existence of a planning function in name is just that—a name—and can best be termed "lip-service planning." Planners functioning under such a system may be able to prevent some mistakes and contribute some pragmatic improvements in isolated projects and problems, but elected officials responsible for permitting and attempting to justify this type of planning are doing themselves, their community, the planning process and planning professionals a great disservice.

Therefore, the greatest disappointment to me, as a result of this research, was to discover the wholesale lack of a planning attitude in the majority of elected officials in almost all of the cities with the exception of Portland and Charlotte, of course. Let me say that it is not totally hopeless in a few places. The revival of Pittsburgh largely resulted from the development of a planning attitude there by the late Mayor Richard Caliguiri and his staff that spread to the entire community, particularly the business sector. The real question now is can it be continued under a weak mayor, district-elected council system?

Minneapolis had a planning attitude for years when more business leaders served on council prior to the same kind of changes in its charter as Pittsburgh. The epitome of the evidence of a lack of such an attitude among city council now is the abolishing of any form of neighborhood planning, which was done for political reasons, and a general lack of support given the planning function. Except for the fact that it is essentially day-to-day, "pragmatic" and special project planning, Saint Paul can be said to at least be aware of and supportive of a planning process. Even my favorite city to criticize, Denver, thanks to excellent efforts of the planning director Bill Lamont, has a spark of a planning attitude. This spark was ignited through community involvement in the development of a new comprehensive plan that resulted in a better understanding of the planning process among those people attending and participating in this process. But these cities aside, my evaluation is that this very desirable characteristic on the part of elected public officials is lacking in Albuquerque, Baltimore, San Antonio, Memphis, New Orleans, San Diego, and Corpus Christi.

Some Evidential Quotes

Just a few examples quoted from some of the interviews serve to support this conclusion. The revitalization of the Baltimore Inner Harbor really started when the private sector Greater Baltimore Committee (GBC) first proposed a plan to redevelop 1,000 acres of the central area of the city. When they approached the mayor, council and the planning commission with the idea that the city take this on, according to the then executive director of the GBC, the response was: "Oh, that is too big of a job, we can't do that." The GBC then did it themselves, first trimming down the size of their initial project to the most central 33 acres. Later on when the GBC proposed to the elected officials that a study be made to determine a way to strengthen the planning department, they were completely rebuffed. The director's comment after recounting this was: "How you get a planner in a city like this to have a dominant role, I don't know. I am not sure that it is possible."

In San Antonio a planning educator told me, "the state highway department has been the major form-giver once you get outside of the central city area." A planning consultant in talking about the elected officials said; "They won't be progressive, they talk good planning, they say they want to do it, but they don't allocate the money and they don't allocate the staff to be able to do it properly. I would call it lip-service, double-standard planning." Another planning consultant reported that "The way it works in San Antonio is that all of the major projects in the CBD are out of the purview of the planning department. They fall under the mayor and city manager who have a separate special projects group and they do a lot of the negotiation and strike the deals." He added, "The planning department in this town is basically doing zoning and platting, housekeeping and is reactive instead of pre-active."

Many similar comments indicating the lack of a planning attitude and support for planning could be included from other cities, but to avoid repetition, I will wrap up with one that is an excellent representative statement of all the cities lacking elected officials with a planning attitude. It comes from an engineering consultant in San Diego in evaluating the city council. "They are all pro-planning provided the planning is coincident with their thinking. You can feed them full of housing theory, transfer of development rights theory and all the rest of the planning theory and they aren't going to pick that up at all. They react to the polls."

Table 1
Profile of Persons Interviewed by Profession

Primary Profession	Total	APA and/or AICP
Public Planner	16	16
Developer	15	4
Planning Consultant	8	8
Public Economic Dev. Official	7	4
Community/Neighborhood Activist	7	2
Educator	5	5
Elected Official	4	–
Attorney	3	–
Planning Commissioner	2	1
Architect	2	1
Private Economic Dev. Official	2	–
Engineer	1	–
Business Person	1	–
Metro Council Official	1	–
Private Preservation Official	1	–
Total	75	41

MAJOR INFLUENCES ON POLICYMAKERS

One of the prime reasons for setting up individual interviews was to obtain the views of local people directly involved with elected officials in order to determine just how these officials were influenced on matters pertaining to planning the urban form. Out of approximately one-hundred local people with whom I had general conversations about their city, seventy-five participated in the scheduled interviews. The interviewees reflected a wide variety of professional backgrounds and interests, but all had some direct involvement with planning and development and their city government. Table 1 shows the professions and interests of those interviewed. Where their prime activity is in another area, but they also are professional planners, this too is indicated.

Each person was asked to offer his or her evaluation of the relative influence of planning on elected policymakers' final decisions on major urban development projects in their community as compared to those of economic development pressure, entrepreneurial sales pressures, or political factors. Since this concentrated on specific actions taken by local officials, some interviewees whose specialties, such as regional concerns, legal matters and business interests, do not provide them with familiarity about day-to-day local policy decisions in the specified areas, either declined to respond or were not asked. Those persons willing to go on record with their personal judgments were given a ranking form containing nine possible sources of influence with each to be given a rating of from 1 to 9, with 1 being the most influential factor and 9 the least. Of the seventy-five interviewed, 64% completed the forms.

As can be seen in table 2, evaluative opinions varied greatly. As might have been expected, economic development sales pitches and political considerations are believed to be most influential. In the top three ranking slots, 60% and 64% respectively believed economic development pressures and political considerations were given the greatest weight by elected officials. Encouragingly, regardless of how truly comprehensive the plan was, 33.3% placed it in the top three influence categories with 18.75% scoring it No. 1. On the other hand, 66.7% felt that the comprehensive plan could be rated no higher than 4, and 25% gave it the lowest ranking. The influence of the existing zoning ordinances did not fare as well as the comprehensive plan, implying that perhaps the existing ordinance had not been made compatible with the plan or, probably more likely, not being supported by the policy makers. Flashy presentations and petitions appear to be the least influential which could be an encouraging sign.

The increasing influence of an organized neighborhood presentation or opinion is evident, although the ranking of the number of objectors is surprising and may bear an important message for consideration by neighborhood organizations. However, the higher ranking of the neighborhood opinion may well be based on the increased election of council members from districts and can carry with it an adverse message about the danger of the loss of citywide concerns and viewpoints and an unfortunate movement to narrow, parochial, neighborhood self-interest. Overall, the ranking analysis emphasizes the need for more effort in developing and preserving an interest in coordinated, comprehensive planning for the building of the urban form. The interview process and the information and results obtained were an interesting and educational experience for me and, if considered carefully by others, could help us to realize how we got where we are, especially in our local communities, and indicate to all of us some areas demanding much more concern and attention.

Table 2
Interview Ranking Tabulations

Ranking Ratings by Numbers*	1	2	3	4	5	6	7	8	9
Comprehensive Plan Proposals	9	2	5	3	3	8	2	4	12
Existing Zoning Ordinance	5	5	7	3	6	6	5	7	4
Neighborhood Org. Opinions	4	7	6	13	7	4	1	4	2
Recommendation of Plan. Off.	3	5	8	14	6	4	5	1	2
Economic Dev. Sales Pitches	10	14	5	2	7	1	2	5	2
Political Considerations	14	10	7	2	8	3	1	1	2
Flashy Presentations	1	3	9	1	2	6	7	9	10
Petitions: Pro & Con	1	0	3	2	4	10	11	8	9
Number of Objectors	0	3	2	6	4	8	12	8	5

*Ratings on scale of 1 to 9 with 1 being the highest

THREE MAJOR FACTORS CONTRIBUTING TO HOW WE GOT WHERE WE ARE

Another objective during my research was to test a firm belief held for many years. The thesis of that conviction has been based on experiences that have shown time and time again our failure to build good cities with attractive, stable urban form, and that clearly defined policy direction for the future rests largely in our own failure to insist on, yes, even demand, good leadership and competency in government. It is much too simplistic to rationalize this failure just by saying that it is the result of apathy by the general public and what is being asked for is impossible. To do so can best be compared to an attitude of doubt many had about the impossibility of space exploration. The irony of this is that until this nation did begin to explore space, the belief was almost universal that it would be impossible to land a human on the moon except for the few scientists and engineers who believed otherwise and *were successful!*

We must stop using these rationalizations as excuses for complacent acceptance of how we have gotten where we are. Instead, we need to begin to take an incisive look at the causes of the malaise with which our society is afflicted. It doesn't take a gifted philosopher to identify the three underlying fundamental causes of this sickness. First and foremost, symptomatic of an affliction, is that which can be best categorized as "me-ism," an unwillingness to accept even a modicum of responsibility for humanity, society, or the kind of urban form being built and instead treating life only as a spectator sport. As Allan Bloom said, "Survivalism has taken the place of heroism as the admired quality,"[4] and, "To sum up, the self is the modern substitute for the soul."[5]

Secondly, what has happened has been nurtured, fertilized, and promulgated by the greed spawned by the selfishness shown most flagrantly in the exploitive portions of the development community. The unscrupulous ones have done such a good job at this that all of us who own property have come to accept the misrepresentation alluded to earlier that land is only a commodity from which each of us, by right, is entitled to the maximum profit. They have thus destroyed an idea that has been axiomatic over centuries that, although there is a right to own land, the use we make of that land should be based on the principle of stewardship. When we begin to use land, we automatically move into a position of affecting others around us: society, nature, and the total community environment. Once we create any type of detrimental, destructive, or costly effect on others beyond the boundaries of the land we own, we have stepped beyond the question of that right and moved into demanding a privilege.

Thirdly, this malaise has now been cultivated and harvested, almost with glee, by the overzealous destructive policy of some forms of media toward anyone who offers a potential for leadership. We may have reached the point where this is not confined to those who might be leaders but extends to damaging or destroying any individual, proposal, or project to whom or which a reporter has taken a personal dislike. They then "report" their feelings under the guise of the freedom-of-the-press privilege, frequently using quotes from unidentified sources or those "who wish to remain anonymous." It is these miscreants who must be singled out as being most responsible and who should be subjected to public pressure. The conviction of those in the media that scandal or exaggerated controversy is the only thing that people will watch, listen to, or read, the only thing that will sell newspapers and advertising or enhance ratings and circulation, has contributed greatly to a debilitating spin-off: the loss of trust and respect for all government.

EVALUATE YOUR ELECTED OFFICIALS

Regardless of the role the press may or may not play in whether effective leaders are now choosing to offer themselves for public service, we cannot afford to give up trying to find them and to encourage their participation. One way to impress yourself with the importance of this might be to take a closer look at the quality and performance of people who presently represent you in local government. To really determine whether your local community is prepared to effectuate planned change for a better future, begin by honestly evaluating the evident philosophy, the indication of concern for the total community, and the planning attitude exemplified by the action taken in the past year by your mayor, council and/or commissioners. If we are sincerely concerned and want to see a change for the better, here is an exercise each of us should undertake.

First, be sure to obtain a list of the names of all the people elected to public office, if you don't know or remember, and who are, by virtue of holding that office, in a position to provide strong leadership. Get to know them as individuals and become familiar with their performance in office by talking with them and asking questions, collecting their past campaign literature and position papers, talking to others about their opinions, and checking their voting record on planning and zoning issues over the past year. Needless to say, it is essential to attend council meetings or other public meetings and observe them in action.

If this is more than you want to take on by yourself, meet with five of your friends, convince them of how important such activity is to the future of your community and get them to assist you. Carefully think about the information gathered about each official and the collective policies, actions, and legislation they support or oppose, particularly regarding their evidenced attitudes about planning for future urban form and development. After this, can you in all good conscience, say that as individuals and as a body politic they represent the best possible choices for determining your personal future and that of your community? Chances are an honest evaluation could lead to surprising conclusions. What possibilities might this offer should you share your thoughtful analysis with just a half dozen more friends who also may be concerned about the direction your community is headed and if the other five people you involved did the same thing with a like number of their friends?

Certainly this is not to imply that all of the people elected are incompetent, unfit, or not doing a good job. As previously indicated, one of the pleasures of my trips was meeting and talking with some sincere, outstanding elected and appointed officials. Granted, these were relatively few in number when compared with the total contacts made, but the fact that there were some illustrates that all is not yet lost in local government. Undoubtedly there are many more of these standouts serving in hundreds of communities not visited and there is no intent here to denigrate them or take away any of the gratitude and appreciation they deserve. However, the experience and knowledge I have gained from forty years of working in planning, and serving as planning consultant for some 300 to 400 other cities not included in this research serves as an excellent comparative base for the conclusion that the sampling can be considered representative. Further, that experience supports my contention about the veracity of judgments made by those interviewed.

LACK OF COORDINATION IN
ALL LEVELS OF GOVERNMENT

Another disturbing influence I have observed over the years, which seems to be on the increase, is that of the lack of coordination in all levels of government. This dilemma within our governmental structure is not confined to the disjointedness resulting from a plethora of special districts. It is all around us at every level of government. Any careful observer of the building or the destruction of urban form over several years will be well aware that one of the biggest obstacles to preserving or creating the kind of urban form that causes people to feel that they are glad to live and work in a particular community is lack of coordination.

This is found in practically every city's internal structural operation and externally between governmental units. As has been pointed out the epitome of this lies at the federal government level. In chapter one, we discussed some of the ways that lack of government coordination is being built into the system by the tendency to increase the number of autonomous authorities. One could almost conclude that elected government at all levels is exercising a submerged death wish in its haste to approve the passing on of anything that in any way appears to be costly or controversial.

Several volumes could be written about one of the most prevalent coordination gaps; however it will be given only a mention here. That is the almost universal lack of coordination between autonomous elected school boards and the governing body and planning function of the community or communities their schools serve. In this situation, because it was included in the Model Planning Enabling Act, almost every state's planning legislation has a mandatory requirement that school boards coordinate their planning, construction or demolition of structures, and buying or disposing of land with the planning arm of the local government. Yet this is almost nonexistent. Try checking this out in your community and it is almost a sure bet that you will find it just doesn't happen.

When all of this is added to the usual split-responsibility assignments pertaining to development within city agencies and departments, it becomes easy to understand why we have failed to build well-planned, coordinated urban form. In all the cities used as examples in this book (with but two exceptions), planning departments lacked a clear definition of a coordinating role. Divided responsibility existed between planning and public works departments, building inspection departments, environmental protection agencies, economic development commissions or departments, urban renewal authorities, ad hoc appointed committees or task forces, and in some cases even the zoning administration. There is conflict rather than coordination, not only between these departments and agencies, but between individual incorporated municipal units. In the majority of places visited there also is evidence of a lack of cooperation between cities and the unincorporated areas of the county in which they were situated and/or a regional planning or economic development agency. The exceptions to almost all of this were Charlotte-Mecklenburg County and Portland.

Comprehensive Planning Equals Coordination

This phenomena of splintering responsibility has been manna from heaven for unscrupulous entrepreneurs, long masters of the divide-and-conquer philosophy. We need to remember that the very basis for the development and acceptance of the need for governmental planning, as well as the justification of that need, is the concept of comprehensive coordination. Never has there been a time where it is more evident that the lack of selling this idea has contributed greatly to poorly planned, unattractive, and expensive urban sprawl than now. The evidence is all around us. We see it every day when we drive to work, walk down the street, or as we look below in the take-offs and landings of any aircraft in which we may fly. The unfortunate part is that it is as if our optic nerves have become deadened; we don't really see the situation for what it is and we accept it without feeling the sense of regret and guilt on our part that we should for the mess we are passing on to future generations. In addition, far too many of us simply still accept it under the mistaken idea that we, as part of government, could not and cannot do anything about it as we can't interfere with "private rights"!

In any process of building for the future, whether it be in business, industry or government, unless there is a centralized authority to ensure coordination, chaos is the likely result. In our society there seems to be an ingrained fear that "coordinated" means big brother-type government and unreasonable superimposed control rather than cooperation between people in a truly democratic way. We need more people willing to work together not only for planned change in physical urban form, but also beneficial planned change at all levels of our governmental operation. If we in America are reaching, or have reached, the Paradise Lost stage, this problem of conflict and lack of coordination unquestionably is one of the reasons. As Dennis O'Harrow said, in his usual prophetic way in a 1956 speech, "The problems resulting from urban growth in the next 40 years will be magnified in direct ratio to the number of independent single-function districts and authorities trying to solve them."[6]

Isn't it time that each of us decided to emulate the actions of the character in the movie *Network*, when he went to a window, raised it to the top, stuck his head out, and yelled at the top of his lungs, "I'm mad as hell and I am not going to take it anymore"? It could well be that the failure to recognize where we are, or to be satisfied with it if we do take an honest look, rather than to make a determined commitment to change and "not take it anymore" could be fatal for our society.

What we need to do is refuse to allow ourselves to be maneuvered to the point where we are in the position of having to ask how we got where we are, but instead concentrate on being concerned first, with *where we want to be and how, working together, we can get there.* This is not the impossible dream any more than have been all the productive past visions of the future about which the ever present pessimistic "aginners" consistently cried, "It's hopeless!"

NOTES

1. Roland L. Warren, *The Community In America* (Chicago: Rand McNally College Publishing Co., 1972).

2. Ibid., p. 16.

3. Ibid., p. 17.

4. Allan Bloom, *The Closing of the American Mind* (New York: Simon and Schuster, 1987), p. 84.

5. Ibid., p. 173.

6. Marjorie S. Berger, ed., *Dennis O'Harrow: Plan Talk and Plain Talk* (Chicago: Planner's Press, American Planning Association, 1981), p. 87.

8

The Planning Profession: Past, Present and, Maybe, Future

Having previously explored some of the outside forces that have had a negative effect on the shaping of the urban form of America today—over which cities have had little or no say—it is appropriate to examine briefly some of the factors directly related to the evolution of the concept of local government planning. It should be restated that any reference to the term "planning" in this book is meant in its most comprehensive sense. This includes future-oriented vision and enhancement of the total community composition—physical, social, economic, and environmental factors—as well as all implementation tools available to local government for achieving a predetermined objective for the built environment based upon adopted goals and policies. Further, it implies that all of the above has been developed with participation of the people of the community and not simply done for them. Dennis O'Harrow in his admirable, aphoristic, no-nonsense style emphasized the importance of this last statement when he said: "Planning in a democracy is not handed down from above. It must come from the people, or it just doesn't come."[1]

THE CITY BEAUTIFUL MOVEMENT

When anyone begins to explore the evolution of the structured governmental planning process, invariably the beginning point is the World's Columbian Exposition of 1893 in Chicago. Occurring as it did at the height of the Industrial Revolution, there was an increasing interest in doing something about the blighted slum-like conditions of many major cities. There can be no doubt from an inspirational standpoint that it did exert an important influence on a number of American cities. Because of the design and splendor of the Exposition buildings, it has been referred to as "the white city" or "the dream city" and later on was popularized through the City Beautiful Movement (CBM). The Exposition's white marble-like structures, plazas, promenades, large gushing fountains, and the magnificence of the overall design were in sharp contrast to the drabness of the existing urban areas of that time in which those who attended actually lived.

This superb example of excellence had such an impact that as America moved into the twentieth century a greater sense of injecting beauty and aesthetics in major cities had been instilled in civic leaders. This resulted in the establishment of municipal art societies, civic center construction of governmental facilities around open space and other focal points of interest across the nation. The movement lasted as the major stimulant for improved public facilities and general beautification until the stock market crash of 1929. Even after this financial debacle, the influence of the movement carried over with some effect into the public works projects built by the unemployed in the programs of both the Work Progress Administration (WPA) and the Civilian Conservation Corps (CCC) during the Depression period of the 1930s and on into the 1940s.

There are many who credit this as the beginning of modern-day city planning. Others, while agreeing that it provided a powerful influence on increasing city attractiveness and quality of design, disagree. Those who do not believe this movement initiated organized local planning point out, with some justification, that while it helped to create a greater civic awareness, close examination reveals that the civic centers, monuments, parks, boulevards, parkways, and other public facilities were only pseudo-facades covering up and ignoring the real ills of cities and the need for future planning of the entire urban area. Regardless of which of these views is more accurate, there is no denying the contribution of the valuable heritage passed on to all of us by those leaders convinced of the merit of the City Beautiful Movement.

Examples of the CBM can still be observed in many of our major cities today, although in some cases overzealous urban renewal projects have destroyed or seriously decreased open space and the beauty of the original design. Cincinnati's Fountain Square and the area around it is one case in point; others include New York, Boston, Saint Louis, Washington, Baltimore, Cleveland and San Francisco. Majestic railroad terminals, parks, and parkways along with other aspects of cultural and aesthetic changes influenced the architects, landscape architects, and engineers in their work during the first four decades of this century and thus mirrored aspects of the CBM. There is hardly a large city in which an example resulting from this powerful model would not be found.

An Example of City Beautiful Influence

Denver is an interesting example of a city in which elected officials and civic leaders of the early 1900s had the foresight to make a deposit of capital into the city's future. Unfortunately, due to the lack of continued forward-thinking leadership, the community has lived off of the interest of that investment and is now seeing an erosion of the principal. While many are critical of some of his personal characteristics and practices, one man has to be credited with being responsible for the original investment in quality development and beauty for the city. He was Mayor Robert W. Speer who was first elected in 1904 and served two terms until 1912 when he chose not to run for a third term, primarily due to strong opposition from the editors of the *Denver Post* and the *Rocky Mountain News* who classified him as being a wasteful spendthrift because of his insistence on money being invested in civic improvements.

He returned, however, by popular request to an active political role in 1916 and was reelected easily. Unfortunately for Denver he died in the middle of his term in 1918. During his three administrations Speer, who had become a dedicated supporter of the City Beautiful even before his first term, was responsible for more cultural and civic improvements for the city than any mayor there since. Among the list of his accomplishments were decorative street lamps, needed storm and sanitary sewers, a municipal auditorium, and a three-element City Beautiful–type master plan, all of which were accomplished. The prongs of Speer's master plan were the Civic Center, parks and parkways, and several mountain parks. Today Denver citizens, as well as those who visit from elsewhere, can enjoy and appreciate all of these amenities. Residents of Denver should regret that there have not been other mayors with the same commitment to the future and the leadership ability to accomplish his objectives that Robert Speer had.

Although comprehensive planning and planners did not play a major role in the earlier days of the City Beautiful Movement the architects, landscape architects, and engineers who did were the majority of those responsible for organizing the first professional institute for city planning. Frederick Law Olmsted and Flavel Shurtleff in 1917 created the American City Planning Institute (later to become the American Institute of Planners), with membership open to anyone who had engaged in any type of city planning work for two years or more. Here again the effect of the City Beautiful Movement has left its mark on both America's urban form and the planning profession.

Historians Barbara Stewart Norgren and Thomas Jacob Noel made a telling point about the Movement's influence in their magnificent book, *Denver the City Beautiful:*

> The City Beautiful was more than aesthetics. It was also an attempt to make cities more efficient. Civic Centers were designed to promote intergovernmental cooperation by clustering city, state, and federal offices in an office park. Landscaping doubled as fire and flood control by putting space between buildings and by changing floodplains to parks. Parks, playgrounds, and recreation centers were also a stock prescription of public health proponents. Civic beautifiers drew inspiration from progressive-era philosophers such as John Dewey and William James. They and other intellectuals contended that improving the urban environment would uplift the entire population.[2]

The value of a community sense of pride in building support for continued improvement in the urban form, whether it is a magnificent arch as in St. Louis, Seattle's towering space needle, or San Francisco's cable cars, has been proof of this over the years.

Some Leaders In The Planning Profession

Just as a sense of pride is an essential element for a community, so it is for a profession. Therefore, in writing about the planning profession's past and present, it is appropriate to mention some of those contributing leadership to that profession based upon my own experiences. One of the more fortunate things about being "older" is that I had the opportunity to enter the profession early enough so that I knew and enjoyed informal bull sessions with some of those people who stood out in the planning field during the 1940s and 1950s. They weren't just active leaders in the profession; they were capable and impressive enough to convince the public that they and the profession had something to offer them.

My first planning job was with Russell VanNest Black from New Hope, Pennsylvania. As a pipe smoker myself, from the time of our first meeting I knew Russ Black was a good guy and a great planner: he too was an inveterate pipe smoker! Like so many of the others at that time, he was trained as a landscape architect and did not have a degree in planning, but he knew and understood its value, always operated with a sense of vision, could inspire people to listen to his ideas, and never hesitated to fight for the profession of planning (and he certainly could raise hell if you weren't doing the best possible job for him). He is lauded in every book recounting the earlier years of planning and the development of a professional organization.

When Harland Bartholomew, a St. Louis–based consultant or Gordon Whitnall, a leading planner from California walked into any room where people were congregated—especially a crowded room at an American Society of Planning Officials (ASPO) Conference—an electrical charge was injected into all discussions taking place. The same was true about Hugh Pomeroy from Westchester County, New York, always with the two cameras he had strung around his neck—a trademark. Another very special person exhibiting leadership was Brysis Whitnall, Gordon's wife, and also a complete, strong person who was a total planner in her own right. Not only was she one of the first notable women planner members of the American Institute of Planners, crusading for deserved equal treatment, but she also fought long and hard for the creation of a Private Practice Department within that organization. Unfortunately, even then AIP was not financially able to provide the necessary support and encouragement and several of us, including Brysis, organized the independent American Society of Consulting Planners (ASCP) which is still in existence, although quite different in its composition now than in those earlier years.

There were many others who truly believed in the professionalism of planning and expounded its merits at every opportunity. Particularly memorable was a true character—and that is the only appropriate way to refer to this loveable curmudgeon—Ladislas Segoe, a consultant from Cincinnati. He had an opinion on any subject pertaining to planning, mostly different from others, usually imaginative and thought provoking, which he never resisted proclaiming. The results of his consulting work continue to be recognized as landmark accomplishments in the development of the planning profession. Others, who influenced many younger planners in those days include Arthur C. Comey from the New England area with his humanistic approach to planning and to life; Frederick P. Clark for his contribution to innovative planning techniques in Rye, New York and to the long list of his consulting clients; and Charles A. Blessing, a continuing major champion of the value of good urban design to city building, represented by the excellent work he did in Detroit and other places.

While many are being left out, mention must be made of T. Ledyard Blakeman, Princeton, New Jersey, who died while this book was being written; not only for what he did for the Detroit Metropolitan Regional Planning Commission and, with VanNest Black, the state planning function in New Jersey, but for his ability to preach the gospel of professional planning and the valuable experiences he passed on to me. A more personal reason for including Tommy, as he was known, leaves me unsure whether to condemn or praise him, for he is the one who taught me to love Jack Daniel's Sour Mash!

Two Voices That Made A Difference

This list of experiences for which I am grateful could be made more exhaustive, but I will conclude with saying how much I do, and the entire profession should, miss two of the greatest voices who ever existed for educating the public on the value of planning and the planning profession. Those came from Walter Blucher and Dennis O'Harrow. For years Blucher was the executive director of the American Society of Planning Officials, as was O'Harrow who followed him. Their positions gave them the greatest opportunity to speak out through the medium of the ASPO *Newsletter* and their speeches were strongly supported by the governing board of directors of that organization. Again, neither one hesitated to say what he thought and believed in even though their public expressions might appear to be critical.

For example, soon after the passage of the Federal Housing Act of 1937 which omitted any reference to requiring referral of the action of local housing agencies to the planning commissions for review or comment, Walter Blucher wrote that the majority of the city planning commissions in the United States had become moribund, were "serving no useful purpose" had "failed to function satisfactorily for many years" and had "made no contribution to community development."[3]

Scott noted that:

In the Newsletter of the American Society of Planning Officials for July, 1952, Walter Blucher pleaded with planning agencies not to shirk their share of responsibility for the local redevelopment program or to feel aggrieved when the Federal Division of Slum Clearance and Urban Development negotiated directly with local redevelopment officials, as the law required it to do. 'Almost universally state redevelopment legislation requires approval of the local planning commission of redevelopment project plans' Blucher noted. 'Obviously, this cannot be done adequately by a planning commission unless such redevelopment project plans are related to a general plan for the locality as a whole.'[4]

Anyone claiming to be a planner who has not read Marjorie S. Berger's book, *Dennis O'Harrow: Plan Talk and Plain Talk* several times is cheating themselves. Among all the highlighted portions in my copy there are thirty-two tabs sticking out representing quotes which would fit perfectly in this book. There are twice as many more which could have been tabbed. Although I have used several and will include others, I did try to stop short of simple plagiarism, but no one could tell it like it is better than O'Harrow could; nor can anyone write a book emphasizing that planners and the entire profession need to look seriously at themselves to determine how to do better without frequent reference to this planning pundit. His reflections of the profession during his time, his candid evaluations, expressions of opinion, and his powerful voice did more, and can still do more, to make us unafraid to honestly evaluate ourselves and, at the same time, instill a sense of camaraderie, community, and pride for all of us in our profession today.

An absolute must for every planner, interested elected and appointed officials and the concerned public, is Chapter 7 of Berger's book, "Communicating: What We Need and What We Don't."[5] Quotes from two speeches Dennis gave, one in 1953 and one in 1959, sum up the thrust of this chapter: "I am sometimes sheepish about the behavior of my fellow planners. I find many of them less than clear in their writing and speaking."[6] Also: "You don't have to write like John Steinbeck or Red Smith, and you don't have to be able to speak as well as Adlai Stevenson II. But unless you can do a better than passable job in both of these, you aren't going to function very well as a planner. And I will say unequivocally that the graduates of city planning schools that I have seen recently have had this part of their training shamefully neglected."[7]

None of these people ever hesitated to stand up and argue profoundly either for or against any topic concerning planners, planning, zoning, and especially planning as a profession; nor did they shy away from being critical when it was called for. They all spoke to the public at every opportunity, attempting to educate as many people as possible about the importance of planning, the need for a planning attitude by elected officials and the importance of the planning profession. These are the very things we are now being criticized for not doing by the public; but these leaders did so in a way that gained the respect of those listening to them.

NATIONAL PLANNING ORGANIZATIONS

For those who are not professional planners, some explanation of the history of the present major national professional organizations may be helpful before going into the results of the opinions expressed on factors influencing local planning. As has been mentioned previously, the beginning was the organization of the American City Planning Institute (ACPI) in 1917 which later became the American Institute of Planners (AIP). At first, membership in both ACPI and AIP was open to anyone participating in the city planning field and calling themselves professional planners, but proof of experience later became necessary with graduation from a "recognized" planning school slightly reducing the experience requirement. In 1934 an organization known as the American Society of Planning Officials (ASPO) was formed primarily for public officials, interested citizens, and those in planning-related fields, although professional planners were also welcome to become members.

The Present Structure

After many months of discussion, not without considerable disagreement as to the advisability of doing so, in 1978 the two organizations merged into the American Planning Association with a subdivision of that umbrella organization becoming the American Institute of Certified Planners (AICP). The APA continues to provide assistance and service for the general public and members of the AICP must also be members of APA. The AICP is now the organization limited to practicing professional planners who must pass a qualifying examination to join. The examination cannot be taken until an applicant has had a minimum of four-years experience in planning or, if that person has a bachelors or a masters degree in planning from an accredited planning school, the experience requirements are reduced by one and two years respectively.

The authority to create a planning school accreditation board was obtained jointly by the APA, AICP and the Association of Collegiate Schools of Planning (ACSP) in the early 1980s. Of more than 20,000 APA members, some 6,500 are AICP members. Since the start of the planning-school accreditation process there have been sixty-one planning programs granted accreditation status each of which is subject to review every five years.

INTERVIEWEES' CRITIQUE OF NATIONAL PLANNING ORGANIZATIONS

Of the 75 interviews conducted, 50 people (67%) were familiar enough with APA and AICP to volunteer their evaluations of the image-building done by both organizations. Of these, 41 (82%) were members of APA or both APA and AICP. Most of those belonging to AICP had been members since its creation with some going back to the days of AIP. All indicated they had been active in chapter affairs, five were involved in the organization of chapters in their areas and seven indicated they had served as officers, board members or as committee chairpersons within a chapter. As was mentioned, a number had involved themselves in national activities with two either elected to a national officer position or as a board member of one of the organizations. The comments made and the opinions expressed by them, therefore, certainly cannot be dismissed as those of "johnny-come-latelys" or individuals not having had exposure in order to know of what they speak.

Support from Others for Discussion

Recent letters printed in *Planning* magazine together with Perry L. Norton's summary of a survey conducted of the presidents for APA chapters in the area designated as Region One by APA substantiate the need for this discussion. Each was asked to respond to the question of what they considered to be the most urgent long-range issues facing the planning profession today. A broad overview of what was determined is included and the opinions expressed are amazingly similar to the concerns of planners contributing to the research conducted for this book. Presented as "AICP Notes", Norton wrote a concise recap of the responses obtained and also included some excellent comments from seven APA chapter presidents in Region One plus another from John A. Humphreys, AICP, director, community development, Breckenridge, Colorado.

This entire section of the magazine should be required reading for all practicing planners, whether members of AICP or not. Excerpts from Norton's summation are: "A surprisingly high priority is a definition of purpose. What are we doing? What kinds of cities are we building? What is our vision? . . . Another concern is the widespread migration of planners to the private sector and the emergence of planning specializations that have become so specialized that those who call themselves hyphenated planners don't seem to have anything in common with other hyphenated planners."[8]

He then says that there was a third concern related to the first two, that of a low esteem for public service. However, he points out that instead of despairing about these we should take heart: "The problems they (the presidents) have shared here are problems to be tackled. The issues are opportunities. What they seem to be saying is 'Let's do a little course correction. Let's get back on track. Let's do what we know we can, and should do.'"[9]

Knowing Perry Norton, I would say that he then turns to his ever present optimistic outlook by concluding: "People like Chapter presidents tend to be optimists, but they're also realists. They know we've got problems, but they all clearly recognize the potential strength in the planning community, the strong sense of belonging. And that, it seems to me, is very good news indeed."[10]

When information like this continues to surface with many more people who write about the need for reexamination and rethinking of the effectiveness and the future of the profession, how can we continue to ignore it? Dennis O'Harrow said in 1955: "The strength of any science or profession or branch of knowledge will be found in the ability of its servants to practice self-criticism."[11]

APA and AICP Education and Promotion

Although there was some divided opinion among planners in this area, the majority were convinced we could do much better. Some favorable comments were made regarding APA, with several finding it valuable, primarily because of the much improved *Planning* magazine. However, even they indicated that, while being helpful to planning practitioners, both national organizations should do more to educate the general public about planning and promote the concept of planning. The work of a number of local APA chapters in both of these important aspects received much favorable comment from several of those interviewed.

An important part of educational and promotional efforts for increasing interest and understanding of planning should be APA and AICP national conferences. In spite of the fact that over 2,700 were in attendance at the 1989 meeting, the APA/AICP national conferences in general drew expressions of concern, primarily because they were not perceived as informative or helpful. Some had attended conferences but felt these had consisted primarily of planners talking to themselves about the same old issues with little concern being evident about the opinion of local elected officials, the importance of the political system, the reaction of the general public or how to successfully involve all of them in the planning function. Many also felt that the format of the conference had been too much the same year after year and that more diversity in content, speakers and discussion leaders was needed. The assistant planning director in San Diego said, "We have taken our planning commissioners to a number of APA conferences and their reaction has been that it was just planners talking to planners and they were not getting a lot of insight from the meetings. They decided they didn't want to go to those any longer. The last five or six years we have been taking them to the ULI meetings. They like those because they are geared to a broader section of people and they feel like they are getting something more out of their trip." Publications, conferences and training sessions of the Urban Land Institute (ULI) and the American Institute of Architects (AIA) were considered to be far more helpful and informative by those who were members of one or the other of these professional organizations, as well as members of AICP.

The APA Journal

Among the 41 professional planners interviewed, the most unanimous expression of concern by far was regarding the APA *Journal*. None indicated that they found it helpful in their professional work nor useful in convincing others of the importance of the planning profession. The general opinions expressed are best indicated by rather strong quotes from two interviews. The director of planning in Charlotte, Martin R. Cramton, Jr., AICP, said: "I don't bother to try to read the *Journal* and I think it is a waste of time. In my opinion the only reason that it is published is so the academics can write articles that they couldn't get published anywhere else and probably can in the *Journal*."

Another comment was provided by Peter Jarvis, AICP, a principal in a private planning consulting firm in Minneapolis: "You pick up the APA *Journal* and you look at the table of contents, you flip a few pages and my reaction is who is kidding whom? Of what particle of value, even from a research standpoint, of what ultimate value, what intellectual value does this have to do with what? I have people in this shop who call themselves planners, even though some don't have a master's degree in city planning, who, when the *Journal* gets routed, laugh at it. When the ULI publication goes around they look at it and they read it. I can see that the reason the *Journal* exists is to give the academic community a place where they may be able to get published and that is the only justification."

While these opinions are somewhat forceful and obviously will not meet with the approval of all responsible for the publication, persons who pay an additional fee to subscribe to it, or those in academia, they do express the general consensus of all AICP members commenting to me about the *Journal*. Unquestionably, there are others who probably hold a different opinion, but there is clear evidence of a sizeable group of professionals sharing the opinion of the people interviewed.

Planning Education

One other area of concern widely expressed was that of where planning education is today and where it is heading. Other than some favorable comments about the training received by those graduating from planning schools at least ten years ago (to which they added concerns about the programs of those schools now), not one person had anything favorable or complimentary to say about planning education. The strongest comments concerned the way planning students are being trained. Twenty-one people commented on the lack of practical training, exposure to real-world problems and the almost complete loss of required participation in an internship program. This reaction was found especially among those who are in a position to hire or closely observe the performance of younger planners in their first positions right out of school. Some went so far as to indicate that the firm or agency with which they were involved had established a policy of not hiring planners unless they had gained several years of experience somewhere else after graduation.

Related to this concern is the widespread belief that schools are not providing enough training or exposure regarding how to communicate with and relate to the public. There seems to be a lack of understanding among recent graduates about the importance of public involvement and how to go about achieving it, and a return to the smug attitude that "we are trained professionals, therefore we know best." Contributing to this problem is the fact that planning education, planning courses and curricula are too theoretical; this is exacerbated by the increasing emphasis placed on pure academic research, which results in obtaining grants to help pay faculty and administrative salaries. No longer is the value of practical applied research considered worthwhile in many planning programs. As a result planning schools are becoming more like liberal arts programs and are moving away from being professional programs or being absorbed into architecture schools which then can say they offer training in planning.

Comments were also made faulting the present deficiency of practical professional planning experience among planning educators and the decreased use of practicing planners as lecturers with others highly critical of the institutional pressure for hiring only those with a Ph.D. This point was expanded on by those who stated they felt that having a masters degree and a Ph.D, but no actual planning practice experience, did not necessarily qualify anyone as a good planning teacher. This belief was not exclusive with those commenting here nor is it a brand new idea. It is amazing that according to Marjorie Berger in an editor's commentary in her book about O'Harrow he felt much the same way: "The 'Fish or Cut Bait' editorial . . . (1966) was equally scatheful on the M.A. to Ph.D to research-teaching progression. It included a suggestion however, a DOH thesis: The Ph.D who has actually done some planning is a better researcher and a better teacher; we should introduce experience as a prerequisite for the planning Ph.D."[12]

Needless to say, this O'Harrow editorial did not meet with enthusiastic agreement from some planning educators even at that time. Expressing support for this concern today, a private consultant in New Orleans, Dr. Anthony J. Mumphrey, AICP, summed up his opinion in this area by saying: "Just knowing all about Lewis Mumford's philosophy is not enough to make a good planner."

Further comments in this area, mainly from planning educators, included the conviction that the Association of Collegiate Schools of Planning (ACSP) was exercising a large amount of influence in the direction planning education is going. This comes through the major role it plays in planning schools' accreditation visitations and, consequently in the training of planning professionals as well as promotion of the idea that all planning educators must have a Ph.D. Other concerns regarded the need for more exposure to the political system and a general understanding of politics. Training in business, economics, public finance and management were thought to be helpful elements of good planning education and others decried the emphasis on specialization. All in all a good deal of dissatisfaction with present day planning programs was evident in the interviews.

Robert Einsweiler, AICP, planning consultant and planning educator in Minneapolis provided an erudite discussion on where planners are now by saying that he sees both good signs and bad signs. The explanation of what he feels to be the bad signs is included in chapter nine. The first bright spot he sees is the work of a numerically small group of planning educators including Richard S. Bolan, Donald Schon, John Forester, Howard Baum and Jerome Kaufman, among others. Their writings and teaching emphasize planning as a process, a strategy for action, but ethically practiced. In short, they have advocated moving away from planning as a collection of social science theories to a theory of planning as producing action and change. Although this approach has earned them the scorn of some planning faculty, Einsweiler says, "It is also the horse I have been on for twenty years." This is confirmed in the interest in recent APA-published books by Bruce W. McClendon and Ray Quay as well as Melvin R. Levin, and William Lucy.

The second bright spot he sees is the forced set of circumstances that closed the federal money spigot, thus making many more planners literate about how the private sector works, about finance, and the market. "Understanding the private sector side of the social equation always has been one of the blind spots in the field and in planning education. If the function of the planner is to intervene when markets fail or when private sector actions are socially unacceptable, that really means intervening in private investments, private decisions and choices. To do that the planner must know how the market and investment systems work and how these decisions are made before sticking a finger into them. Such knowledge enables planners to make markets work more in the social interest, or to improve the social effects of private investment decisions, rather than automatically substituting public programs for them."

In specifically addressing planning education, Einsweiler's opinion is that planners are never taught enough about the three main complementary systems of decision making in our society—the economic system, the political system, and the legal system. "Most decisions are made in the private sector. The political system is the social means to lead that sector, to intervene and alter or stop unacceptable practices, and to do the things the private sector cannot or will not do. The legal system is the set of rules and means whereby the political system and its citizens intervene in public and private decisions, primarily through property rights, but also personal or human rights."

"If the planning schools offered a good course focusing on the interaction of these systems and the interaction among governments, we would be a long way down the road to improved effectiveness. Students want to know more than what constitutes a "good" plan, or whether this is a "good" housing policy. They want to know how to *do* planning, and how to produce effective change. For that, they must understand these larger systems."

THE PLANNING PROFESSION'S PRESENT—AND FUTURE?

Reference has been made several times thus far to the planning process, planners, and the planning profession. In the remainder of this chapter, attention will be focused on a discussion of planning at the local level and some conceptions of it from planners, local officials and public representatives. Emphasis will be placed on the importance of each of these in relating, or not relating, to the general public and to the role that relationship should play both in the community and the planning profession. Most of the discussion will be based on interviews described elsewhere. I would note that although each interviewee was informed that the purpose of the interview was to elicit their opinions for material to be used later in a published book, they nevertheless responded with surprising candor to the questions asked.

Understanding of The Planning Process

As someone with years of experience in community planning, I have long known that we have not provided a strong, commonly accepted base of understanding of the planning process and its importance. This has contributed to a ready willingness to criticize planning and the professionals involved in its practice since it is always easier to be critical of something about which you have little, if any, clearly stated, factual information. Listening to the many tapes and transcribing the pertinent comments, a goodly number of which were less than complimentary about the process of planning and planners in their cities, provided impressive support as to the accuracy of my previous conclusion.

While this gives reason to pause and reflect, it also causes one to wonder if some of these comments come from the time-worn lack of understanding of planning or from an unwillingness to be personally involved in seeking to improve that with which they are dissatisfied in their community or the planning profession. Regardless of the reason, I am firmly convinced that it behooves all professional planners to listen, discuss and seek answers as to how to overcome *any* adverse or critical expression. The worst things we can do are to pretend that criticism does not exist or else try to ignore it; however, I would note there is an encouraging trend from the number of published articles and books, some by APA, pointing out our need for rethinking and evaluation. All bona fide professions must, from time to time, reexamine themselves to look for and correct any weaknesses or failures that may exist in both a present process and/or perception by those they must be prepared to serve. That was the hope in undertaking this project and what I have indicated as being important now to all of us.

Fortunately there were other viewpoints expressed that showed a better understanding of the planning process and recognized the contribution planning and planners had made even with less than enthusiastic support from elected officials.

Summary of Interview Comments

The next area for consideration will include further comments from the seventy-five interviews. Although a large majority of those interviewed provided information on their impressions of planners and to some extent the success of the profession in gaining public acceptance and understanding, almost all of what was said about APA and AICP internal activities, functions, publications, and conferences came from members. After visiting with these people, I am convinced that most of them spoke from a genuine interest and concern and were reflecting sincere feelings about ways we can improve ourselves as effective planners and as a planning profession. At least from the cities I visited, there is an evident honest hunger by planners to be part of a professional organization that does a good job in educating the public about planning and planners, provides excellent information to its members, has developed a widespread national recognition of its existence and acceptance as a voice worthy of being listened to.

The Need For Definition of the Planning Profession

When two or more persons are engaged in any discussion, one of the things contributing to the difficulty of consensus is the ambiguity of the English language. Like Alice In Wonderland we each know what we intend a word to mean, but the odds are great that the word may be interpreted as meaning something entirely different by another person. In no word does that problem exist more than in that of "planning" when it is applied to cities. At present, planning can mean anything to those to whom we are supposed to be supplying a service—from the idea that it is "communistic," to street sweeping, installing sewer lines, planting trees, or simply idealistic, impractical dreaming. For years we in the planning field have not understood this nor have we developed the ability or willingness to agree among ourselves on a common objective of what we are trying to do and what we are all about so that it can be easily understood by elected officials and the general public. There is ample evidence that even within the profession some of those performing as planners do not understand just what planning entails.

A simple, understandable definition would be very helpful in establishing the much needed fraternity-like bond among the many diversified interests represented by those considering themselves to be planners and, perhaps, even help to pull us together more as a profession and thereby become more effective. To make the argument for the need for this definition more dramatically supportable, how many of the 226,549,010 people reported in the 1980 census for the United States and the 6,300,063 persons in the cities included in this study would you estimate have any understanding of what we as planners should hope is recognized as our common purpose? Even two percent would be 4,530,980 and 126,001 respectively. If anyone who has attended city council or planning commission meetings, or represented a planning viewpoint in lectures or at a gathering of citizens considers even these lower figures realistic, they are much more optimistic than I.

Yet, as the Minneapolis planning director, Oliver Byrum, said: "Most of the public just assumes what planners are doing, if they care at all, and the planning profession has not done much to overcome this." The former planning director in New Orleans, Robert W. Becker, along with several others interviewed, was not convinced that we as planners have defined the planning profession adequately for public acceptance, or even decided whether or not planning truly is a profession. His rather pessimistic comment was: "I am not certain we can ever get around this syllogism unless a way is found for those in the profession to lay claim to some extraordinary, unique block of knowledge which our training gives us that no one else has. Unfortunately, I do not see that happening and planning schools in general certainly are not imparting it. The present value of planning seems to be that of combining multi-disciplines into a problem solving mode and any profession can do that."

The Image of Planners

Just as important as the question of defining planning and the profession effectively is that of recognizing the image some planners have created in the minds of the public as well as in those of some professionals from other fields with whom I spoke. On this subject the non-planners had no hesitation remarking on the areas where they feel we can and should do a better job on the general image we create. One of the areas commented on most frequently was that of developing, either through educational training or by self-improvement, a better ability and a greater willingness to communicate ideas and their value as well as the planning process in general to elected officials, lay planners, and the citizenry. Suggestions included listening to and giving consideration to the viewpoints of others: the general public, the business community, neighborhood organizations and other professionals including department heads within city government. Eric Damian Kelly, AICP, and a nationally reputed land use attorney has submitted a proposal to APA regarding preparing a series of videotaped educational planning sessions for public officials, public schools, and even the planning profession itself—something that would be most helpful in this regard.

In addition, another thing we need to overcome to improve our image is the impression that some planners have an attitude of "I am right, and you are wrong," "It is us versus them," or believe that there is a single right answer to every problem. We have also created a feeling among some of the public, as well as other planners, that there is too much of a sense of turning inward within the profession, that we are clannish and talk to ourselves about the same things year after year and spend more time trying to impress others within the profession rather than communicating with and impressing those whom we profess to serve.

This matter of better communication applies not only to verbal expression, but also to our writing. In this latter, it is imperative that we realize who our audience is. As the assistant planning director in San Diego, Michael J. Stepner, said: "As far as writing is concerned we have to decide who our audience is. We are not writing for the classroom anymore, but for a general public audience, many of whom are uninformed about the planning process, to whom we are trying to sell the value of the planning functions and our proposals. When you are trying to sell any product to anybody, you have to make it meaningful to that person or those persons. In order to do so we need to develop better our ability to speak, write, and prepare illustrations in the language and a manner that can be understood by those whom we are trying to convince. It is important to remember that, generally, people act in what they perceive to be their own best interests and it is very difficult to convince them otherwise."

There are a number of interviews from which quotes could be taken emphasizing these points, but only a few others will be used. The first is the most disturbing, but perhaps the best summary of the dilemma in which we may well find ourselves unless we work to discover ways to improve our image. It came from Edward Martin, a former city manager of Corpus Christi with some twenty years of governmental administrative experience, who said: "Unless planners begin to overcome their isolation image they will become the least effective group in shaping the urban form while the accounting, engineering, and architectural firms will increasingly apply for and receive planning contracts to advise on planning decisions. Unless some changes are made within the profession, planners and planning as a profession will become extinct within five years."

Although I, too, am somewhat pessimistic about the profession unless we listen to criticism and institute improvements, I do not entirely believe that the last part of that quote will prove to be correct, or at least I hope not. However, Dr. Michael Brooks in his article on the planning profession in the APA *Journal*, while sharing that hope with me, lends credence for our being somewhat concerned. He said: "When the last planner becomes primarily a 'facilitator' in service to the activities of the private sector, we will have lost a profession. Strong forces impel us in that direction at present. One hopes that we will have sufficient strength of professional character to resist those forces."[13]

On the other hand, Robert Worthington, AICP, of Minneapolis, agreed somewhat more strongly with Martin when he said: "I think that in the next five years, maybe the next ten at the most, if we don't reverse what I see to be a negative trend, all of the positive benefit we have achieved is going to be lost."

The Role of Planners

A lot has been said about the need for more leadership capability in those we elect to public office as mayors and council members. Along with a number of other qualities such as vision, intelligence, personality, and dedication, there are two qualities absolutely essential for defining good leadership. In order to be a good leader, a person must be inspired themselves and thus inspiring to others. Just as this is a definite need in local government officials so it is for planners and the planning profession.

This is not to say that planners in local communities should try to assume the role of setting policy, speak out against adopted policy, or become involved personally in day-to-day politics. Instead, it is my firm belief that good leadership can be reflected in the way planners deal with elected officials, planning commission members, zoning board members, other professionals with whom they must work, and the general public. I strongly believe that planners must learn more about politics and politicians; what they think, how they operate and how the political system works. Politicians are, after all, the people who set policy, legislate effectuation tools, supervise planning and zoning administration as well as oversee the way all other departments are managed. They can see that coordination is an enforced policy and ultimately pass on any plan or proposal coming from planners. Also, they determine just what role will be assigned to planning and planners in every community.

A planning director or even an entry-level planner can show that they are inspired and can inspire others by the way they present themselves, whether to their supervisors, co-workers, politicians, business people, or members of the general public. We can inspire by showing a strong dedication and belief in the planning process, in the profession, and in ourselves. All of these comments apply equally to our professional organizations and to the people we elect to office and entrust with administration at the national and chapter level just as they do to local, county, state, and national elected officials. As we should expect those elected or appointed to a public political office to provide inspired and inspiring leadership, so should we expect it at all levels in our professional organizations.

Where there is a lack of commitment to the planning process or a lack of understanding of the role a planning department or individual planner should play, the role assigned today in many cities does not speak well for either public officials or the inspiring capabilities of planners. Many of those interviewed who were both qualified and willing to evaluate the role of planners did not indicate an encouraging situation for professional planners, at least in their cities. While not refraining from criticizing planners and the profession in general, it is not surprising that comments were favorable in Portland and Charlotte regarding their own planners and the role they are playing. The same is true in Minneapolis, especially pertaining to downtown planning, although several indicated disapproval about the constraints placed on the planners by the city council; beyond that, several of the non-planners were critical of planners as a professional group as a whole.

In Pittsburgh a lot of concern was evident regarding the future role of planning under the new form of government. Evaluation of the planners' image and role in other places did not fare as well. Saint Paul's mayor and council are believers in pragmatic, action-oriented planning and have established this as their policy for planning in their city. This met with enthusiastic support from the planning director who indicated she was in the management business and said; "Planning is a practicing profession. If we want visionaries, I think that is a role for professors." In the remaining cities the role assigned to the planning department and planners was not indicative of a strong professional position.

While no one questions the capability, dedication and professionalism of the planning director in Baltimore, several expressed disapproval of the lack of a planning attitude evident from the elected officials, the role assigned to the planning department, and the lack of official support for long-range planning there. Like Baltimore, New Orleans has had the active involvement of the business community in the central city downtown area, but similar positive participation is absent from the rest of the city. Furthermore, with the council using the excuses of difficult economic times and a revenue shortage, the planning department is understaffed and constrained from updating the comprehensive plan; it basically fulfills a housekeeping function by reviewing zoning changes and pragmatic project proposals. In Denver, before 1983 the planning department was merely abided by the mayor and council and remained in existence primarily because it had been established in the city charter. Federico Pena, the current mayor, ran on a platform of restoring effective planning and improving the role of the planning department and, to a large extent, this has been done.

Planners in San Diego, San Antonio, Corpus Christi, and Memphis are not highly regarded as influential professionals by the officials and the general public. However, it should again be noted that Corpus Christi voters have now approved a city charter amendment mandating the preparation of a comprehensive plan with periodic updating. Nevertheless, through all of this comes the unfortunate picture of professional planners being cast into the role of crisis responders, doing housekeeping chores and providing routine information while the governing body assures everyone that they are all for planning. This type of planning, if it can be called that, is not only harmful to the planners forced to contend with less than a challenging opportunity, it is not aiding the profession's reputation, is a disservice to the citizens of the community and is reflective of a mediocre or worse leadership quality in elected officials.

Who must share the blame for this? To some extent those of us in the planning profession are responsible for not having contributed sufficiently to educating the general public about what good planning is all about in order to place them in the position of being able to recognize when they are being hoodwinked. The remaining responsibility rests on those people of the electorate who, on their own, have not insisted upon the kinds of leaders capable of putting community interest ahead of selfish vested interests or have a contorted idea of how the political system in a democratic society should be used.

The most strikingly descriptive statement about this misuse of planning and planners came from John H. Shanahan, Jr., an experienced planning consultant in Corpus Christi who shared some of Brooks's concerns. He stated that "Planners have begun to see themselves as facilitators, luggage carriers between community groups, politicians, and business interests. If we are, in fact, a profession supposedly having studied an organized body of knowledge and are tested for that knowledge in order to be granted AICP membership, is it really sufficient for us to be characterized no better than a bunch of

Red Cap porters lugging suitcases? Planners certainly can, and must, do better than that!"

Perhaps this provides some basis for the reason why all seven persons interviewed in the city agreed, although not using the exact same words, that Corpus Christi officials and residents lack any real understanding of planning and exhibit no planning attitude in spite of the charter revision. There can be a big difference between mandating planning and seeing that it becomes truly effective.

In commenting on the role of planners, Susan Powers, AICP, executive director of the Denver Urban Renewal Authority made an interesting point that differed from the approach taken by others. This was done by pointing out that planners themselves, to some extent, contribute to their own problems by accepting a role less than appropriate for a trained professional and then are simply not aggressive enough. She believes that "Planning professionals in the traditional planning office find their roles to be narrowly defined. They have done this to themselves by not realizing people define their own lives. They create a product that is a policy recommendation, but they don't think it is their business to help see that it is implemented. Therefore, they certainly are not out there representing that the profession cares beyond making recommendations."

Each Planner Mirrors The Profession To Others

There is more than a grain of truth in this statement, and it is worthy of careful analysis with regards to our own professional performance. Each of us presents a reflected image of the profession or organization with which we are associated to those with whom we come in contact. If a member of any profession—but especially planning—is relegated without protest to playing a minor role, or is prevented from practicing real planning, it soon becomes easy for others to conclude that placid acceptance of "housekeeping" assignments must be what the profession is about. Certainly people who have never met or talked with someone called a planner are very likely to form a mental image of what they believe all planners to be like from the behavior or performance of just one planner.

CONCLUSION

Some, no doubt, will find fault with this project and many of the opinions expressed in this book. However, had it not been done or been written differently, I would not be true to the need discussed in the introduction for an objective, analytical examination and discussion of the failures, as well as the successes, of planners and the planning profession over the years. Although I indicated earlier that including the interview comments is not necessarily indicating agreement with them, I do agree strongly with the main impression that we have created an unfortunate image that has become prevalent as a result of our inactivity, improperly directed emphasis, and, in effect, acting almost as a secret society, rather than a truly professional organization.

As many of those interviewed have said, the prime reason for this lies in our failure to produce and support the kind of leaders and the leadership absolutely essential to developing a meaningful, saleable definition of planning and the role of the profession, strengthening our organizations so they are capable of gaining people's understanding of who we are, what we are, and why our profession is important to them. Instead, those serving in the positions where they could develop that kind of organization have evidently believed when taking office that the profession has already arrived and that public acceptance can be taken for granted. Yet, it is clear from the interviews that in the minds of many, including planners, the planning profession does not demonstrate that it cares enough about what the public thinks, even though that should be the major reason for our having an organization. Consequently, while not agreeing entirely, I am seriously concerned about the frightening prediction made that if we, as individual planners and as a profession, do not reexamine our purpose and direction, establish more of a sense of community within the profession, and concentrate, not only on doing a better job in our planning, but even more on changing our image in the minds of the general public, the profession will become extinct.

Two interesting observations should be noted. The first is that almost all of the planners interviewed were in agreement and, in fact, stated their opinions with almost the same words as appear above. The second is that interview comments from those who are not planners frequently reflected a lack of knowledge about the fundamental purpose of local government planning. Although playing an important role in shaping urban form, these people generally had no firsthand experience with the process or planners as individuals, and often appeared to have accepted ill-founded adverse opinions advanced by others with questionable motivations. Most apparent was the almost complete lack of knowledge about planning's professional organizations, both now and in the past.

An encouraging aspect was that this obviously did not reflect a lack of curiosity or interest as questions asked necessitated explaining the former existence of the American Society of Planning Officials and the American Institute of Planners and their consolidation in 1978. However, many had trouble understanding the difference between the resulting American Planning Association and the American Institute of Certified Planners while knowledge about planner certification and accreditation of planning schools was nonexistent among the non-planners. A real need was thus manifested for greater public information about APA and AICP as organizations and the membership criteria for both.

In summary the principal issues commented on by both planners and non-planners were:

1. The apparent inability of planners to reach agreement on understandable definitions of planning and the planning profession which are meaningful enough to the average person to be accepted as important to them and their future.

2. The unwillingness, or lack of ability, of planners to communicate their ideas and the value of the planning process to elected officials, lay-planners, and the citizenry.

3. The reluctance of some planners to listen to and give consideration to the viewpoints of other people.

4. The trend of planning schools to shift toward the academic pattern of the liberal arts educators' emphasis on pure research at the cost of practical professional training such as offered in engineering, law, medicine, architecture, and other professions. This situation results in the loss of people-oriented practical exposure.

5. An expressed dissatisfaction with the role played by national planning organizations in the education of practicing planners as well as the populace. Publication of practical and helpful materials, profession-promoting brochures, and media materials need to be developed. Comments from members of APA and AICP, as well as local officials and the public, indicated dissatisfaction with the format and content provided at training sessions and conferences.

Whether we choose to consider the opinions expressed as constructive concerns worthy of thoughtful discussion and providing justification for taking steps to improve our image in the eyes of the public or whether they are viewed simply as undeserved and unjustified criticism is entirely up to us, but it could be determinative of the future of our profession.

POSTSCRIPT

Throughout this book I have avoided two important elements that are the foundation for building the kind of urban form we should be seeking to leave for future generations: one, a clearer definition of what I consider today's comprehensive plan to be, and two, the much-overlooked, under-used capital improvements program process. If there are any tools more essential to laying the foundation for good, future-oriented development, I have yet to hear of them.

Suppose I were still a planning consultant. A planning director, the planning commission and, in the best of all worlds, even the governing body of one of the fifteen cities studied had stated that they wanted my firm's help in updating a long-outdated plan. However, it was made clear that budget constraints were such that a major outside project was out of the question, so what would I advise?

I would explain why the traditional, specifically stated master plan, regardless of the fact that it may be named a "comprehensive plan," has some serious shortcomings. Far too many things have changed, e.g., community structures and community development have become increasingly complicated, while economic forces and pressures are shifting much too rapidly for the specificity of the traditional master plan. When events and forces were more stable in the past, these elements comprised a solid base to approach building the urban form. This is not to say, or even imply, that I no longer believe in comprehensive, long-range future planning with a vision, but rather that the process needs to be in touch with the times.

Secondly, I would provide a detailed explanation of the Capital Improvements Program (CIP): how it is prepared, how it is kept current, and why it is frequently overlooked as an important tool in effectuating any comprehensive plan and therefore its role in shaping the future of the city. This would include a discussion of the CIP as a financial checks-and-balances system for all major public improvements needed in the future (in specific time frames) based upon the projected ability to pay either cash or the bonded indebtedness necessary to meet the yearly costs of the outstanding bonds. Next, I would explain how the CIP is reviewed each year or, at the most, every two years and then further projected into the future for that time and estimated cost. This would then become an accounting reference for all capital investment based upon the expressed needs and desires of the comprehensive plan and, in many ways, the method of achieving the goals and objectives of that plan. Any city operating without a well-considered, thorough CIP, continually reviewed and kept current, is like a ship without a compass and a rudder.

Next, I would ensure that the following conditions exist before even bothering to go into this project.

1. The local elected officials have a planning attitude and pledge their complete support throughout the project including attending additional meetings and participating in public discussions. The same kind of commitment must come from the planning commission.

2. There is a determination to involve people, to listen to them, to seek their help in deciding what the plan will be. In addition, private sector contribution in both time and financial assistance, if necessary, will be enlisted.

3. It is understood that this process will take a lot of input and commitment from a large number of people over a period of from eighteen to twenty-four months.

4. The professional planners, whether staff or consultant, understand the political process and will work closely with the elected officials, especially providing them sufficient information to justify their commitment and continued support for facing those who may oppose the idea of a plan.

5. The elected officials recognize that no plan can be effective without commitment to appropriate policy decision making of implementation and enforcement provisions. The planning commission members are equally committed to assist in seeing that the principles of the plan are upheld by their recommendations and that the plan becomes a "working document," and is followed up on and carefully considered before action is taken.

Further, the development of the plan itself has to be people oriented, which means it is built upon the results of their input and modified only where necessary based upon what is possible and feasible. This should be accomplished by the use of the planning commission, an advisory steering committee and a broadly representative comprehensive plan advisory committee composed of both elected and appointed officials and citizens. The assignment for the advisory steering committee would be to work closely with the planning commission and planning staff, to identify the major areas to be addressed for the future and to develop a list of preliminary goals and objectives. The steering committee then organizes the larger citizens' group into task forces, which are assigned the responsibility of exploring thoroughly the problems to be faced as well as action and solutions for each of the several major areas designated by the steering committee. Each member of the planning commission should serve as a member of one or two of the task forces. This was the pattern followed in development of the newly adopted Denver Comprehensive Plan, to some extent by Charlotte and Portland, and to a lesser degree by Corpus Christi. In Denver the following task forces were established: economic development, land use and urban design, mobility, living quality and social services (including housing, education, cultural affairs and air quality), governance, and strategic planning. To this I would add that each task force would be given the charge to follow a three-step process in examining their assigned areas of responsibility. This would be started by determining: (1) what is it that we now like and want to keep and preserve; (2) what is bad, inadequate, and destructive that we want to correct or change; (3) how do we propose to achieve *planned change*, the steps to be taken both short- and long-range, and who is to be responsible.

After this work has been done, including input all along the way from professionals in each task force area as well as from citizens who may have experience, interest and/or expertise in specific subjects, a preliminary draft of the comprehensive plan is written together with graphics as needed. At this point, widespread publicity and a mailing to neighborhood organizations should occur informing the general public, which hopefully has been informed frequently of what was happening, that the draft is available and comments are welcome.

All organized groups—business, industry, civic, and neighborhood—should specifically be asked to name three people who will agree to serve as readers and participants. Each reader would study the document, ask questions of those preparing it, report to their organization members on their opinions and recommendations and send a written summary of these to the planning staff assigned to work with the advisory groups. A series of neighborhood meetings should be organized and scheduled at times and in locations convenient for attendance throughout the entire geographic area of the city or town. After the stated period of time for comments to be submitted to the planning commission, the task forces would review the comments and prepare a second draft, revised where necessary and desirable, for the portion of the plan for which they are responsible. This would then be assembled into another draft including both a short-range and a long-range action agenda. Ultimately, of course both the planning commission and the city council should conduct official public hearings on the plan which have been scheduled well in advance and highly publicized.

At the time of each official public hearing, those involved in its preparation will attend and express their supportive views. In fact, one additional assignment for the advisory steering committee and the members of the general advisory committee will be to attempt to gain support from their associates, friends and neighbors and seek to have them appear at the hearings and provide their endorsement. The desired next step is adoption by the planning commission and the governing body or—if adoption is not the proper procedure according to state laws or governing body policy—at least an adopted resolution of strong endorsement and support. Thereafter the job becomes that of maintaining citizen interest, constant vigilance regarding implementation and necessary revisions, and making certain that both the planning commission and the elected officials are determined that the plan will be an effective working document, not something consigned to a shelf and forgotten.

The vision statement developed for the Denver plan is a good example of what a comprehensive plan should be and is impressive enough to be included in your plan. It reads:

> An overall plan for a great city must answer the question 'what do we really want this city to be, and to become?' This isn't a simple question. Any city and its people are both the beneficiaries of special opportunities and, in a sense, the victims of special circumstances suggested by a particular history and geography. The core of this Comprehensive Plan lies in our attempt to agree on Denver's purposes for the future, to think through the effect of Denver's special inheritance on those purposes, and then to apply our consensus in specific plan suggestions.
>
> The fundamental thing we want Denver to both be and to become is a city that's livable for all its people. A city in which they can learn, move about, work and play in safety and comfort, with pleasure and pride, and in a spirit of openness and opportunity.
>
> It is essential that living quality for all the people of Denver be perceived as this plan's central purpose. The question 'Does this action improve the quality of life for people?' is the challenge the plan poses to future civic leaders.[14]

Believe me, in this scenario my firm would be pleased to have the opportunity to serve as general and technical consultants to this city throughout this project and as facilitators for the work meetings of the advisory steering committee and your subcommittee task forces. A more detailed outline of the type of plan development proposed, the steps involved together with a suggested time schedule and a range of the fees for our services would be forthcoming within ten days of the receipt of a request to do so from you.

Ladies and gentlemen, the future of your city, your community, is far too important to be left to chance or to try to rely on an outdated master plan. The future and the well-being of all residents, as well as those yet to come, is at present in your hands. It is my belief that effective, people-based comprehensive planning is the best approach, the only way to effectively meld people together in a common purpose in a democratic society so that they are prepared to face the future. You may be assured I wish you well in doing so.

NOTES

1. Marjorie S. Berger, ed., *Dennis O'Harrow: Plan Talk and Plain Talk* (Chicago: Planner's Press, American Planning Association, 1981), p. 3.

2. Thomas J. Noel and Barbara S. Norgren, *Denver The City Beautiful* (Denver: Historic Denver, Inc., 1987), p. 27.

3. Walter Blucher, quoted in Mel Scott, *American City Planning Since 1890* (Berkeley: University of California Press, 1969), p. 330.

4. Ibid., p. 495.

5. Berger, pp. 205–220.

6. Berger, p. 206.

7. Berger, p. 216.

8. Perry L. Norton, "AICP Notes," *Planning*, Vol. 55, No. 9 (September 1989), p. 54A.

9. Ibid.

10. Ibid.

11. Berger, p. 289.

12. Berger, p. 282.

13. Michael P. Brooks, "Four Critical Junctures in the History of the Urban Planning Profession," *The Journal*, American Planning Association (Spring 1988), p. 246.

14. The Denver Planning Office, *1989 Denver Comprehensive Plan*, chap. 3, p. 1.

9

Quo Vadis?

It seems that the most appropriate title for this chapter is Quo Vadis, which, as you know, means "Wither Goest Thou?" It is fitting because that is the question about American cities underlying this entire book. Although much has been written about planning in America, primarily regarding specific concerns or success stories, no one has attempted an analysis of its effectiveness over the years in influencing our urban form. Support for doing this—as compared to most of what has been written about planners in the past—comes from the foreword, written by Anthony James Cantanese, for the book *Mastering Change:*

> In order for planning to work better, there will have to be a number of major changes. These changes have to do with process, techniques, organization, and management. Perhaps most importantly, planning must be more concerned with effectiveness and implementation rather than principles and theory. A major problem has been that precious little can be found in the literature dealing with such changes. Most of the planning literature tends to be utopian, radical, theoretical, or dogmatic—all of which provide for good reading but little applicability. In the world of *realpolitik*, most planning books are met with mild disdain.[1]

Perhaps with the diversity in regions, cities, and towns in this country it is foolhardy to think that conclusive evidence for such an analysis can be obtained from a sample of a few cities. My contention, however, is that this is not true; that it is a rationalizing escape for doubting Thomases, and those unwilling to face the facts. Even if this were so, such a sampling most certainly provides a strong basis for questioning present day application of the planning process, its successes and failures, those responsible for applying it, and, most importantly, to stimulate thought and discussion among municipal officials and the planning profession. This has been my objective throughout these pages.

THE IMPORTANCE OF URBAN FORM DECISION MAKING

The first sentence of the Introduction provides the basis for all of the rest of what has been reviewed, examined and discussed. Everyone involved in the day-to-day operation of city government, as well as any interested and concerned citizen, knows the truth about the fact that the thousands of decisions made every twenty-four hours more or less permanently place or deny some type of land use as a part of the urban form. With this as a given and with the observable condition of how in building that urban form we have been moving into more of a Paradise Lost condition, it seems almost imperative to start asking the question of who and what has the most influence on the policymakers responsible for those land development decisions. It then follows that the question of the role that planning and planners have played needs to be examined. Has it been effective? If not, why not, and how can that effectiveness be improved? Have we as members of the planning profession really concerned ourselves enough about how we have or have not been influential in building our cities and towns?

The reason for visiting and writing about the fifteen representative cities has been to gather information regarding these questions of whether the major problems lie with planning, with the elected policymakers, and/or an uninformed, apathetic public. The next logical step, assuming a reasonable basis has been laid for a conclusion that things can and should be better, is to accept that and start some serious discussion on how to improve the only course of action available in a democratic, capitalistic society for trying to regain Paradise Found—effective comprehensive city planning.

We have at least come far enough and seen the results of both direction and misdirection to know that great cities do not just happen. Neither do they occur from leaving all decision-making for land use development to the marketplace and economic forces. Where better city building has taken place it becomes apparent that the reason has been that a workable partnership between governmental forces and the private sector, understood and supported by the populace, has been achieved. Sometimes this has been voluntary, but mostly it has resulted from a governing body of elected officials imbued with a planning attitude, a sense of vision and a concern for the future.

Building cities is very much like putting together a jigsaw puzzle. You start with a good base at an identifiable corner upon which to build, check colors, design and shape, find another piece that fits and continue on one piece at a time making sure that they fit nicely together. When you are successful in doing this, assuming one or more pieces are not missing, you have a marvelous, coordinated picture and a feeling of pride in what has been accomplished. Every building, every subdivision, and every public facility is an important piece of the urban form jigsaw puzzle and like any such dilemma the important thing is making sure that the end results comprehensively and beneficially fit together. Where this is not the case you have chaos, hodgepodge growth that is expensive to service, and also inefficient and detrimental to the total quality of life now and in the future. To prevent this, organized city planning was started, has continued to exist, and is supposed to be it doing now. I submit that planning is not doing all it should do and believe that we had better spend a lot more time and thought on how to make this happen; otherwise the future is bleak.

The Society and System With Which We Live

There is no question that the improvement of planning effectiveness will be difficult and that there are many impediments making it so built into our society over which local governments, even those committed to planning, have little if any control. That is the reason for as much emphasis on outside forces as was expressed in the earlier chapters. In them it is brought to the fore that we live in a society and an economic environment where it is most difficult to make comprehensive urban planning work. These difficulties do not exist in any other nation in the world. In some of those where there is totalitarianism and dictatorship, what happens to development is easy to control; however, we never want to live under those forms of government. Nevertheless, other countries such as Great Britain, Australia, Norway, Sweden, France, and our neighbor to the north, Canada have retained a much greater sense of land as a community asset rather than a commodity. In fact, as has been said many times by many people, the Europeans, as well as some in other countries, have more respect for how land is used and make certain more public interest is reflected than we have ever shown or can seem to develop.

In addition to the influence of federal and state forces, we also have seen that the very political system under which we operate, especially at the local level where control of land use largely has been placed, is simply not conducive to long-range planning because of the limited terms of office provided in our governmental system. This is further complicated by the slothful light in which most of us regard political campaigns and elections. The most frightening aspect of this is that television's thirty-second election sound bite is becoming the deciding factor in how we vote instead of us demanding in-depth candidate positions. Also, it has been indicated that all forms of the media, especially newspapers, are not guiltless in seeking out and concentrating on personal lives rather than personal beliefs, capabilities and dedication to public service.

All of this makes it clear that in addition to examining the professional practice of planning and those who participate in it there is just as much, if not a greater, need for scrutinizing the political system, societal changes, and our philosophies as individual members of a collective society. We must give serious thought to where this has led and is leading us. No doubt some will say that statements such as this have no place in a book devoted to the effectiveness of planning implementation in local communities. I disagree strongly. Remember that one of the fundamental reasons for organizing governmental planning for urban and suburban development was the belief that its prime function should be to achieve cooperation and coordination of all aspects of community building. No one can question that the major components of comprehensive planning and successful urban development are the people with whom we plan for the future. If we as professionals don't understand our society, the people comprising it, their strengths and weaknesses, how can we expect to impress upon them the necessity of a sense of community? If such a sense is developed, it can be the motivation for citizens to become educated about why planning is important to them, their children, and the country in general.

Not Tolerance, But Insight

At a retreat I attended recently at a resort in Colorado, known as "The Nature Place," several most impressive sayings were displayed on the walls in various gathering places. One of the most thought–provoking of these unfortunately did not attribute the source but it bears repeating here. "We are all different, but we are all interrelated in search for meaning. It is not uniformity that we need, but understanding—not points of view as much as points of connection—not tolerance but insight."

Is community planning perhaps the only way that these points of connection and insight can be achieved in advance of a crisis in our society? My answer has been, and is, *"Yes!"* Through such an effort collective discussion, problem analysis and the development of solutions become possible.

The society in which we live illustrates the important changes that have occurred in mores and attitudes, as well as the diversity of ethnic, cultural, and religious backgrounds of all of us comprising that society. In such a situation, nothing is more important for a planner than insight and a bulging vault-full of common sense. The diversity of people can be paradoxical in that it offers many advantages, but we must find a way to meld them into supporting a common cause, a connotation of community and pride in being a part of it. Otherwise, like election by wards, the potential for divisiveness can flourish. This has already happened to such an extent that we seem unable to respond together to develop solutions for problems that many consider to be only minor irritants, if they are concerned at all. This situation changes only during times of war, a major catastrophe or because of our fanatical support fixation for a winning professional, college or high school sports team. Although difficult to accomplish in what our society is today, when the situation is carefully thought through, planning with people instead of for them is the only way to provide the cohesion melding to pull our diversity together and turn it into the advantageous asset it could be.

Few will argue that we have not become more and more apathetic to almost everything involving community life unless it appears to affect our own ideas, our personal selves or family, our pocketbooks, or the lifestyle we have grown to love and enjoy. To a large extent we are suffering from the nuclear-age-family philosophy. This, plus the luxuries we enjoy and to which we feel we are entitled are the major factors contributing to the apathetic condition that I have labeled "Me-ism." By believing in this philosophy, we have almost completely convinced ourselves that the only thing important is that "I get mine" and then be left alone to view life as a spectator sport.

Think of the social gatherings and cocktail parties you have attended and try to remember one where two or more people joined together to discuss the problems of the present, much less what the
future holds. My bet is that not many of us could think of even one
such event. Furthermore, if you want to cut down on your invitations
to such affairs, just try to start such a conversation at the next social
function you attend. Is it any wonder that the majority of our cities,
our urban form, and our schools have reached a "messopolis" state
and that we have begun to see Paradise Found turned into Paradise
Lost? As Elizabeth Wright Ingraham, architect and educator once
said; "Of course, the public is apathetic—it is the way we maintain our
mental health." While this is true about American life today, that is no
excuse for us to continue to accept, condone, or ignore it instead of
trying to change it. Regrettably, I have to say that I have seen this in
the younger generations of my own family members who feel that
they must live for today as tomorrow might not come. They refuse to
even discuss such matters as the mess we face as a society and in our
cities. Being rather stubborn, I have not, and do not intend to, give up
trying to discuss these issues with them and others.

Planners As A Societal Voice of Conscience

To counteract this me-ism, it is my conviction that the measure of an
effective planner today is whether or not she or he is committed to
being a voice of conscience for society, always patiently prodding and
poking people at every opportunity to help them realize where we are
in building our future environment and how all of us working together can do *better* and we *better* start to try to do so. This should be
the credo for the profession and for each member thereof. This is not
to say that planners have a direct connection with the Almighty, always know best, or always are right. Rather, it means simply being
aware of what is happening all around us, being able to point that out
in a clearly intelligible way with supportive information and documentation, then suggest ideas and methodology for making it better
or doing the same thing better the next time.

This is where conviction, commitment, and communication become so very important for anyone trained as a planner. Remember, it
has been pointed out that there are still a multitude of people who
have no idea what planning is all about, what a planner does, or that
individuals, working with their local policymakers, have the legal
right to represent the community interest in all land development,

public and private. A good planner has the opportunity and, in my opinion the responsibility, to act as that voice of conscience to his or her non-planner friends or in presentations to various groups.

The Loss of Connection Focal Points

In addition to Warren's indication of the loss of a "horizontal" community, there are two other important factors resulting from societal changes that are detrimental to the cohesiveness of people. In our earlier history there were two major sources of focus in our city building. One was the major central business district even though there also may have been neighborhood single purpose convenience stores. Not only vital business activity centered here, but so did churches, cultural facilities, movies, and general fraternizing.

The central business district focal point lost out, however, thanks to the highway engineers, the evolution of the automobile and its attendant problems such as parking, some unfortunate planning and zoning decisions, and the me-ism of pride of possession and an enjoyment of self-expression available from fancy, high-powered cars. As our cities grew, some of this was inevitable with first the shopping center and later the shopping mall taking over from the central area. Where these were well located, well planned and designed and they established cores or activity centers, the effects were not totally destructive and could even be beneficial.

The worst scenario has been the plethora of such outlying shopping areas together with urban fringe strip commercial centers and unduly disruptive, misplaced mixed-use, high-rise buildings. Many of these were highly speculative endeavors with questionable survival capabilities, some already have turned into new slums, most were improperly located and lacked quality of design. Beyond that, they were destructive of desirable neighborhood characteristics. In many cases the destructive features were the result of non-cooperation between cities and counties in land use controls. Land and taxes were usually cheaper in the county, and too many county officials—in their rush to grab onto what they considered economic development and tax ratables—ignored the fact that city residents were also taxpaying residents of the county.

The other focal point was the neighborhood school. In years past, the kids walked to school, parents assembled and participated there, and school sports activities were all strong forces binding a neighborhood together. Today, all that has changed, other than in the rural communities and small towns. The loss of the neighborhood school can be credited to a number of causes including actions by the federal government already covered rather thoroughly. Some of this loss resulted from increased growth that was probably inevitable; however, the FHA's housing policies, the interstate highway program of the Department of Transportation (DOT), and the court-ordered busing resulting from the Supreme Court decisions, unquestionably were major contributors. In addition, forced busing exacerbated the innate desire of many to escape from what they considered as the evils of the inner city and provided the looked-for excuse for doing so.

THE BRIGHT SIDE

Fortunately there are signs that there may be brighter things ahead for both the central business districts and the schools, all of which need to be encouraged. There is a sense of rebirth in many inner cities, some of which can reluctantly be credited to urban renewal, but most result from the Commonity Development Block Grant (CDBG) and Urban Development Action Grant (UDAG) programs, initiated much later than they should have been by the federal government. An even more encouraging sign is that the cities themselves are fighting back. Recognition is rising of the facts that survival requires concentrated effort, encouragement of economic development that conforms to planning and design standards, and active and effective promotion as well as the public sector's responsibility for infrastructure improvements, addition, and maintenance. The private sector is beginning to realize that their investments in the inner city are also at stake and they are assuming a more pro-active, participatory role. With the exception of the lack of city–generated planning leadership, the Baltimore experience is a good example of this. All of the above also apply to Portland and Charlotte, where public/private partnership has become an accepted practice. Pittsburgh and Minneapolis have experienced the value of this, as has Saint Paul to some extent. While the other cities included here at least recognize the need for fighting back, it is regrettable to note that much needed coordinated, comprehensive planning cannot be held up as shining examples.

Similar things can be said about neighborhoods. If they have not been able to overcome the effect of bigotry where it exists, they, too, have at least recognized that preservation and improvement of their neighborhood requires getting organized and fighting back. In every city visited, the power of an organized neighborhood is being realized, and, if not yet a bright flame, the glow of an ember can be seen. One thing contributing to this, referred to by many derogatorily as "gentrification," is the return to the inner city by many younger middle-class people. The newcomers along with the remaining residents are developing a common interest in protecting their investments and improving the quality of the neighborhood in which they live.

Another factor that is beginning to be overcome is the seeming disregard elected officials have for neighborhood protection. In the past, there have been far too many approvals of zoning changes and variances allowing types of uses and increases in density that are contrary to the wishes of the residents; in most cases they have been destructive to the neighborhood. One of the major causes of such action has been the drunken binge of "economic development" we have been caught up in throughout the country. This failure to serve the neighborhoods has extended to neglect in public facilities installation and improvements such as street paving, street sweeping, sidewalk repair, sewer and water lines, street lighting, crime prevention, and adequate public safety.

As a result, when it comes to the narrow issue of neighborhood interests, residents who have become tired of politicians not listening to or working with them have become determined and even militant in their reaction. So far, unfortunately, this grassroots groundswell of power primarily has been confined to parochial, single neighborhood interests. Individual community residents, in most cases, have not yet seen the importance of extending their concerns to the entire city and exercising their power in a comprehensive way for the betterment of the entire populace, as well as their own neighborhood.

Neighborhoods: The Secret Power Base

It is my belief that this extension of interest is going to develop in the very near future. It has already happened in some of the cities studied, even in Corpus Christi, where the charter amendment was adopted forcing the development and continuing maintenance of a citywide comprehensive master plan. My experience in government causes me to believe that the most powerful influence on elected officials can come from united, organized neighborhood action when it is exercised constructively. This kind of a cooperative outburst of public sentiment is the only thing powerful enough to overcome favor granting, and even payoffs, made by politicians to large campaign contributors, special political power influences, and vested interests. In cities such as Corpus Christi and Denver, where the mayor and entire council are elected at the same time, if all neighborhoods within the election districts organized, selected capable candidates with leadership ability, and united to work together with a commitment to the total city's well-being, they could change the entire composition of the elected governing body at one election.

This brings us back to two themes stressed throughout. The first is leadership, whether it be in elected officials, the planning profession, civic organizations, or the neighborhoods. It is an essential element in our need for preventing or correcting Paradise Lost and returning to the development of Paradise Found. This is what our urban form might once have been, should be now, and could be if we all became concerned and involved. That leads to the second of the two themes I have tried to impart: the important requisite of people to consider government as our business. As Joseph de Maistre said, "Every country has the government it deserves."[2] People in America have frequently altered this slightly by saying, "We get better government than we deserve." But, again the quote from John F. Kennedy in the same book better says what I believe and try to impart: "No government is better than the men [and women] who compose it."[3]

To repeat a cardinal principle stressed in this book, no organized, effective planning or desirable urban form building can be successful without committed, determined leadership from those holding public office. Isn't it time we all took stock, began looking at our leadership and our government as reflective of how involved and effective we, the people, have been, and resolve to do something about it? I believe the time has come when it is necessary to do this and we *can* do it, even though there are many who would say that it is an impossible dream. A giant step in the direction of achieving this dream would be for each of us to resolve to become more involved, to get others in our neighborhood interested and committed in constructively utilizing this high–potential power base for citywide, as well as neighborhood, interest. Just imagine the reawakening among present and possible future elected officials if each neighborhood group first individually, then collectively, publicly declared its intent to work toward assuring that the entire community structure is based on these four principles:

1. To commit ourselves and then persuade others to look for, encourage, and support inspirational leadership in those we elect to represent us in government as well as in our civic and neighborhood or

professional organizations—perhaps even be willing to run for office or accept responsibility and provide it ourselves.

2. To promote a permeating sense of vision and concern about the future and to insist that anyone elected to office or accepting a civic or professional responsibility has displayed this characteristic and capability.

3. To reject and combat the stupid "all growth is good" economic development craze and seek to prevent the selling out of our city's future for a mess of porridge.

4. To never give up in the resolve to stimulate and expand a community spirit built on pride of place or a profession, so that when the question is asked of anyone "Why do you like this town or city?" the immediate response will be, "Because I am proud of being a resident (or a member of a profession)—we know where we are going and how we are going to get there!"

The Technique For Action

This kind of activist program, while aimed here at local communities, could be just as effectively applied to a professional organization. In my opinion, there are similarities between community structures and professional organizations. In both, many people will say that all this sounds nice, but it can't be done, I can't do anything by myself and there are no groups willing to take on those kinds of things even if they are organized. This certainly is true if you aren't interested, if you don't care about the future of your community or organization, and if you admit to being a member of the me-ism part of society and treat the rest of life, other than your own little private world, totally as a spectator sport.

On the other hand, if you are willing to ask yourself why my professional organization isn't as effective as it should be; why our downtown looks uninviting and seedy; why we can't get good businesses and industries to locate here so there can be more jobs and fewer people on welfare; or, most important of all, if my kids want to stay here, what will this town or city be like ten or twenty years from now—then you are ready for the suggestion I am about to give containing a technique that can be adapted for a neighborhood, a city, or a professional organization.

Several times I have mentioned the National Civic League (NCL) and the process it has developed and promoted called "The Civic Index." It is appropriate now to look at more details about what it is, how it works, and how it can be useful in your city. Actually, it is a process for initiating studies very similar to the basic studies of a comprehensive city plan, but you will notice that they don't call it city planning or even refer much to the governmental planning process. My speculation is that there are three reasons for this. The first is that they were smart enough to suspect that the idea of local governmental planning still is not understood, and has not been properly defined so that people really know why it is important. Further, the term "governmental planning" still connotes a mistaken image in the minds of many people. Even more importantly, there is one very important difference in the index process from that of most cities' efforts to do comprehensive planning; it is started at the grassroots level and remains a citizen function until it is concluded and, hopefully, thereafter.

The Civic Index Program of the National Civic League

The NCL defines its index as a self-evaluation tool with the purpose of generating community-wide discussion about the civic infrastructure of a city or region. The components of the index are the elements the NCL considers to be the critical underpinnings of a community's ability to resolve problems, meet challenges, and set directions for the future. In their opinion, whether the specific issue is economic development, low-income housing, or transportation planning—the skills, processes, and values described in the index are necessary ingredients for success. With the advice and assistance of the NCL the index process is started by a single individual or organization, newly formed or already in existence, to serve as a catalyst to begin discussion about applying the index to their city.

The second step is the formation of a planning (not governmental city planning) group representing a diverse cross-section of the community's leadership. Its job is to design a community-wide, consensus-based, strategic planning process using the index and to select the 35–45 community leaders who will make up the task force that will incorporate public outreach into their endeavors. From all this comes a final report and an action plan.

To give a clearer picture of how this can pull a community together and ultimately strengthen its governmental planning process, here are brief summaries of the ten parts comprising the elements of the index taken from some of the NCL's material:

1. *Citizen Participation.* Citizen involvement in local affairs is a crucial component of civic health. Questions that communities may ask in evaluating the level and quality of local citizen participation fall into the four general categories of opportunities, preparation, involvement, and types of involvement.

2. *Community Leadership.* The public, private, and nonprofit sectors must all develop leaders who can cooperate with each other in enhancing the long-term future of a community.

3. *Government Influence.* While government cannot solve all community problems, it must be a positive force in addressing community needs and providing services effectively and efficiently.

4. *Volunteerism and Philanthropy.* Caring about, and sharing resources to help one another and the community as a whole, is essential to community life.

5. *Intergroup Relations.* As communities experience more ethnic, racial, and religious diversity, programs are needed to increase communication and appreciation between different groups and within the community as a whole.

6. *Civic Education.* To preserve a strong civic infrastructure, young people need to develop knowledge, values, and skills to contribute to community life.

7. *Community Information Sharing.* To be informed about issues, citizens require access to adequate information through their government, schools, libraries, civic organizations, and the media.

8. *Capacity For Cooperation and Consensus Building.* The growing number and complexity of problems faced by local communities demand that government, business, and the nonprofit sector work closely together in setting common goals and then working together to achieve them.

9. *Strategic/Long-Range Planning.* Apart from the comprehensive planning that many communities undertake, there is a broader approach to planning that incorporates a community's vision of its long-term future.

10. *Inter-Community Cooperation.* To solve problems and be successful, metropolitan and rural areas must find ways for jurisdictions to work together. Individual communities need to cooperate with each other in planning for their future and addressing regional needs.

This process has been used and found helpful in melding diverse groups together and stimulating effective, citizen-involved planning in a number of communities, including Charlotte and Philadelphia as well as helping various organizations in Georgia, California, and Kentucky. It could be well worth looking into for your city or town in order to stimulate citizen interest. Further information can be obtained by contacting the National Civic League, Inc.[4]

PLANNERS AND THE PLANNING PROFESSION

Having examined the general conditions of the society with which we have to deal, governmental structure and leadership, and people involvement, we turn now to a summary of the problems and opportunities I see for planners and the planning profession. Again, it is important to recognize the impediments, both from outside forces of national and state governments and the local governments within which the planners must work. It is worth repeating that planning by itself is not going to solve anything, cure a city's problems, or assure that changes for the better will be made, nor are planners responsible for making policy and implementing plans. Instead, the first problem I see is that planners have to learn to work with the impediments that exist, use them to the best of their advantage, or work around them. This is where activism and leadership from planners can be most effective, providing they are willing to explain to people what they are doing in a clear and understandable manner. In addition, their proposals must be sufficiently exciting to inspire vision, and the way they are presented should build confidence in themselves and the profession. In other words, to be activists in generating planned change and in helping to prevent changed plans.

George W. Spasyk, executive director, Lambda Chi Alpha fraternity, drew an analogy between thermometers and thermostats and chapter members of the fraternity. This can very aptly apply to professional planners as well as elected and appointed officials:

> I grew up in New England, where winters were cold and the snowdrifts sometimes came up to the second-floor windows. In the cellar was this enormous coal furnace, and on the living room wall was a thermometer. Now this thermometer told us what the temperature was, and when it registered below a certain level, my Dad, or one of my brothers or I would go down to the cellar to shovel more coal in the furnace. At night, when we were going to bed and didn't need as much heat, one of us would go down to bank the fire, and that would keep it going until morning. The thermometer didn't do anything but report the conditions around it.
>
> Some years later, my Dad bought a new oil furnace, and with it came one of the most fantastic gadgets I'd ever seen. It was called a thermostat. You just set it at whatever temperature you wanted to maintain, and when the temperature in the living room went below that, the thermostat went

to work. It kicked the furnace on, and when the desired temperature was reached, it turned the furnace off. In other words, the thermostat didn't just report the conditions around it, it made things happen to *change* the condition to the desired level.[5]

What an effective example this could be for all of us: planners, local officials, and the public. For planners it should have a special message, perhaps even a warning. Unless we can train and inspire people in the planning profession to be activists, both with politicians and the public, we are not going to be effective with those for whom we work or in making the profession meaningful to the public. Certainly it is becoming more obvious that we need more "thermostats" who can change conditions to the desired level among planners and our profession.

I have found several examples of planners who understand these precepts. They have learned to accept that the name of the game is politics, and how politicians think, what motivates them, and how to work with and gain the confidence of both them and the public they serve. (Almost all of these planning leaders, however, had misgivings about their professional organization, even to the point of non-involvement or, at best, tacit participation.)

You Can't Be All Things to All People

The next problem for the planning profession that became clear is the Statue of Liberty complex. Like the inscription on the statue of the famous lady, our profession has adopted an open arms policy to all those who wish to be called professionals, and thus we are trying to be all things to all people. As a result we have a multitude of interests with little, if any, sense of common purpose or common bond. To try to satisfy various special interest groups a total of fifteen special purpose divisions have been created within APA which can detract from a unified membership as well as a sense of common purpose among all of us. Many of the planners commented on this, especially members of AICP, and expressed frustration over the lack of a definition of what it means to be a professional planner.

Two of the most telling comments came from AICP members, both coincidentally located in Minneapolis. The first from Peter Jarvis is: "Planning has tried to be any and everything for the twenty or twenty-five years since it went through the self-critical movement of 'we have got to stop being physical planners because there are other things that are more important.' So the advent of social planning, health planning, policy planning, international planning, transportation planning and all of the other adjectives that get attached to the word planning have led to almost a paralysis of thinking and very little development of a product that is communicated to the public in a way they can understand. As a result, it has almost no impact."

Robert Einsweiler, AICP, expressed the same type of concerns. He stated that "the really worrisome sign is the move by some members of APA to require all planners to be bound by the reformists' agenda, to be *advocates* for the poor. The general electorate does not share this view. Therefore, many elected officials resent being positioned on an issue that lacks political support. This does not mean planners should have no concern for the poor; rather, the profession should not impose a requirement that sets the planner at odds with duly elected or appointed officials. This is a democracy. They are elected to represent the public interest. No other profession has hung such a millstone around the neck of its members; neither can we and survive."

Both of these quotes emphasize the importance of planners being practical, maintaining a sense of vision and recognizing that planning, to be effective, must be part of the political process. It cannot try to be all things to all people.

Practical Problems Must Be Faced

I recognize that both APA and AICP have to be concerned with maintaining a financial base sufficient to allow their continuing operation, and I do not quarrel with APA broadening its membership base as one means of doing so. I do not believe, however, that AICP should follow the same course. In fact, I am convinced that it is time for AICP to abandon the idea of increasing membership by broadening or lowering its standards for membership, to encourage all types of hyphenated planners and "allied professions." Rather, my conversations with members of AICP and planners who are non-members support the conclusion that there would be fewer dropouts and more interest in becoming members if there were higher standards of membership requirements for those who may call themselves professional planners.

We say that we are a profession and that AICP is a professional institute. If strengthening membership requirements should, in spite of my argument otherwise, result in fewer membership additions, then we should concentrate on efforts to make membership more valuable and beneficial to those who do belong and change the fee structure accordingly. In addition, just as APA does, AICP could develop other services and materials aimed more directly at the planning professional for which charges can be levied to supplement the present dependency upon membership dues. Preparing and marketing the video-training session tapes such as those suggested by Eric Kelly would be yet another way to supplement needed income.

If planning is a profession and we want to maintain a professional organization, the cost of doing so must be recognized. It might be helpful to examine the fee structure and other ways of generating sufficient revenue used by other professional organizations such as the American Bar Association, American Medical Association, American Institute of Architects, and American Society of Civil Engineers. We surely aren't going to do it by increasing membership just for the sake of increased numbers.

Facing Reality is Never Easy

Another concern is the need for planners and AICP to become better educators and public-relations purveyors to local officials and the general public. Only by doing so can we offer a readily acceptable understanding of planners, the planning process, and the profession. We haven't even begun to approach the point reached by other professional organizations in promoting the value of using the services of their members. Granted they have the advantage of having a "licensed profession," but AICP has indicated it wants to have members use the title of "certified planner"; thus members will become licensed professionals. In addition, we do not provide our members with the helpful, practical materials they need and want, services that would help justify their AICP membership.

The litany recited by planners during this project indicates a serious concern about our planning organizations. Whether fully justified or not, a sincere feeling of the need for improvement exists. Comments regarding such things as more useful publications, more exciting, interesting and informative conferences and workshops, a better definition of planning and the planning profession, and a reexamination of planning education were repeated to me over and over. Based on my investigation, several recommendations appear to be worthy of consideration. Some of these pertain to APA and AICP as organizations while others are ways each of us as individual planners can help improve the recognition and image of ourselves and our profession.

Some Challenging Suggestions

The first concern should be the development of an understanding among planners that, whether we like it or not, planning works only where it reflects the political climate in any city, public organization or private firm. We must understand this and realize, while we should not lose a sense of vision, it is the political power structure that must understand and support what we do to make it work. As this book is concerned primarily about public sector planning at the local level, we should urge APA chapters and the national organizations to put more time, effort and money on working with, even lobbying, elected officials at the local and state levels as compared with the effort and money now spent providing testimony before Congressional committees and lobbying members of Congress. In the long run we would be better off affecting national policy by convincing local and state politicians of the importance of planning since they are the ones who can really influence elected national representatives more than we can do as a national lobbying organization. In addition, many local elected officials and politicians of today may well be the national representatives of tomorrow.

This leads to the second theme in these pages, that of working more effectively in educating the public we serve about the importance of planning and how it benefits them and their families. There are two aspects to this. The first is that both APA and AICP in their publication programs should place more emphasis on the importance of leadership ability as the prime asset of persons seeking public office. Beyond that, the public should be more concerned with a candidate's interest and attitude about planning for the future. Nor do I see anything wrong with individual planners stressing the importance of both neighborhood groups and individual voters searching out people who have exhibited leadership ability and commitment and convincing them to step forward and run for office. In our work we have the opportunity to get to know such people and should, if we are not doing it now, encourage them to promote a planning attitude on the part of elected officials and the voters. If this is playing politics, so be it, for planning is not going to succeed unless we begin to recognize that politics always has called and will continue to call the shots. Such practical endeavors would at least serve us better in having an effect on the future of America's urban form than publishing theoretical, scholarly, and academic tomes which are read by few people and understood by even fewer.

What Do Our Members Think?

The next suggestion is that APA and AICP conduct detailed, but separate, surveys of their membership, just as the Urban Land Institute has done. The survey would be somewhat like the one Perry Norton did of APA chapter presidents in the planning region in which he lives. It would ask members' opinions about what they think of their organization in general (including the present structuring of APA and AICP), what it is not doing that they would like to see it do, what it is doing of which they don't approve, what they see as the major problems facing the organization in the future and how it can better serve them as members.

This survey should also include questions regarding what members see as the major planning issues they as planners, as well as the profession as a whole, will have to face in the 21st century. A question might be included about the financing of both organizations by asking whether members would pay more if services are improved. What could be more logical than finding out what the members of each organization think about the association or institute that exists to serve them?

Chapter Conferences

I would further propose that APA chapters organize conferences of APA members and AICP members so that each group could meet separately, then jointly in each planning region to examine and discuss the survey results. From this should come a representative group from both organizations within each region which would meet together with the governing bodies of each organization in a national conference to examine structure, organization and purpose and, based upon the survey and conference results, determine whether or not changes should be made. A complete report would then be prepared covering the deliberations, conclusions and recommendations. As a final step, the report would be submitted to each chapter for discussion and a vote taken by members of each unit on any recommendations for changes in their respective organizations. After all, we do say we live in a democracy and isn't this the most democratic way for something like this to be accomplished?

Planning Education Involvement

Another area needing further exploration is the trend in planning education. Among the planners I spoke to, most of them AICP members, this was one of the most commonly expressed criticisms and it centered on two concerns. The first was the increased emphasis on grant-funded research, academic publications, and the publish or perish syndrome, which are primarily the result of inadequate funding by state legislatures of public educational institutions. I doubt that planners and planning organizations can do very much about their legislatures other than to recognize the situation and try to encourage alumni funding earmarked for planning practical experience internships or applied research projects.

The second area is the increasing emphasis on a Ph.D degree as the terminal degree for educators in graduate planning programs along with the lack of any required practical experience. The resulting product, the graduating student, is therefore not equipped to deal with the real world by making a meaningful contribution in a public planning position or private consulting office. Many also decried the lack of use of practicing professionals as instructors and adjunct professors as well as the limited use made of them on accreditation visitation teams.

These site visit teams represent the only method, other than a document prepared by the schools themselves, provided for recommending approval or denial of accreditation of planning programs to the accreditation board, and they also exercise considerable influence on the curricula and course content of the subjects being taught. This is something about which AICP should be concerned. My proposal would be that AICP attempt to get the Association of Collegiate Schools of Planning to agree to each organization forming a task force of seven or nine members to meet together and explore this important matter. It would seem logical that the AICP task force should be comprised of a majority of professional planners who are in positions of hiring planning school graduates.

The work of this group should include examination and discussion of planning education as it is today, the forces affecting it, where it appears to be heading, and what its purpose should be. There should be serious discussion about what educational training is needed in today's world and how education can become more effective in furthering the profession. The most important element would be a determination regarding how a better balance can be achieved between research and practical exposure. It is interesting that none of these concerns are startlingly new, they have only become more widespread. In an ASPO *Newsletter* of December 1958, Dennis O'Harrow listed four simple requirements he felt determinative of a good planner: (1) a sense of responsibility to the community; (2) be intellectually honest; (3) ability to see one's actions in the proper scale; and (4) a good planner has courage. He then states; "Of these criteria of a good planner, not one is taught in planning schools."[6]

THE NEED FOR CHANGE

The direction planning is headed is being questioned by more and more people, planners and others involved in community development. William Fulton in an article in *Governing*, after quoting from Edmond Bacon's, Michael Brooks's and others' expressions of concerns and fears, says:

> In part, these fears represent a crisis of self-definition among planners, but such crises are not new to the field. No other public policy field is so eternally obsessed with the question of what it is because none is so chameleon-like. Unlike engineers or architects, planners have no basic body of technical knowledge to fall back on, and when they have attempted to define themselves as policy experts, they have been regarded by public administrators as interlopers. Over the past 60 years, planners have played the roles at one time or another, of architect, city manager, policy analyst and social worker. Academic planning faculties often include geographers, economists, architects and political scientists, along with a few social workers, historians and labor experts.[7]

Later in his conclusion, Fulton adds,

> But today's impatient politics and restless real estate markets demand short-term results. In planning now, the cloud-niner is likely to find himself not just out of the loop, but out of a job, no matter how good his ideas are. Ultimately, to survive, planners must learn to bridge the gap. They must solve the problem of self-definition by adapting themselves to the political tenor of the times—serving, essentially, as architects, social workers, city managers, real estate developers or whatever else is called for. Yet they still must somehow remain planners at heart, bringing to government the long-term perspective, idealism and concern for the pub-

lic agenda they have historically exhibited. It is a dilemma that would arise only for an oddly idealistic, oddly ill-defined profession such as urban planning.[8]

I don't agree completely with Fulton in his apparent write-off of the idea of better defining who and what planners are, nor do I care for his implication that we should settle for the quick fix. Overall, however, his article states the problems of planning well, says things that needed saying and substantiates my argument that the time has come for examination, discussion, and action. Indeed, it is time for all of us in planning to examine ourselves and perhaps change the direction we and the profession are going. Our strategy could come from McClendon's and Quay's book:

> Strategy can be defined as skillful management in getting the better of an adversary or attaining an end. We have found that the most dangerous adversaries to the goal of effective planning are the status quo, complacency, and outright resistance to change. Planners must be willing to change. In fact, they must aggressively embrace change if they are going to make a difference in this world. How planners respond to the opportunities and risks presented by change will determine their ultimate success or failure.[9]

I have attempted to show some of the problems we in planning face, both from forces outside the community in which we are working and within it. Almost as much, if not more, space has been occupied by discussion of the society in which we live and an examination of those of us comprising it. Elected officials in general have been criticized generously throughout this book. The reason for this is the obvious lack of a planning attitude on the part of many and their responding to expressed emotional diatribes or pressures not reflective of community interest. At the same time, the general public has failed to be concerned, to recognize the importance of giving thought to our communities' futures, and to insist on good planning support by those elected.

From all of this I have concluded that the blame for our having Paradise Lost instead of preserving and building Paradise Found must rest more on the ills of our society, especially the lack of farsighted, inspiring elected leadership, rather than on planners and planning. Nevertheless, we do need to think about changing our strategy since planning otherwise does work when there is a concerned public and strong leadership. It is not the system that has failed, but we the people who have failed the system, and this is where my role for planners as a voice of conscience for society comes into play. I am not alone in the concern I have for our urban form, our cities, the attitudes of elected officials and the general public—many of us wonder why we have failed the system and perhaps even democratic government.

Roger K. Lewis, a practicing architect and planner as well as a professor of architecture at the University of Maryland, expresses this opinion:

> Too many towns, cities, and counties have been timid about taking the longer, more visionary view. Too many mayors and executives, councils and legislatures, boards and commissions have been unwilling to exercise fully their legal authority—and duty—both to articulate and to achieve land use goals through wise planning, budgeting, and regulating. Governments have spent too much time getting themselves elected, coping with emergencies, reacting to ad hoc proposals, and generally oiling the system's squeakiest wheels. Too often public officials, whether elected or appointed, have not taken the time—and capitalized on the expertise needed and available—to reexamine and modify policies, plans, and regulations in a proactive, prospective mode.[10]

Another of my favorite pundits, former Governor Lamm of Colorado, could have been writing about the planning profession when he said: "There is not far in our future a time of testing: a period of dislocation that will test the tensile strength of our society. We have not been tested as a nation since World War II. I believe we will pass that test but not without immense self-imposed traumas. We have made our time of testing incredibly more difficult by our political, economic and social mistakes. We have become an overindulged and undermotivated society. We have forgotten our duty to our children to pass on to them a world equal to or better than that which we inherited. We are wasting our most precious resource: time."

That is exactly the message I hope that I have imparted in these pages about our society, our governments, all of us as planners and our profession. We cannot afford to further waste our time!

A Britain who has long been dubbed a missionary for environmental quality, Michael Middleton, stated:

> Planning is more than remedial; it can offer alternative futures. But there is more to the question even than that. It is a matter of what we ourselves

want to be. If standards are allowed to slip in one direction, they soon being to slip in others too. With pride of place goes confidence. With loss of pride of place goes a little of our self-respect, a little of our national, and local, and personal identity.

We end, then, as we began: with recognition that the city is ourselves, mirroring with precision our needs and our activities, our values and our aspirations, our confusions and our contradictions.[11]

And now a final benediction:

There can be no vulnerability without risk; there can be no community without vulnerability; there can be no peace—and ultimately no life— without community. Since integrity is never painless, so community is never painless. It does not seek to avoid conflict but to reconcile it. Community always pushes its members to empty themselves sufficiently to make room for the other point of view, the new and different understanding. Community continually urges both itself and its individual members painfully, yet joyously, into ever deeper levels of integrity.[12]

NOTES

1. Anthony James Cantanese, "Foreword" in *Mastering Change* (Chicago: Planners Press, American Planning Association, 1988), p. xv.

2. Charles Henning, *The Wit & Wisdom of Politics* (Golden Colo., Fulcrum, Inc. 1989), p. 87.

3. Ibid., p. 91.

4. For information contact: National Civic League, Inc., 1601 Grant Street, Suite 250, Denver, Colorado 80203.

5. George W. Spasyk, "On Thermometers and Thermostats," *Cross and Crescent*, Lambda Chi Alpha fraternity, (Spring 1988), p. 3.

6. Marjorie S. Berger, ed., *Dennis O'Harrow: Plan Talk and Plain Talk* (Chicago: Planners Press, American Planning Association, 1981), p. 287.

7. William Fulton, "Visionaries, Deal Makers, Incrementalists: The Divided World of Urban Planning," *Governing* (June 1989), p. 52.

8. Ibid., p. 58.

9. Bruce W. McClendon and Ray Quay, *Mastering Change* (Chicago: Planners Press, American Planning Association, 1988), p. 253.

10. Roger K. Lewis, "Planning Is A More Sensible Choice," *Urban Land* (September 1989), pp. 35 and 37.

11. Michael Middleton, *Man Made The Town* (New York: St. Martin's Press, 1987), p. 220.

12. M. Scott Peck, *The Different Drum* (New York: Simon & Schuster, Touchstone Books, 1988), p. 235.

Index

Abbey, Edward, 63
Abbott, Norman A., 95-96
Abdullah, Sharif, 101, 102
ACPI. *See* American City Planning Institute (ACPI)
Adolph Coors Company, 174
Agins v. *City of Tiburon*, 82
AIA. *See* American Institute of Architects (AIA)
AIP. *See* American Institute of Planners (AIP)
Albright, Robert, 101-2
Albuquerque, New Mexico, 164-69
    district system in, 179
    form of government in, 166-67, 178
    home-rule authority in, 20
    as horizontal urban form, 166
    leadership in, 167-69, 184
    planning attitude in, 186
    potential in, 165-66
    problems of rapid growth in, 165
    special interests in, 169
Albuquerque Convention Center, 169
Alinsky, Saul, 156
American City Planning Institute (ACPI), 200, 204
    education and promotion functions of, 206-7
    membership of, 242
    need for membership survey, 245
American Institute of Architects (AIA), 207
American Institute of Certified Planners (AICP), 204, 221

American Institute of Planners (AIP), 200, 204, 221
American Planning Association (APA), 204, 221
    chapter conferences in, 245
    education and promotion functions of, 206-7
    membership base of, 242
    need for membership survey, 245
American Society of Consulting Planners (ASCP), 201
American Society of Planning Officials (ASPO), 201, 202, 204, 221
Amicus curiae (friend of the court) brief, 80
Anheuser-Busch Company, 174
APA. *See* American Planning Association (APA)
APA Journal, 207-8
Appeal process, 77
ASCP. *See* American Society of Consulting Planners (ASCP)
ASPO. *See* American Society of Planning Officials (ASPO)
Association of Collegiate Schools of Planning (ACSP), 205, 209-10, 246
Attorneys, as land use expert witnesses, 71-72
Autonomous authorities, as special districts, 31-33

"Back-Room" scenario, 77-79
Baltimore, Maryland, 119-30, 173

attempts to strengthen role of
planning rebuffed, 129-30
capital improvement program
in, 122-23
city beautiful movement in, 199
coordination of economic
development and planning
in, 127
district system in, 179
economic development in,
125-26
governmental structure in,
121-23
influences on development in,
124-25
Inner Harbor development in,
120, 128-29, 187
leadership in, 184
new challenge in, 130
planners in, 217
planning attitude in, 186, 187
planning background of, 120-21
role of the Greater Baltimore
Committee in, 127-28
strong mayor/council system in,
178
views of others in, 123-24
Baltimore Economic Development
Corporation (BEDCO), 126
Barr Lake Village Metropolitan
District, 36
Bartholomew, Harland, 160, 201
Baum, Howard, 210
Baumbach, Richard O., Jr., 147
Beck, Mark H., 123, 124-25
Becker, Robert, 145, 214
Berger, Marjorie S., 203, 209
Bergholz, David, 113
Berkowitz, Bernard, 125, 127
Bettman, Alfred, 80
Black, Russell VanNest, 201, 202
Blackmun, Harry A., 84
Blakeman, T. Ledyard, 202

Blessing, Charles A., 202
Bloom, Allan, 191
Blucher, Walter, 202
Blumenauer, Earl, 184
Bolan, Richard S., 210
Borah, William E., 147
Boston, Massachusetts
city beautiful movement in,
199
height restrictions in, 12
Boucher, William, 121, 127
Boudreaux, Ray, 146
Boulder, Colorado
adoption of growth
management plan in, 58
planning in, 57-60
Breen, Ann, 150
Brennan, William, 66
Brooks, Michael, 3, 151, 215-16, 247
Brown v. Board of Education, 18, 68
Buck stops here principal of
government, 182-84
Bureau of Public Roads, 15
Busing, court-mandated, 17, 18
Byrum, Oliver, 109, 213-14

California Environmental Quality
Act, 29
Caliguiri, Richard, 111, 113, 114,
182, 184, 186
Cantanese, Anthony James, 227
Capital improvement programs, 2,
222-23
in Baltimore, 122-23
Carrot and big stick approach, 9,
40-41
Carter, Jimmy, 178
Center City Commission (CCC), in
Memphis, 158
Center City Development
Corporation (CCDC)
in Memphis, 158, 159-60
in San Diego, 132, 134-35

Center City Planning Committee, in San Diego, 132
Center City Revenue Finance Corporation, in Memphis, 158, 160
Central 21 (San Antonio), 151
Central business district, 233, 234
See also Downtown planning
in Denver, 26, 27, 137-38
Central Business Improvement District (CBID), in Memphis, 158
Central City Association (CCA), in San Diego, 132
Charles Center (Baltimore), 120
Charles Center Development Group (Baltimore), 124
Charleston, South Carolina, 144
Charlotte, North Carolina, 98-106, 173
annexation in, 102-3
citizen's forum in, 101
citizen-involved planning in, 239
city council/city manager system in, 178
Civic Index Project, 185
as community in action, 100-2
community leadership in, 185
cooperation, coordination, plus consolidation, 99-100
economic development in Uptown, 105-6
form of government in, 103, 178
Generalized Land Plan in, 103
importance of planning function in, 102-3
planners in, 217
planning attitude in, 104-5, 144
population of, 99
power of the neighborhoods in, 103-4
Project Catalyst in, 101
public/private partnership in, 104-5
term of office in, 180

Charlotte-Mecklenburg Citizen's Forum, 100, 185
Charlotte-Mecklenburg Government Center, 99
Chicago, Illinois, Columbian Exposition (1893) in, 12, 181, 197-98
Churchill, Henry S., 90
Cincinnati, Ohio, city beautiful movement in, 199
Cisneros, Henry G., 150-51, 155, 156, 178, 183
Citizen, reaction to taxing policy, 53-54
Citizen participation, 238-39
Citizen's Forum (Charlotte), 101
City Beautiful movement, 12, 180-81, 197-204
City commission method, 177
City council/city manager system, 178
Civic education, 239
Civic Index Program, 100, 237, 238-40
Civilian Conservation Corps (CCC), 198
Civil Rights Act (1964), 17
Clark, Bud, 183
Clark, Frederick P., 202
Clark, William A. V., 19
Cleveland, Ohio, city beautiful movement in, 199
Cockrell, Lila, 151, 152
Colorado
abuse of petition and referendum process in, 24-28
special districts in, 34-36
state land use commission in, 23
and withdrawal of federal funding, 22-23
Colorado Front Range Plan, 54-56
Colorado Public Expenditure Council, 34

Colorado Springs, Colorado, 10, 174
Columbian Exposition (1893) in Chicago, 12, 197-98
Comey, Arthur C., 202
Commodity, land as, 11-12
Community Development Block Grant (CDBG), 234
Community information sharing, 239
Community involvement, corporate roles in, 174-75
Community leadership, 239
Community Organized for Public Service (COPS), 156
Comprehensive planning, 194-95, 222
  in Denver, 139, 224-25
  in Pittsburgh, 115
  trend away from, 51
Condemnation, power of, 70
Consensus building, capacity for, 239
Cooperation, capacity for, 239
Coordination, lack of, in government, 193-95
Corporate roles, in community involvement, 174-75
Corpus Christi, Texas, 161, 180
  charter amendment in, 235
  city council/city manager system in, 178
  comprehensive planning in, 162-63
  encouraging signs in, 162-64
  leadership in, 184
  neighborhood involvement in, 163, 164
  planners in, 218
  planning attitude in, 161-62, 186
  term of office in, 180
  zoning in, 164
Corpus Christi, 90, 162

Courts, role of, in land use planning, 65-87
Cox, Thomas, 113-14
Cramton, Martin R., Jr., 102, 185, 207
Crump, E. H. "Boss," 160, 181
Cullick, Robert, 152, 156
Curley, James M., 181

Daley, Richard, 181
Dallas, Texas, master plan for, 14
Danish, Paul, 58-59
de Maistre, Joseph, 236
Demonstration Cities and Metropolitan Development Act, 41
Denver, Colorado, 136-39, 174
  annexation of surrounding land by, 24-25
  central business district in, 26, 27, 137-38
  city beautiful movement in, 199-200
  comprehensive plan in, 139, 224-25
  council district election system in, 137
  creation of, 24
  high rise development in, 26-27
  investment in, 27-28
  leadership in, 27, 184
  optimistic signs in, 138-39
  planners in, 218
  planning attitude in, 26, 27, 28, 186
  "Poundstone Amendment" in, 25, 26, 28
  school desegregation in, 25
  strong mayor/council system in, 177
  zoning ordinances in, 138
Denver Housing Authority, 137
Denver Urban Renewal Authority, 219

Design Review Board, in Memphis, 160

Detroit, Michigan, school integration in, 18

District system, 179

Downtown Marketing Consortium (DMC) (San Diego), 132

Downtown planning. *See also* Central business district
in Memphis, 159-60
in San Diego, 133-35

Duke Power Company, 99

Dully, Larry, 93

DuPuy, Carla, 99, 100, 183

Economic development quality, 52-56

Economic pressure, impact of, on local governments, 49-52

Economy, building strong, lasting, 56-63

Edwards Aquifer, 153

Edwards Underground Water District, 153

Einsweiler, Robert, 109-10, 210, 211, 242

Eisenhower, Dwight D., 40

Elected officials
evaluation of, 192-93
leadership of, 175-76

Elementary Education Act (1965), 17

Eminent domain, 70-71

Environmental Protection Agency, 13

Expert witnesses
attorneys as land use, 71-72
tips for, on testifying, 73-75

Fair-share doctrine, 72, 75-76

Federal Aid Highway Act (1956), 14, 15-17

Federal Emergency Management Agency (FEMA), 83, 84

Federal Express, 157

Federal government
cumulative effect of programs of, 17-19
lack of coordination of, in local development, 8-19
withdrawal of funding, 21-23

Federal Highway Act (1956), 39-40, 41

Federal Housing Act (1937), 202

Federal Housing Act (1954), 39-46

Federal Housing Administration, 14-15

Federal Model Enabling Acts, 12-13

First English Evangelical Lutheran Church of Glendale v. *County of Los Angeles*, 80-85

First Union National Bank, 99, 104

Floor area ratio (FAR) requirement, 26

Forester, John, 210

Fort Collins, Colorado, 174

Frazer, Donald M., 108-9, 184

Fulton, William, 247-48

Gantt, Harvey B., 183

Garden State Parkway, 32

Gates Corporation, 174

General and Block Grant Revenue Sharing, 41

Giles, Kathy, 133, 136

Golden, Colorado, 174

Goldschmidt, Neil, 91, 92, 97, 177, 178, 181, 182, 183

Government. *See also* Federal government; State government
form and structure of, 176-80
influence of, 239
lack of coordination in, 193-95

Greater Baltimore Committee (GBC), 124, 127-28, 187

Growth management
in Boulder, 58, 61

in New Orleans, 148
in San Diego, 29, 131-32

Hagge, Michael, 159
Hague, Frank, 181
Hahn, Ernie, 132
Hall, Frederick, 66
Hammond, Mary Ann, 103-4
Hartford, Connecticut, planning in, 12
Heher, Harry, 66
Hewlett Packard, 174
Highway 280/University Avenue Redevelopment Plan (Saint Paul), 140
Home-rule, 20
Homestead Act (1862), 11
Hoover, Herbert, 12, 41
Horizontal pattern, 172-73
Hornby, Bill, 47-48
Housing and Community Development Acts, 41
Housing and Home Finance Agency (HHFA), 41
Housing and Urban Development, U.S. Department of (HUD), 41
Howard, John T., 16
Hughes, Richard, 66
Humphreys, John A., 206

Ickes, Harold L., 9
Ingraham, Elizabeth Wright, 232
Inter-Community Cooperation, 239
Intergroup relations, 239
Interior Department, U.S. Department of, 9-10
Interpretive changes, in planning, 66-68

Jacobs, Jane, 4
Jarvis, Peter, 110, 208, 241-42
Jefferson, Thomas, 115
Johnson C. Smith University, 101

Kaufman, Jerome, 210
Kelly, Eric Damian, 214, 243
Keystone Bituminous Coal Assn. v. *DeBenedictis*, 86
Kodak, 174
Kopca, Chris, 93
Kubat, Charles A., 125

Lamm, Richard D., 22-23, 54, 182, 249
Lamont, William, 138, 186
Land, philosophy of as a commodity, 11-12
Land ownership, as right, 11, 68
Land use attorneys, as land use experts, 71-72
Land use planning, courts' role in, 65-87
Latimer, George, 183-84
Lawrence, David, 111
Lawson, Simpson, 121
Leadership
of elected officials, 175
political and community, 180-85
Levin, Melvin R., 3, 38, 210
Lewis, David, 115
Lewis, Roger K., 249
Littleton, Colorado
contrast between Boulder and, 60-61
planning in, 61-63
Local government, impact of economic pressure on, 49-52
Local planning, 7-8
role of federal government in, 8-19
Long-range plan, developing, 70-71
Lorch, Robert S., 22-23
Lucy, William, 210
Lugar, 182

Majeed, Nasif, 102
Mandelker, Daniel R., 85

Manville Corporation, 174
Martin, Edward, 215
Martin Marietta, 174
Mason-Dixon line, impact of, on
    planning attitudes, 143-44
Master plan, 76-77
Matter, David, 114
Mayor's Development Council
    (Pittsburgh), 114
McCall, Tom, 91, 182
McClendon, Bruce W., 210, 248
McKeldin, Theodore, 121, 129
Mecklenburg County, 99. *See also*
    Charlotte, North Carolina
Media, power of, 175-76
Memphis, Tennessee, 156-61
    Center City Commission in, 158
    Center City Development in,
        158, 159-60
    Center City Development Plan
        in, 160
    Center City Revenue Finance
        Corporation in, 158, 160
    Central Business Improvement
        District in, 158
    Design Review Board in, 160
    downtown planning in, 159-60
    leadership in, 184
    Mid-America Mall, 158-59
    planners in, 218
    planning attitude in, 186
    policy plan in, 160-61
Memphis 2000 Policy Plan,
    160-61
Merriam, Dwight H., 81, 83
Metro 2000 (Minneapolis), 108-9
Metropolitan Council
    (Minneapolis/Saint Paul), 33,
    110
Mid-America Mall (Memphis),
    158-59
Middleton, Michael, 249-50
Miller, Jeff, 129

Millspaugh, Martin, 122
Minneapolis, Minnesota, 106-11,
    173
    brighter side in, 107-9
    central city in, 107
    choice ahead in, 111
    citywide and regional planning
        in, 110-11
    cooperation between Saint Paul
        and, 109
    current evaluation of, 109-10
    dilemma in, 106-7
    district system in, 179
    governmental relationship and
        cooperation in, 109
    leadership in, 184
    Metro 2000 in, 108-9
    neighborhood planning in, 108
    planners in, 217
    planning attitude in, 106-7, 186
    planning commission in, 109-10
    planning philosophy in, 107-8
    strong mayor/council system in,
        178
Mitchell, Robert B., 40
Model Cities Act (1966), 39-40
Model Cities Program, 13
Model Planning Enabling Act, 194
Modesto, California, zoning in, 12
Moses, Robert, 147
Mt. Laurel I, 72
Mt. Laurel II, 72, 75
Mumford, Lewis, 209
Mumphrey, Anthony J., 209
Municipal attorney, 78

Naisbitt, John, 48-49
Naito, William, 97
National Civic League (NCL),
    Civic Index Program of, 100,
    237, 238-40
National Conference of City
    Planning, 80

National Flood Insurance Program, 84
National land use policy
    absence of, 10
    failure of, 21
National Planning Board, 9
National planning organizations, 204-5
    critique of, 205-11
National Resources Committee, 9
National Resources Planning Board, 9
National Trust for Historic Preservation (NTHP), 83, 84
NCNB National Bank, 99
Neighborhood(s), 234-35
    increasing influence of, 189
    interests, 235
    in Minneapolis, 108
    as power base, 235-37
    power of, in Charlotte, 103-4
Neighborhood organizations, relative influence of, 185
Neighborhood Partnership Program (Saint Paul), 141
Neighborhood planning
    in Cincinnati, 113-14
    in Portland, 95
    in Saint Paul, 140-41
    in San Diego, 133
Neighborhood school, 233-34
New Federalism, 41
New Jersey, requirement for master plans in, 76-77
New Jersey Council on Affordable Housing, 76
New Jersey Turnpike, 32
New Orleans, Louisiana, 144-49, 173, 180
    downtown development district in, 148-49
    French Quarter in, 146-48
    leadership in, 184

neighborhoods in, 145
planners in, 217-18
planning attitude in, 145-46, 186
strong mayor/council system in, 178
zoning moratorium in, 145
New York City, city beautiful movement in, 199
New York Expressway, 32
Noel, Thomas Jacob, 200
Nolan, John, 131
Nollan v. California Coastal Commission, 85-86
Norgren, Barbara Stewart, 200
Norman, Jerry, 163
Norton, Perry, 205, 206, 245

O'Connor, Sandra Day, 84
O'Harrow, Dennis, 3, 11-12, 43, 181, 195, 197, 202, 203, 206, 209, 247
Oliver, Gordon, 98
Olmsted, Frederick Law, 200
One Financial Center (Portland), 96
Operation Breakthrough Program, 41
Oregon, 95

Peabody Hotel (Memphis), 157
Peirce, Neal, 60-61
Pena, Federico, 138
Pennsylvania Turnpike, 32
Petaluma, California, adoption of growth management plan in, 58
Petition, 23-30
    abuse of, in Colorado, 24-28
Philadelphia, Pennsylvania, citizen-involved planning in, 239
Philanthropy, 239
Pioneer Courthouse Square (Portland, Oregon), 92-93
Pittsburgh, Pennsylvania, 111-15, 173, 180

community concerns in, 112-13
community/neighborhood
  planning concerns in, 113-14
comprehensive planning in, 115
district system in, 179
leadership in, 114-15, 184
planners in, 217
planning attitude in, 186
strong mayor/council system in,
  178
Planner(s)
  image of, 214-16
  problems and opportunities for,
    240-47
  role of, 216-19
  as societal voice of conscience,
    232-33
Planning
  concept of, 2-3
  decreasing stability of, 51-52
  interpretive changes in, 66-68
  need for change in, 247-50
Planning attitude
  impact of Mason-Dixon line on,
    143-44
  in Baltimore, 187
  in Charlotte, 104-5
  in Corpus Christi, 161-62
  in Denver, 26, 27, 28
  in Minneapolis, 106-7
  in New Orleans, 145-46
  in San Antonio, 187
  in San Diego, 187
  of public officials, 185-87
Planning education, 208-11
  trends in, 246-47
Planning magazine, 206-7
Planning process, understanding
  of, 211-12
Planning profession
  leadership in, 200-2
  need for definition of, 213-14
  present and future of, 211-19

Plough Chemical Company, 157
Police power, 69-70, 71, 80
Policymakers, major influences on,
  188-89
Pomeroy, Hugh, 201
Pontalba case (New Orleans), 147
Portland, Oregon, 90-98, 173, 177,
  179
  central city plan in, 97-98
  city commission form of
    government in, 177
  community leadership in, 185
  comparison of, with Seattle,
    94-96
  comprehensive plan in, 95
  downtown housing policy in, 92
  land use policy in, 91, 94
  leadership and support of
    design community in, 91-92
  leadership in, 184
  neighborhood groups in, 95
  planners in, 217
  planning as process in, 97-98
  planning attitude in, 96-97
  planning policy performance in,
    90
  private-sector viewpoint in,
    96-97
  public support of planning in,
    92-93
  public transportation in, 90-91
  revitalization of, under
    Goldschmidt, 181
  sense of community in, 91-92
  successful policies in, 93-94
  term of office in, 180
  urban renewal in, 93
Port of New York Authority, 32
Potter, Roy, 134, 143
Poundstone, Freda, 24, 25
"Poundstone Amendment," 25, 26,
  28
Powell, Cathy, 150, 154

Powers, Susan, 219
PPG Industries, 114
Prendergast, Pat, 96-97
Presley, Elvis, 158
Project Catalyst (Charlotte), 101, 185
Proposition 13, 28-29, 131
Prosperity shopping center, fable of, 50-51
Proxmire, William, 161
Public health, safety and general welfare, 69
Public officials, planning attitudes of, 185-87

Quality Urban Environment Study Teams (QUEST), 121
Quay, Ray, 210, 248

Raabe, Steve, 58
Red-lining, 17
Referendum, 23-30
abuse of, in Colorado, 24-28
Rehnquist, William, 82
Reich, Larry, 122, 125-26, 127, 130
Rigby, Dick, 150
Riverwalk (San Antonio), 149-50
Roosevelt, Franklin, 68
Rouse, James, 121, 124, 127, 150

Saavadra, Louis E., 168
Saint Louis, Missouri, city beautiful movement in, 199
Saint Paul, Minnesota, 139-41
cooperation between Minneapolis and, 109
district system in, 179
government form in, 140
leadership in, 184
neighborhood planning in, 140-41
planning attitude in, 186

strong mayor/council system in, 178
San Antonio, Texas, 149-56, 180
Central 21 in, 151
city council/city manager system in, 178
Community Organized for Public Service in, 156
comprehensive vision for the future in, 150-51
district system in, 179
diversity in, 152
HemisFair World's Fair in, 149-50
highways and transportation in, 154-55
leadership in, 184
planners in, 218
planning attitude in, 186, 187
policies plan in, 155-56
post Cisneros, 151-52
public education in, 155
Riverwalk in, 149-50
Target 90 in, 155
under Cisneros as mayor, 150-51, 183
water supply as issue in, 153-54
Zoning Board of Adjustment in, 152
San Diego, California, 130-36
city council/city manager system in, 178
community and neighborhood planning, 133
district system in, 179
future of, 135-36
growth pressure results and reaction, 131-32
lack of coordination in, 132-33
leadership in, 184
petitions and referenda in, 28-30
planners in, 218
planning attitude in, 143, 186, 187

planning policy in, 29-30
real power in downtown
    planning in, 133-35
San Diego Port Authority, 134
San Francisco, California
    city beautiful movement in, 199
    planning attitude in, 143
Schaefer, Donald, 121, 126
Schaefer, William, 178, 184
Schering-Plough corporation, 157
Schiro, Victor H., 147
Schmoke, Kurt L., 130
Schneiderman, Michael, 105-6
Schon, Donald, 210
School desegregation, 17, 18, 68
Scott, Mel, 14, 202-3
Seattle, Washington, comparison
    of, with Portland, 94-96
Segoe, Ladislas, 201-2
Shanahan, John H., Jr., 218
Sherburne, Harriet, 94-95
Shurtleff, Flavel, 200
Societal changes, effects of, 47-49
Spasyk, George W., 240-41
Special districts, 30-31
    autonomous authorities in, 31-33
    financing of, 36-37
    illustrations of, 34-36
    why and how of, 33-34
Speer, Robert, 180, 184, 199
Standard City Planning Enabling
    Act (1927), 12
State government, in local
    development, 19-38
States' rights, 67-68
Stepner, Michael, 130-31, 132, 133,
    215
Stevens, John Paul, 84-85
Strachan, Margaret, 98
Strategic/long-range planning, 239
Strong mayor/council government,
    177-78
    in Albuquerque, 166-68

    in Baltimore, 121
    in Saint Paul, 140
Subdivision regulations, 2
Sun Belt, 48-49
Superconducting Super Collider
    Project, 10
Sutherland, George, 80

Taking issue, 80-86
Target 90 (San Antonio), 155
Taxing policies, effect of, 46-47
Telford, William L., 152, 155
Terms-of-office complication,
    179-80
Testifying, tips on, 73-75
Texas Water Commission, 153
Tocqueville, Alexis de, 87
Turner, Betty, 162

U.S. Supreme Court, 67-68
University of North Carolina at
    Charlotte, 102
Urban Development Action Grant
    (UDAG), 234
Urban form
    adverse forces affecting, 13-17
    building, 56
    decision making, 1, 228-34
    factors contributing to failure in
        building, 190-91
    horizontal, 172-73
    vertical, 173-74
Urban Growth and Community
    Development Act, 41
Urban Land Institute (ULI), 207, 245
Urban Renewal Administration
    (URA), 41, 43
Urban Revitalization Action
    Program (Saint Paul), 141
Urbco'Lat Purser, 104
Utter, Tom, 162

Value judgments, 1

Vertical pattern, 173-74
Veteran's Administration, 14
Vieux Carre Commission (New Orleans), 146
Village of Euclid v. *Ambler Realty Co.*, 79-80
Volpe, John A., 147
Volunteerism, 239

Wallace, David, 121, 128, 129, 130
Wallace, George, 68
Warren, Roland L., 172-73, 233
Washington, D.C.
   city beautiful movement in, 199
   height restrictions in, 12
Watershed Management Organization (Saint Paul), 140
Whitnall, Brysis, 201
Whitnall, Gordon, 201

Wilentz, Robert, 67
Wilson, Pete, 184
Wilson, Woodrow, 177
Winchester, James, 156
Workable Program for Community Improvement (WPCI), 40-41, 44, 45
Works Progress Administration (WPA), 150, 198
World Trade Center (Baltimore), 120
Worthington, Robert A., 107, 216
Wright, Frank Lloyd, 16-17

Young, Robert, 104-5

Zoning, 2, 12, 65-66
   decreasing stability of, 51-52
   and *Euclid* v. *Ambler*, 79-80